Reconceptualizing India Studies

RECONCEPTUALIZING
INDIA
STUDIES

S.N. BALAGANGADHARA

OXFORD
UNIVERSITY PRESS

OXFORD
UNIVERSITY PRESS

Oxford University Press is a department of the University of Oxford.
It furthers the University's objective of excellence in research, scholarship,
and education by publishing worldwide. Oxford is a registered trademark of
Oxford University Press in the UK and in certain other countries

Published in India by
Oxford University Press
YMCA Library Building, 1 Jai Singh Road, New Delhi 110 001, India

© Oxford University Press 2012

The moral rights of the author have been asserted

First published in 2012

ISBN-13: 978-0-19-808296-5
ISBN-10: 0-19-808296-7

Typeset in Dante MT Std 10.8/12.8,
at MAP Systems, Bengaluru 560 082, India

Dedication

'Should you be able to overhear what people say about you after your death, what would move you the most in the way people judge you?' This was my question on one of our familiar evenings, after he and I had had a good dinner, few glasses of excellent Bordeaux wine, and, as philosophers, reflected and discussed. He thought for a long time, longer than he normally does, and said: 'It would move me the most if people found that I was fair and reasonable throughout my life.' Immediately, he burst into a loud laughter: 'Of course, I would not believe that because I have not always been fair and reasonable.' Ethical actions and goals grip him deeply; it would mean much to him should he live up to them. He is also objective enough to know that he has fallen short of these goals. Instead of making him sad, the question elicits laughter from him. What amuses him about this? I have asked myself many a time since. Is he delighted at his own cleverness? Is he thrilled by his insight into himself? Is he, perhaps, laughing at the condition humaine?

No, the human predicament does not make him laugh. I have scarcely met someone who is more or even equally intense and passionate about his humanism. About thirty-two years ago, I, an Indian, knocked at his door asking in English for help and guidance. Since then, much has changed. Now I neither speak in English with him nor knock at his office door. I am now a Belgian who speaks more 'Flenglish' than Flemish, and, having retired, he has no door at the University. What has not changed is that I still ask his help and guidance. What has also not changed is that he is always there with help and suggestions.

This extraordinary kindness to people, whatever their size, shape, colour, or circumstance, marks him deeply. He is consistently kind. He is consistent in other ways too: in his thought, in his tolerance of human variety, and in his almost naïve acceptance of individual failings as mere idiosyncrasies. It is almost as though he loathes to judge people. Is it his Jesuit and Christian training, or his uncompromising commitment to humanism that makes him value human beings so much? Sometimes, it appears to me, he tries to mix the unmixable: a reasoned rejection of the Christian God together with *a uniquely Christian attitude that places the value of human life beyond human judgement. In his criticisms of what he considers wrong thinking and wrong actions, he spares no words. In his judgement of people, however he is the very embodiment of Christian charity. I have often wondered about this strange mixture; sometimes well into the early hours of the morning after our late dinners. At the same time, I also wonder at my good own fortune of having known well enough to call him my friend. I feel proud as well, because I realize that, all said and done, I have met someone who is an extraordinary asset: to any people, at any time, in any age, for any culture, and anywhere in the world.*

He is Etienne Vermeersch: a Belgian, a professor, a former vice-rector, and a friend. He is my teacher. This book is for him.

Contents

Acknowledgements

I am grateful to the following for giving me permission to reproduce from my previously published works.

Sage Publications and Taylor and Francis for parts of chapters 2 and 3 published earlier in 'The Future of the Present', *Cultural Dynamics*, 10(2), pp. 101–21, 1998, London: Sage Publishers; and (with Marianne Keppens) as 'Reconceptualizing the Postcolonial Project: Beyond the Strictures and Structures of Orientalism', *Interventions* 11(1), pp. 50–68, 2009, London: Taylor and Francis.

Pencraft International for an earlier version of Chapter 4, which was published as 'Rethinking Colonialism and Colonial Consciousness: The Case of Modern India' (with Esther Bloch and Jakob De Roover) in S. Raval (ed.), *Rethinking Forms of Knowledge in India* (Delhi: Pencraft International, 2008), pp. 179–212.

Journal for the Study of Religions and Ideologies for an earlier version of Chapter 6 (with Sarah Claerhout) previously published as 'Are Dialogues Antidotes to Violence? Two Recent Examples from Hinduism Studies', *Journal for the Study of Religions and Ideologies*, 7(19), 2008, pp. 118–143.

Wiley-Blackwell for an earlier version of Chapter 8, published as 'The Secular State and Religious Conflict: Liberal Neutrality and the Indian Case of Pluralism' (with Jakob De Roover) in *The Journal of Political Philosophy*, 15(1), 2007, pp. 67–92.

Introduction

What can India offer to the world of today and tomorrow? In one sense, a reconceptualization of India studies would be the answer to this question. In this book, I take a first step in clearing away the intellectual deadwood that prevents us from formulating this question adequately. Before I discuss how I aim to accomplish my task, we need to understand why the above question is both important and intriguing.

For the first time in the last four to five hundred years, non-Western cultures have the opportunity to make a significant impact on the affairs of mankind. India will be a global player of considerable political and economic impact. As a result, the need to explicate what it means to be Indian (or, what makes Indian culture 'Indian' and not, say, just 'modern') will soon become a task for the intelligentsia of India. In this process, it will face the challenge of responding to what Europe has so far thought and written about India. A response is required because, in the last three hundred years, the theoretical and textual study of Indian culture has been undertaken mostly by Europe. What is more, it will also be a challenge because, as I will argue, the study of India has largely occurred within the cultural framework of Europe.

In fulfilling this task, the Indian intelligentsia of tomorrow will have to solve a puzzle: what were the earlier generations of Indian thinkers busy with? Surely they were busy with many things in the course of the last two to three thousand years? Let me use European culture as a contrast to explain why this is a puzzle, and also its nature and importance.

Intellectual Labour and Its Results

What were European intellectuals engaged in during the last two thousand years? It is almost impossible to answer this question without relating the history of Europe; still, we can say that they produced theologies, philosophies, fine arts, and the natural and the social sciences. The list is so varied, so diverse and so long, that one does not know where to begin or how to end. Perhaps the most interesting theories about human beings, their cultures and societies, which we use today, are products of European intellectuals. So, too, are the institutions and practices that we find desirable: democratic institutions and courts of law, for instance. The sheer scope, variety, and quality of European contribution to humanity are overwhelming.

What were Indian thinkers doing during the same period? The standard textbook story—which has schooled multiple generations, including mine—goes as follows: the caste system has dominated India; women have been discriminated against; the practice of widow-burning still exists; corruption is rampant; most people believe in astrology, karma, and reincarnation. If these properties characterize the India of today and yesterday, the question about what the earlier generation of Indian thinkers was doing gives rise to a very painful realization: these thinkers were busy instituting and defending atrocious practices. Of course, there is our Buddha and there is our Gandhi, but that, apparently, is all we have: exactly one Buddha and one Gandhi. When the intellectuals of one culture—the European culture—were challenging and changing the world, most thinkers from another culture—the Indian—were, to all purposes, sustaining and defending undesirable and immoral practices. If that portrayal is true, the Indians of today have but one task, which is to modernize India; and Indian culture has but one goal: to become like the West as quickly as possible.

However, what if this portrayal is false? What if these descriptions of India are wrong? In that case, the questions about what India can

offer to the world and what Indian thinkers were doing become
important. For the first time, the dominant knowledge about India
will be subjected to a kind of test it has never faced before. Why
'for the first time'? The answer is obvious: knowledge of India
was generated primarily during colonial rule in India. Subsequent
to Independence, India went through a period of poverty and
backwardness. In tomorrow's world, Indian intellectuals will be able
to speak back with a newly found confidence, and they will challenge
the European descriptions of India. That is, for the first time, they
will test European knowledge of India and not just accept it as God's
own truth. This has not happened earlier. The results of this test will
not be merely of scientific interest; they will also have serious social,
political, and economic repercussions on European and Indian society.
If this is the case, the question that now rises is: what is the nature of
the European 'knowledge' about India that will be tested?

A Redescription

As an example, consider one of the things that Europe 'knows'
about India: the Indian caste system. Almost everyone I know
has very firm moral opinions on the subject. The caste system
is considered as the origin of all kinds of evils in India: it is held
responsible for the denial of human rights and oppression, and seen
as an obstacle to progress and modernization, and so on. I suppose
we can all agree that we need to understand a phenomenon before
making moral judgements, and that the firmer the moral opinion,
the more certain is our knowledge of the phenomenon. With this
in mind, if we try and find out what this infamous caste system is,
and why people either attack or defend it, we discover the following:
our firm but conflicting moral opinions on the subject are not based
on consensual scientific clarity. In that case, how can anyone be so
firmly pro or contra the caste system?

To spell out this question more clearly, let us engage in a thought
experiment. Let us accept the standard textbook descriptions of the
caste system, but, let us turn them upside down. What happens then?
While emphasizing that I do not wish to attack, much less defend, the
caste system, let us take a look at both the existing descriptions and
the consequences of turning them upside down.

Caste is supposed to be an antiquated social system that arose in the dim past of India. If this is true, the system has survived many challenges: the onslaught of Buddhism and the Bhakti movement; the process of colonization; Indian Independence and world capitalism and it might survive even 'globalization'. From these considerations, follows that the caste system must be a very stable social organization

There exists no centralized authority for enforcing the caste system across the length and breadth of India. There is, of course, the story about the conquering Aryans imposing 'the caste system' on India Irrespective of the truth or falsity of this story, it speaks of a time long gone and not, say, of the last thousand years or more. In that case, the caste system must be an autonomous and decentralized organization No social or political regulations—whether promulgated by the British or by the Indians—have been able to eradicate this system. If this true it implies that the caste system is a self-reproducing social structure.

The caste system exists, in one form or another, among Hindu Sikhs, Jains, Christians, and Muslims. It has also existed in different environments. It means that this system adapts itself to the environments in which it finds itself. Since new castes have risen and disappeared over the centuries, this system must also be dynamic Since the caste system is present in different political organizations and has survived under different political regimes, it is also neutral with respect to political ideologies.

Even though more can be said, this is enough for us. A simple re description of what we think we know about the caste system tells us that it is an autonomous, decentralized, stable, adaptive, dynamic, self reproducing, social organization. It is also neutral as regards political religious and economic doctrines and environments. If indeed such a system ever existed, would it also not be the most ideal form of social organization one could ever think of? As I have just shown, this consequence is derivable from the current descriptions of the Indian 'caste system'.

There is a good reason why I have spent time on this issue. And that is to signal in the direction of a problem which has very far reaching consequences. If, what Europe knows about India resemble what it claims to know about the caste system, what exactly does Europe know about India or her culture? Not very much, I am afraid Precisely at a time when knowledge of other cultures and people a pre-requisite to surviving in a 'globalizing' world, it appears as though Europe knows very little about either of the two. Perhaps, the absence of knowledge is felt most acutely by the Europeans who invest in India. Today, they are rediscovering what people already knew before: they are not well-equipped to do business in India. They understand neither the culture nor the role of cultural differences in management structures and organizations.

In other words, I am suggesting the following: what the Europeans think they know of India tells us more about Europe than it does about India. This 'knowledge' will be tested during this century. If that is the status of the standard textbook descriptions of India, quite obviously, the earlier generations of Indian thinkers were not merely busy instituting and defending immoral practices. What else were they doing, then? Now, the puzzle becomes very intriguing: what exactly were Indian thinkers doing in the course of the last two to three thousand years? What did they think and write about? Did they make contributions to human knowledge? If yes, what are those contributions? Answering these and allied questions will be one of the primary preoccupations of the Indian intelligentsia in the course of the twenty-first century. This puzzle is important for Europeans, too. To understand why, we need to study the context first.

Learning from Each Other

Let me sketch the context by raising a question: what has the world to learn from Europe? Here are the familiar answers: science and technology; democracy and the rule of law; respect for human rights and ecological awareness; becoming modern and cosmopolitan. When such answers are given, it does not mean that the rest of the world has to learn from Europe this or that scientific theory; or, a solution to this or that mathematical problem. What is meant is something like this: Indians have to learn from European culture a particular way of going about in the world. That, one believes, is the unique contribution of European culture, something that is absent in other cultures.

Let us now reverse the question: what has Europe to learn from India? In the thirty and more years that I have spent in Europe and in all the books I have read, I have not come across any satisfactory answer. Most do not even raise the issue; those who do, mumble vaguely about 'learning' things that Europe once knew but has forgotten since. How do we understand this situation?

The first possibility is that there is nothing to learn from India. This is logically possible, but implausible. It is possible that, like the 'chosen people' which Jews believe they are, Europe is the 'chosen' culture from all the cultures that populate the planet. However, it is implausible because I have not come across any explanation for this 'European miracle'. Nevertheless, if there is nothing to learn from India, we can all sleep peacefully: the world, as we know it, will not be disturbed. This is the first possibility.

Consider the second possibility now. Europe has 'something' to learn from India, but Europeans do not yet know what. Some give the following answers: meditation, yoga, notions of karma, Vedic astrology, spirituality. These answers will not do: not only are there native meditative and astrological traditions in Europe, but such answers are also inadequate for another reason. It is like saying that one has to learn partial differential equations from Europe. So, let me push the question: what is this 'something' Europe has to learn from India?

At this stage, we usually encounter silence because there does not appear to be any answer to give. Surely, this is strange: Europe has been studying India for centuries; it has colonized her territories and people; it has told Indians what is wrong with their society and culture. And yet, no answer is forthcoming. Indians know what they have to learn from Europe and they have been learning it for centuries on end. Europe, by contrast, apparently has given no thought to the question and certainly has no proper answer.

By virtue of this, the second possibility—that Europe has something to learn from India but does not know what—is very disturbing. One culture, the Indian, has been learning for generations and centuries; the other culture, the European, does not know what to learn or even whether there is anything to learn in the first place. For the first time in so many hundred years, these cultures will meet with each other on the world arena as equals and as competitors. What will the outcome be?

Setting the Stage

Whatever the outcome, the meeting between these two cultures sets the context for the puzzle of which I have spoken. To this puzzle, we have one set of indirect answers. In the course of the last three hundred years or so, the mainstream theories in the social sciences and the humanities have been carrying on as though Indian thinkers have made no substantial contribution to human knowledge. At the same time, almost without exception, this splendid corpus of writing about human beings embodies specific assumptions of Western culture. Not only have Western intellectuals created these theories in the humanities and the social sciences; the theories also express how this culture has looked at the human world so far. Generations of Indian intellectuals have accepted these answers as more or less true. Future generations will not be so accommodating: they will test these answers for their truth. I say this with confidence because I find that more and more people in India are gravitating towards this kind of research.

Even a limited acquaintance with Indian culture tells us that its thinkers, too, have produced multiple 'theories' about human beings. For example, think of the claims made by the Advaita traditions, the Buddhist traditions, the Jain, the Saivist and the Vaishnavite traditions. These, too, express the way Indian culture has looked at the human world. (Here, one can think of many examples: from the philosophical arguments of the pre-carvaka or lokayata varieties of Indian materialism through the various Dharmashastra literatures to individual treatises on economics, the arts, and language.) These theories are contributions to human knowledge. This knowledge is about many things: the nature of human beings; the nature of ethics and morality; how human beings learn; what happiness is and how to attain it; what we can learn about human beings, their language and speech. In short, this is knowledge about us; it is also about what we can know, what we may hope for, and what we should be doing. Just as Indian and European cultures differ from each other, so do their views about human beings.

In the currently dominant social sciences and humanities, European intellectuals have so far been elaborating on their stories. Indian intellectuals (more generally, the Asian intellectuals, because what I say about India is true of them as well) will start doing the same in the course of this century. These two sets of theories will meet on the world arena, too, as equals and as competitors. Today, we believe that the European story about human beings constitutes knowledge; that is because there is no competition to this story as yet. How about tomorrow, when there is going to be competition in the marketplace of ideas, where Indians and Asians will come up with other and different theories? By the end of this century, there will be at least two different sets of stories about human beings, their societies and cultures. One which the West has produced, and the other, which India and Asia will. Which one of these sets will turn out to be true? Could one of them be false, or will both be transcended by a better alternative? Will neither of these sets (qua sets) be true because only one or the other element from either of the sets is true? These are not our issues yet; they are for tomorrow. Today, all we can do is set the stage for an intellectual development that will tackle these, and allied, questions.

An Overview

What I hope to do in this book: to set the stage for this intellectual endeavour which, I believe, will be carried out by the coming generations. I am aware that what I do in these chapters—compared to what needs to be done—will not do justice to the nature of the task. My only consolation is that, before a beautiful mansion can be built, someone has to prepare the ground. This happens to be my allocated job and I plan to execute it in the following way.

As must be obvious, the imminent intellectual development about which I discuss is premised on the fact that there are different cultures present in the world, and that it is both interesting and illuminating to talk about cultural differences. However, this premise does not represent the consensus in today's academic community. In fact, some anthropologists challenge the very use of the concept of 'culture' in studying human societies. Therefore, I begin by looking at the controversy about this concept. Today, it is almost sacrilegious to 'other the other' while doing anthropology. Because the notion of culture itself has become suspect, apparently, one cannot even suggest that cultures different from one's own are these 'others'.

In Chapter 1, I show that most arguments that advocate jettisoning the concept of culture are cognitively inadmissible: none of these arguments establishes the need to reject the concept of culture or shows its undesirability. Subsequently, I will examine a suggestion to look at the adjectival uses of the word 'cultural'. Here, I will formulate and answer the following question: what makes some difference—any difference—into a cultural difference and not a social, biological, or psychological difference? This question lies at the basis of anthropological practice, and I suggest that the current debates bring that to the surface. Instead of a wholesale rejection of the notion of culture, I will show that it is possible to explore the nature of cultural difference in new ways, provided we come up with interesting hypotheses about their nature.

Critics of Orientalism and scholars from the discipline of post-colonial studies have challenged the colonial nature of anthropology before me. Consequently, I will focus on their challenge in the following two chapters. Through a critical meta-examination, I will look at the need to go beyond criticisms of Orientalist discourse and turn our attention towards a critical examination of the nature of the social sciences. In these chapters, I will also clarify the nature of the post-colonial predicament by explicating the notion of 'colonial consciousness'.

More concretely, Chapter 2 probes the phenomenon of Orientalism in order to answer the question: what is next after Edward Said's Orientalism? Said's works have been of crucial importance to Indian intellectuals, allowing them to raise the following issue: if we know India through the organization effected by Western intellectual tradition, how would it look if organized otherwise? Of course, this issue lies at the heart of the reconceptualization of Indian studies. However, to begin answering this issue, we need to examine Said's insight that Orientalist discourse is the result of a particular form of constrained thinking, which transforms non-Western cultures into pale and erring variants of Western culture. This chapter argues that the social sciences and Orientalism constrain each other. To understand the way Western culture has described both itself and others is to begin understanding this culture. The challenge of Orientalism is to understand Western culture itself. Consequently, I conclude, a critique of Orientalism becomes coterminous with the task of creating alternative theories in the different domains of the humanities and the social sciences.

In Chapter 3, I look at some of the methodological problems confronting such new ways of developing alternative theories about cultures—a research programme that I call 'comparative science of cultures'. This new research programme is intended to challenge the current anthropological theories and practice and, here, I show why it is new and interesting. In a sense, these three chapters function as a prolegomenon to what is to come.

Why can the current social sciences not provide an alternative to Orientalism? After all, Said believed otherwise. Many subscribe to his view as well. One of the reasons why we cannot rely on current social sciences is because of the fact that many of their theories also embody and express what I call 'colonial consciousness'.

Chapter 4 focuses on the Indian experience and argues that colonial consciousness pervades both colonial and modern theoretical and empirical social-scientific descriptions of India. The persistent colonial ways of describing the world reveals a lack of adequate understanding of colonialism and explains why the colonial project was immoral. This persistence is indicated by way of an interdisciplinary survey into descriptions of India as a corrupt, immoral and caste-ridden society. Colonial consciousness denies the presence of morality in the Indian tradition. Moreover, it takes the superiority of Western culture both as its presupposition and its conclusion. This stance towards Indian culture can be traced back to the Christian theological understanding of 'heathen religions'. The conclusions of this theological understanding have become the foundation of the descriptions of India as developed by later generations of social scientists. This characterization of colonial consciousness also allows me to explain why colonialism is intrinsically immoral and why it has been perceived as an educational project. Colonialism modifies the Indian experience and replaces it with a framework which is rationally unjustified and unjustifiable, and must, therefore, be imposed with violence.

The remaining chapters grapple with this phenomenon of colonial consciousness: they examine the violence involved in the imposition of an unjustifiable framework, the reactions to such violations, and the fact that independence from colonial rule does not make for an automatic disappearance of this consciousness.

Chapter 5 begins by focusing on the last point: contemporary writings on modern India by Western authors. It comprises an open letter to Jeffrey Kripal. He uses a version of Freudian psychoanalysis to study the person of Ramakrishna and his mysticism. I show how violence is involved in this study of Ramakrishna Paramahamsa. I analyse his book from two different perspectives and demonstrate that violence emerges in the course of using such 'secular' discourses. One could argue that what is at fault is not the discourse itself but Kripal's use of psychoanalysis. I suggest that it is wrong to view the problem in this way. The problem lies elsewhere: it lies in the very nature of some intercultural dialogues.

In religious studies and elsewhere, there is a strong conviction about the role that dialogues play: by emphasizing and fulfilling the need for mutual understanding between people, such dialogues are supposed to reduce violence. In Chapter 6, two recent examples from Hinduism studies in the United States are analysed to show that precisely the opposite is true: dialogues about religion are often the harbingers of violence. This happens not because 'outsiders' have studied Hinduism or because the Hindu participants in the dialogue are religious 'fundamentalists', but because of the requirements of reason as they are embodied in such dialogues. The chapter generalizes this argument to show that there is no prima facie harmony between the requirements of reason and the requirements of symmetry in certain dialogical situations. Where religious violence is on the rise, thoughtless slogans are no substitutes for a study of the history of religious dialogues in a different way.

Chapter 7 pushes the general argument about intercultural dialogues further. It shows that the conclusions of the previous chapter hold good in many intercultural settings as well and, in so doing, raise questions about the implications for political theory and its dominant attempts to deal with cultural and religious diversity. Currently, political liberalism is seen as one of the best solutions to the problems of diversity. I try to argue that, by not reflecting seriously on the nature of rational dialogues, the different models of political liberalism of thinkers like John Rawls and Charles Larmore end up being hopelessly compromised. They are not capable of doing what they intend and promise.

What they promise, of course, is that a 'secular' liberal state will enable the containment of religious violence, because it can function as a neutral arbiter grounded in non-religious principles. In Chapter 8, I show that this is not the case by taking the Indian secular state as an example. There are few places in the contemporary world where the problems of religious pluralism are as acute as they are on the subcontinent. The Indian situation poses some fundamental

challenges to the existing political theory concerning religiou
toleration. As Indian society consists of both 'pagan traditions' an
'Semitic religions', the secular state confronts a set of difficultie
unknown to the Western cultural setting from which it originall
emerged. More specifically, by tackling the problem of religiou
conversion, this chapter shows that the dominant way of conceivin
state neutrality becomes problematic in the Indian context. Th
argument suggests that the post-Independence Indian state, modelle
after the liberal democracies of the West, is the harbinger of religiou
violence in India because of the way it conceives of state neutralit
More 'secularism' in India will end up feeding what it fights: the so
called 'Hindu fundamentalism'. Secularism breeds religious violence

In the Conclusion, I show why the attempt to reconceptualize Indi
studies is so important to all of us, including the Indian 'diaspora'.
show that the problems I have discussed in these chapters are also rea
issues for Indians living abroad, and why we should begin to tackl
them. I also indicate why, in this process, we so urgently need t
understand Western culture in a different way from before.

Taken together, this collection of essays—although writte
separately over the last decade—is unified. They introduce the reade
to a research programme that has been under development for th
last three decades. The essays do so using different styles and differen
formats. Even then, I hope they fulfil the author's ambition: to sho
why we need to reconceptualize India studies today.

CHAPTER 1

Culture and the Cultural
Problems, Pitfalls, and a Proposal

Unlike half a century ago, today, we can no longer state that 'virtually all cultural anthropologists take it for granted, no doubt, that culture is the basic and central concept of their science'. Among those anthropologists who do, though, there is still 'a disturbing lack of agreement as to what they mean by this term' (White 1959: 227). In the second half of the twentieth century, the bane of some of the social sciences has been the unending disputes about definitions. Anthropology has not been an exception to this trend. Like some other disciplines in the social sciences, debates about the concept of culture have generated much heat without shedding any light on the issue. Most of the methodological and philosophical arguments that some anthropologists use do not withstand serious scrutiny. In this sense, one cannot but think that much of this debate has to do with conceptual confusions. However, instead of countering these confusions at their root, many practitioners have tended to either beat a full-scale retreat into obscurantism, or come up with 'ever newer' definitions. Even though no one has counted their number after Kroeber and Kluckhohn (1952) identified 164 definitions of culture, one suspects that, today, there must be at least tenfold. I would like to begin this chapter by examining the theoretical solidity of the criticisms of the concept of culture.

Problems of the Culture Concept?

Instead of giving an overview of the objections against the concept (Brightman 1995) and rebutting them *ad seriatim*, in this section, I would like to identify some of the major problems underlying the arguments. I illustrate these problems by analysing citations from some recent debates. It will be the conclusion in this section that none of these forces us to abandon the concept of culture.

Words, Objects, and Definitions

Let me begin with the following claim from an edited volume which intends to argue that anthropology can have a life beyond culture:

> We have become increasingly dissatisfied with the traditional definition of culture within anthropology, by which culture is a highly patterned and consistent set of representations (or beliefs) that constitute a people's perception of reality and that get reproduced relatively intact across generations through enculturation. (Fox and King 2002: 1)

Despite a certain ambiguity in the formulation, one could justifiably suggest that, here, Fox and King are dissatisfied with the definition of the English word 'culture' in traditional anthropology. Under this interpretation, consider how they continue: 'The homogeneity and continuity that this traditional definition assumes, along with its failure to address social inequality and individual agency, distresses many anthropologists' (ibid.). In this citation, they suggest that this definition assumes 'homogeneity and continuity'. Of what, though? The only defensible and consistent interpretation of the above citation is to say the following: the traditional definition assumes that culture (in the world) is homogeneous and continuous. Further, it is also their suggestion that this definition fails to address the real issues (in the world, again) of social inequality and individual agency. What is wrong with this set of criticisms?

First, it is important to note what the definition of a word from some language or another does: it identifies what requires defining (the English word 'culture' in our case), and provides a definition of that word (say, 'a highly patterned and consistent set of interpretations'). Such a definition merely stipulates how some theorist or another uses a particular word and lays down its meaning. It cannot do anything else. Therefore, in so far as Fox and King talk about the 'assumption' of the traditional definition, they can speak only about (some) anthropologists assuming 'the truth' of some set of statements that are independent of the definition of the English word 'culture'. Even if we want to say that the anthropologists, who use this traditional definition, *assume* that culture in the world is 'homogeneous and continuous', such an assumption is not a part of the definition of the word. Such statements either define the word 'culture' (that is, they belong to the *definiens*), or they do not: in *neither* of the two cases, are they *assumptions* of the definition of the word 'culture'. In the first case, it is a part of the definition of the word 'culture'; in the second case, it is not.

Second, a definition assumes nothing about whether or not there exist entities or processes in the world that provide a reference to that word. For instance, one can define logical connectives like 'and', 'or', 'if ... then'. These definitions carry no ontological assumptions in the sense of asserting that these connectives refer to some or another entity or process in the world. Equally, one can define mathematical operations such as addition, subtraction, multiplication and division with respect to real numbers. If, and only if, there is a one-to-one mapping *explicitly postulated* between the domain of numbers, its structure and the mathematical operations, and the domain of a set of objects in the real world, only then can we claim, for example, that the mathematical operation of, say, addition, is mapped to the operation of concatenation in the real world. Otherwise, we cannot. After all, if definitions *carry* ontological assumptions, then one will have to say that all mathematical entities—from numbers to sets—also exist. Yet, centuries of discussions in both mathematics and philosophy of mathematics about the existence of mathematical entities tell us that using a definition does not entail (or presuppose) a specific ontological thesis about the existence of such entities. That is to say, this traditional definition cannot be said to 'assume' that culture—in the world—is either homogeneous or continuous; only an *ancillary hypothesis* can make such a claim. The practitioners, who use this definition, might or might not assent to the truth of such a hypothesis; there is no logical compulsion on them to do either of the two. For instance, they could say that they 'do not know whether culture is homogeneous and/or continuous', and yet continue to use the traditional definition.

Third, Fox and King further speak of the failure of this definition to address social inequality and individual agency. Edward Said (1978: 325) and Lila Abu-Lughod (1991: 137–8) anticipate this charge. 'Social inequality' is a normative judgement about some states of affairs in the world. Even if we were to believe that norms and facts are intertwined, what does it mean to demand that the definition of an English word address the issue of social inequality? What would it mean for some definition of 'culture' to address these problems? Are the authors demanding that such a definition should either formulate the problem of social inequality in the world or solve it? How can any definition ever do this? In the same rhetorical vein as Fox and King, one could also ask further questions: why just social inequality? Why not also address ecological imbalance, dietary deficiencies, the problem of AIDS, and so on? Clearly, this demand makes no sense at all.

Similar comments apply to their demand that the definition should address individual agency. Among other things, the notion of individual agency is a part of a philosophical and/or psychological theory about the nature of human beings. What does the 'failure to address itself' to a moral judgement and a philosophical/psychological theory mean when formulated as a criticism of the definition of a word from the English language? (See also Sydel Silverman, 2002.)

Analogous confusions abound in many discussions about the failure of the so-called traditional definition of culture: there is a total lack of clarity about what definitions are and what we should expect them to do. As one further example, consider the following remark by Ingold (1993: 212):

In effect, the concept of culture operates as a distancing device, setting up a radical disjunction between ourselves, rational observers of the human condition, and those other people ...

Obviously, Ingold is not merely criticizing some or the other definition of the English word 'culture'. He is saying something else as well, for which there is no shred of proof: any and every definition of the word 'culture' (this is why he speaks about *the* concept of culture) functions as a 'distancing device' that sets up a 'radical disjunction'. Read literally, this thesis makes no sense: between any two discrete entities (whether between objects in the world, or among a set of ideas, or in the continuum of natural numbers, or between a *word* and its *definition*, or whatever else), there is 'distance'. The only object that is not 'distant' from itself is the object in question: as long as there are two objects in the world, there is 'distance' between them. How 'radical' the disjunction is between any two objects in the world depends, not upon the definition of a word from a natural language, but upon a theory which tells us about the nature of that 'distance' and 'disjunction'. In short, this is the first problem in contemporary discussions about the concept of culture: *There is no clarity on what a definition is and what it should or can do.*

Multiple Meanings

The second major problem in the discussions is the following: *One argues for the rejection of the word 'culture' because of the multiple meanings the word carries.* Terry Eagleton (2000: 32) takes a step in this direction: 'It is hard to resist the conclusion that the word "culture" is both too broad and too narrow to be greatly useful. Its anthropological meaning covers everything from hairstyles and drinking habits to how to address your husband's second cousin ...' The basic problem is about the very intelligibility of the first sentence: How can a word from a natural language be either broad or narrow? A charitable reading of Eagleton might make one want to say that he does not mean the word (even though he explicitly speaks about the word) but has its anthropological meaning (whatever that might mean) in mind. Even then, one needs more arguments to reject the use of a word from a language than to simply notice that the word carries multiple meanings.

Clausen (1996: 383) tries to provide us with one such argument: 'What [the] contradictory uses of culture suggest is that the objects the word used to identify, which were always more fluid and slippery than many anthropologists liked to admit, are now close to moribund.' This citation is hardly a model of clarity: it is simply impossible to figure out how contradictory 'uses' of any word can suggest to us that the objects to which the word refers are close to 'dying'. Is this some kind of a thesis on how people use language, the relation between language-use and what exists in the world? If language speakers use some word in contradictory ways, should we assume that such contradictory use suggests that the entities to which these words refer in the world are 'close to moribund'?

Consider the word 'eel', where the word identifies a slippery object, and 'water' which identifies a fluid. The sentence, 'eels in water', identifies slippery and fluid objects. What is wrong with this 'identification', irrespective of whether or not the eel is 'more slippery' than we care to admit? Surely, this is an irrelevant consideration. (Of course, Clausen is using a metaphor here. I shall shortly take up the issue of the use of metaphors.) As far as identifying 'moribund' objects is concerned, just because ancient Greek is moribund, this does not create any special identification problems, does it?

Furthermore, it is difficult to understand what Clausen means by 'contradictory uses'. We use 'pipe' to refer to a certain kind of device for smoking tobacco; a tubular wind instrument; a hollow cylinder or tube through which something may pass; a hollow instrument used for suturing wounds; and a large container of definite capacity for storing solids or liquids. The word refers to many other objects in scientific terminology and in slang. Naturally, many of these objects have mutually exclusive properties, but this does not make our *use* of the word 'pipe' contradictory. The multiplicity of meanings might sometimes give rise to the fallacy of equivocation: using a word in more than one sense, while convinced that one is being consistent. This, however, is the mistake of particular minds, which has nothing to do with the fact that a word has many meanings.

Can one really argue in favour of abandoning the use of a word because it has many meanings? Imagine how poor the English language would become if one were to abandon the use of a word because it carried multiple meanings! Formulated as a demand, this idea of meaning is an antiquated philosophical story: James Mill, for instance, used this 'theory' to trash the Sanskrit language because, Mill said, unlike English, Sanskrit words often carried multiple meanings.

Language and Philosophy

Then there are the philosophical sins: reification and essentialism. The charge that the concept of culture leads us into reification goes back more than five decades (Radcliffe-Brown 1940: 10–11; Bennett 1954: 172; White 1959: 239; Brightman 1995: 512; Stolcke 1995: 12). Recently, Keesing (1994: 302) reminded us that 'our conception of culture almost irresistibly leads us into reification and essentialism'. What are the issues here?

Reification is the process of transforming a process or a relationship (both of which are in the world) into a substance (also in the world) in real time. While this is one interpretation of 'reification', this process requires an active intervention by an agent in the world. One does not quite see what is objectionable about this intervention, or why. If transforming a process into a substance is required for some purpose or another, what is intrinsically wrong with it?

Quite possibly, these authors are referring to something else, namely to a cognitive process, when they talk of reification. Here, there are three possibilities; it refers to: (a) conceiving relations between people in terms of properties (or attributes) of people; or (b) conceiving relations between people as relations between objects; or (c) conceiving a process as an object. There is nothing intrinsically objectionable in the first case: we say that magnets attract iron filings, while we know that attraction is a force that a magnetic field exerts on iron filings. Equally, what is wrong with calling someone a father (that is, attributing the property of 'fatherhood' to an individual) when 'being a father of' is a relation between two individual human beings?

This brings us to the second possibility. Reification looks at relations between people as relations between objects. Even if we assume that this is objectionable, we need to figure out how the definition of a word (which is what a 'conception' is) could lead us almost irresistibly to committing this sin. What is involved here is a cognitive process. Hence, there is only one possible way: the conception logically compels us to reify. ('Logical compulsion' is the only possible way for us to be 'almost irresistibly' led in a cognitive process.) Such a logical compulsion could conceivably operate on us if, and only if, reification were a *logical consequence* of some definition or the other. However, this is impossible: *definitions have no logical consequences; only the theories that embed them, do*. Because of this, *contra* Keesing and others, we can conclude that 'our conception of culture' definitely cannot be guilty of the sin of reification.

Let us take up the third possibility: conceiving a process as an object together with the other philosophical sin, namely, essentialism, because the objections are pretty much the same. Essentialism is an ontological thesis on what exists in the world and on the nature of that existence. The objection against essentialism often amounts to the claim that the concept of culture ignores the internal variety of human social existence: 'The most dangerously misleading quality of

the notion of culture is that it literally flattens out the extremely varied
ways in which the production of meaning occurs in the contested
field of social existence' (Friedman 1994: 207). On the one hand, it
is unclear how the notion of culture can be guilty of such a sin. If
the biological notions of 'species' (in the singular) and '*Homo sapiens
sapiens*' do not flatten out biological variety, why should 'culture' do
so? On the other hand, this type of criticism confronts an obvious
question: Why not provide a definition of the word 'culture' that does
not have this 'misleading quality'? Why can Friedman not say that
'culture' means 'the extremely *varied ways* in which the production of
meaning occurs in the contested field of social existence'?

The second fear about essentialism is that it does not allow for
dynamics and internal development because it requires static essences.
This is philosophical nonsense: nothing prevents a philosopher from
postulating 'dynamic essences' that can grow and develop. In fact,
even Aristotle speaks of 'dynamic entelechy', while speaking about
individual essences. However, instead of pursuing the path of making
sense of dynamic essences, let us look at how this worry is expressed
in anthropological literature.

One suggests that the notion of culture generates the illusion
that 'cultural sets' are fixed, unitary and bounded: 'Once we locate
the reality of society in historically changing, imperfectly bounded,
multiple and branching social alignments ... the concept of a fixed,
unitary, and bounded culture must give way to a sense of the fluidity
and permeability of cultural sets' (Wolf 1982: 387; see also, Kahn
1989). In his spirited defence of the concept of culture, Christoph
Brumann (1999: s1) summarizes this concern of the critics of 'culture'
as follows: 'The major concern of the skeptical discourse on culture
is that the concept suggests boundedness, homogeneity, coherence,
stability, and structure, whereas the social reality is characterized by
variability, inconsistencies, change and individual agency ...'

Let us focus on these supposed defects of the concept of culture.
The first is that it is 'bounded'. However, this is true of all concepts:
any and every concept (that is, the meaning of a word) is 'bounded'
if the language in question (whether artificial or natural) contains
more than one word and gives more than one meaning to that
word. The second defect of the culture concept is supposed to be its
'homogeneity'. However, this is not a property of words or concepts

or example, it makes no sense to say that the meaning of the word
:ar' is homogeneous. Nor could one say that the word 'car' has the
ame meaning across the globe: there are languages where 'car' means
 trolley and 'auto' means a car. (An 'auto', in India and Sri Lanka,
n the other hand, refers to an 'autorickshaw'.) The third defect of
ie culture concept is supposed to be its 'coherence'. Asking whether
ne preferred an incoherent to a coherent concept might smack of
ietoric. Instead, let us note that coherence is mostly a property of
 structured set of sentences. However, reading charitably, it could
iean that the words used to define the meaning of some word (the
efiniens) should not be internally contradictory. The fourth defect
f the concept of culture is supposed to be its stability. This could
iean that the meaning of the word 'culture' is either synchronically
r diachronically unchanging. No word in any language has the
:cond kind of stability. Regarding the fifth defect, it is unclear what
emanding a structure for the meaning of a word means. In other
vords, to the extent that these five defects form a coherent set, they
re not 'defects' in any sense of the term: these properties are true of
ny and every word, whether from a natural or an artificial language.
Iow do these properties—which all concepts have—become defects
f the culture concept?

Further, if we look at the contrast set in Brumann's summary, 'the
ocial reality', the situation is more puzzling: What is more bounded
ian individual agency? Surely, the word 'individual' distinguishes
etween several agents. When one speaks of 'variability', what
aries? Because temperature varies across the globe, this does not
iean that some measured temperature at some particular time
nd place does not exist. Temperatures do change, but this does not
iean that the concept of temperature has to be rejected because it
 'bounded' or 'stable'. More than anything else, here, one rejects
ie definition of a word (namely, 'culture') because some other
henomenon (referred to by the word 'social reality') exhibits other
roperties.

In short, this is the third major problem in the discussions: while
uthors appeal to theories from philosophy, they do not attempt to
mulate its rigour. In this sense, the problem emerges not because
eople reject philosophical theses but because *they make use of them*
) casually.

Saving 'Culture' from Its Critics

In the 1920s, anthropologists and sociologists defended the validity of the culture concept against psychologists and other sceptics (Willey 1929). In the following fifty years, they continued to argue for a science of culture (White 1949; Weiss 1973). In the late 1970s and 1980s, when it was stated that 'the concept died in American anthropology, or at least is now in the process of dying' (Moore 1974: 546), and that 'the old culture concept is moribund'(Wolf 1980), anthropologists at least mourned the potential loss and tried to revive the concept (Bohannan 1973; Peterson 1979; Flannery 1982; Yengoyan 1986). In the last two decades, however, many of their inheritors have renounced one of the main contributions of American anthropology to the human sciences: 'It may be true that the culture concept has served its time' (Clifford 1988: 274); 'perhaps anthropologists should consider strategies for writing against culture' (Abu-Lughod 1991: 147). Anyway, 'the concept of culture ... will have to go' (Ingold 1993: 230). Or, as Adam Kuper puts it, 'the more one considers the best modern work on culture by anthropologists, the more advisable it must appear to avoid the hyper-referential word altogether ...'

This is how Geertz (1995: 45) talks about the issue: '... it took ... a little ... longer to realize that a conception of culture as a massive causal force shaping belief and behavior to an abstractable pattern ... was not very useful ... Something a good deal less muscular is needed, something a good deal more reactive, quizzical, watchful, better attuned to hints, uncertainties, contingencies, and incompletions.' Three different issues are combined in these thoughts. First, there is the definition of the word 'culture': a massive causal force that shapes belief and behaviour into a pattern. Second, there are independent ontological assumptions about the existence and nature of this causal force: such a causal force exists in the world; it gives a shape to belief and behaviour; and, perhaps, such a shape is 'abstractable'. It is unclear whether Geertz wants to say that such a pattern is 'abstractable' by the mind (and, therefore, exists only 'in the mind'); or whether he claims that such an 'abstractable' pattern ('abstractable' in the sense that the pattern is capable of being described in the abstract, that is, structurally) is a part of the world.

The third issue is about the difference between mixing metaphors and committing category mistakes. One can perhaps understand (in some vague sense) the metaphor that we need a less 'muscular' notion of culture. However, when he describes the nature of the 'concepts' which we do need—namely, 'reactive, quizzical, watchful, better attuned to hints, uncertainties, contingencies, and incompletions'—many problems arise. 'Reactive' is a notion applicable to many chemical substances and biological organisms; 'quizzical' and 'watchful' are used to speak of biological organisms, normally those with a developed nervous system; 'hints' can be understood only by those creatures which understand intentional behaviour; 'uncertainties' can be extended metaphorically to organisms with a highly evolved nervous system; 'contingencies' is a notion understandable only by those beings who possess the concept of 'necessity'; 'incompletions' is understandable only by those beings who understand the contrast set of 'completions'. To use them as though they were the properties of words from a natural language, or as though they were properties of concepts, is to commit a huge set of category mistakes. Such usage cannot be considered 'metaphorical' anymore because Geertz draws conclusions—scientific and philosophical—based on such ascriptions.

On the Nature of Confusions

The citations we have seen so far reflect confusions—from the linguistic to the philosophical. Some of these linguistic confusions, first, have to do with not distinguishing between the 'use' and the 'mention' of a word, a distinction that has been in place for more than a century in Western intellectual tradition: how the word 'culture' is used in the anthropological discourses is distinct from mentioning the culture in question. Second, an equally old distinction between a word and a concept is lost sight of: one might criticize the definition of a word (say, the English word 'culture'), but to call for 'abandoning the concept of culture' is to argue that the word 'culture' has to be divested of all meanings *because* some meanings are 'contested'.

As though these linguistic confusions were not enough, there are also philosophical confusions. First, one confuses a word in a language (or even its meaning) with the world. We use language to talk about the world but our words are not co-extensive with the world. Second, one does not seem to realize that nothing about any definition either guarantees or precludes reference: we may define the word 'culture' as 'a stable pattern in society'. However, on its own, this definition does not tell us whether there is such a stable pattern, or tell us how to go about finding such a stable pattern. Even if we were to fail to find such a stable pattern, this would not damage the definition because, in a manner of speaking, all definitions stipulate: they tell us how someone uses the word 'culture'. Third, because of the above two considerations, one fails to notice that the definitions of a word are ontologically neutral: if we define 'unicorn' as 'a magical horse with a single horn that only virgins can see', there is no existential claim that either such a magical horse does exist or that it can be seen only by virgins. The same applies to the definitions of the word 'culture'. Fourth, the definition of a word in a language does not tell us what the world is like, unless such a definition is part of a theory that claims to describe the world. The suggestion, therefore, that a definition 'ignores' the reality that the world is, or that it ignores 'inequalities, power and agency', makes no sense.

One could go on thus, but I trust that the point has been made. Largely, all tall claims notwithstanding, most of the above citations identify pseudo-problems arising out of conceptual confusions. If these are the 'failures' of the concept of culture, then it is no failure: *none of these problems requires the jettisoning of the concept of culture.*

However, the concerns about the culture concept have also given rise to an interesting suggestion, namely, the suggestion to shift from 'culture' to the 'cultural':

One possible escape ... might be to abandon the talk of different 'cultures' altogether, because of its taint of essentialism, but to retain some of the uses of the adjectival 'cultural' (Barnard and Spencer 1996: 142). (C)ultural ... (t)he adjectival form downplays culture as some innate essence, as some living, material thing. (Borofsky 1994: 245)

Brightman (1995: 510) indicates that this preference for the 'cultural' instead of 'culture' is widespread in contemporary anthropology. I will explore the benefits of this suggestion; in doing so, we will also move beyond the disputes about the definitions.

Culturality and Cultural Difference

Even though I have focused on tracing some conceptual confusion surrounding the debate about the definition of the word 'culture', it does not suffice to explain away the unease of all these anthropologists as though it were all a matter of doing 'good philosophy'. There is a reason why such an explanation is not acceptable. Most of these, and other, anthropologists are not only well known in their domain but are also practitioners with many decades of fieldwork experience. Their dissatisfaction, then, stems from this expert-knowledge as well. That is to say, not being novices in the field (like, say, a recently graduated medical student), they express the discomfort of experts (say, of people with many decades of medical experience). Even if one has not articulated one's expert-knowledge adequately, it remains true that these experts converge on two points: (a) a negative judgement regarding the notion of 'culture'; and (b) a positive endorsement of the adjectival use of 'cultural'. We have seen that their negative judgements do not withstand scrutiny. However, I think that their positive endorsement has merit. Therefore, I will now focus on elaborating on the second of their two judgements in one particular direction.

The Question of Cultural Difference

Consider the question that Moore raises in the italicized part of the following citation:

Mapping a region, delineating a culture area, or shading the regions in distinctive colors ... distorted reality because the cultural differences were conditional, not permanent, and shifting, not clear-cut. Yet there were distinctive differences between Serbs and Nuer and Sinhalese and French Canadians. *What makes them different?* (Moore 2004: 287; italics added.)

In order to see precisely what Moore's question is, let us assume that the French Canadians and the Sinhalese constitute two different cultures. One way of formulating his question (*using his words*) would then be: What makes these two cultures different? If the question is asked this way, we can come up with a whole laundry list of differences and, in the process, encounter almost every objection that has been raised in anthropological literature. Let me just mention some of these differences: the French Canadians use a heating system during winter whereas the Sinhalese do not; the Sinhalese eat spicy food whereas the French Canadians hardly use any spice; many Sinhalese believe in astrology and reincarnation, whereas the French Canadians are largely sceptical; many Sinhalese worship deities and figures of Indian origin, whereas the French Canadians usually either worship the Christian God or are agnostic; Sinhalese are usually brown-skinned, whereas the French Canadians are primarily white-skinned; family bonds play a very important role among the Sinhalese, whereas the French Canadians are individualistic; most Sinhalese are shy and non-aggressive, whereas most French Canadians are friendly but fiercely competitive; and so on and so forth.

While such talk—which has dominated colonial ethnography—could pass muster in a social gathering and is common in contemporary literature on cross-cultural management, no living anthropologist is likely to be caught dead with such descriptions. Why? From the many reasons that we could give, let me pick out one that is of importance to the argument. Some of the mentioned differences are climatological in nature; some are social; some differences are biological; yet others are psychological differences, and so on. In other words, there are many kinds of differences between cultures, but not all of them are *cultural differences*. Moore is not asking about 'the differences that exist' between the Sinhalese and the French Canadians alone. Instead, he is asking a question about the existence of cultural differences, if any, between these two communities. That is to say, he is suggesting that the notion of 'differences between cultures' is *not identical in meaning* with the notion of cultural differences. We can adequately capture this sense in the form of a question: *What makes a difference, any difference, into a cultural difference and not a social, psychological or biological difference?*

Of course, there is always a tendency to assume that cultural difference is the same as 'difference between cultures'. As an illustration, let us take Sir Edmund Leach. Consider what this leading exponent of British anthropology writes in his *Glimpses of the Unmentionable in the History of British Social Anthropology* (1984):

Anthropological accounts are derived from aspects of the personality of the author. How could it be otherwise? When Malinowski writes about Trobriand Islanders he is writing about himself. When Evans-Pritchard writes about the Nuer he is writing about himself. *Cultural Differences, though sometimes convenient, are temporary fictions.* (Cited in Merryl Davies 2002: 156)

Why does Leach make anthropological accounts derivative of the *personality* of the anthropologists and not, say, their sociality? Even better put, *why cannot an anthropological account also be derivative of the culturality of the individual anthropologist* instead being a derivative only of that individual's 'personality'?

The Notion of Culturality

An old insight from anthropology tells us that 'in a literal sense cultures have never met nor will ever meet' (Hallowell 1945: 175). Any contact or communication between cultures occurs only when individuals meet each other (Boas 1928: 236; Radcliffe-Brown 1940: 10–11). It is at that point of contact that we notice cultural differences. Whether as a tourist or as an anthropologist, it is only when in contact with some individuals that one is forced to exclaim: 'Oh! They are culturally different'. However, what do we notice when we notice 'cultural differences'? Here is the first approximation of an answer: we notice the *culturality* of individuals when we notice cultural differences.

This might strike us a bit mysterious at first glance. However, this has to do with our unfamiliarity with the terminology. Therefore, I will use this word for a while before trying to make theoretical sense of the same. When we meet individual human beings, we routinely talk of being struck by their 'physicality', their 'intellectuality', and, of course, their 'personality'. We perceive individual persons through their personality; why then can we not say we perceive culturized individuals through their culturality?

Let us assume in the rest of what follows that, in any individual, many elements are fused together: her genetic predispositions, her psychological uniqueness, her sociality, her culturality ... In this sense, an individual exemplifies, at the least, three things which have come together: her sociality, her culturality, and her personality. I will not talk here of the first, but only very briefly of the other two.

The relation between the 'culturality' and the 'personality' of an individual is not a matter of definition but requires theoretical and empirical research. In the way that some processes in individuals eventuate in their becoming persons, and thereby acquire their personalities, so do other processes eventuate in individuals acquiring their culturality. How a person acquires her personality is a research question in psychology. Similarly, I would suggest that anthropological theory and practice should study the development of culturality. That is to say, the issue is not one of providing adequate definitions of personality and culturality; instead, it is a *problem for research in both cases.*

When we talk about the culturality of individuals, we are always confronted with the following question: How much of the difference between individuals is 'psychological' and how much of it is 'cultural'? At this stage, without further research, none can answer this question. Nevertheless, it draws our attention to an important issue that clarifies the meaning of the word 'culturality' in a preliminary way, namely, that culturality involves at least two dimensions: a dimension which is, in one sense, experiential (that is, the unique way in which an individual experiences the world); and in another—which is both learnable and teachable and, in this sense—socially shared.

When one speaks of the 'learnable' and the 'teachable', the standard way of approaching this issue has been to *focus on the what*. That is to say, research has asked the question of what is taught and what is learnt in a specific community. To this, there is but one possible answer: one is taught, and one learns attitudes and beliefs. Consequently, the anthropological discipline has concentrated on studying the beliefs of specific communities while assuming that the attitudes are embodiments of certain types of beliefs. I suggest concentrating *on the how*. Culturized individuals have not only learnt some things but they have also learnt to learn.

Theorizing Cultural Difference

We need some conceptual apparatus to go further: a hypothesis about cultural differences (Balagangadhara 1994). In broad terms, we can conceive learning as the way in which an organism makes its environment habitable: learning is the activity of making a habitat. Compared to other animals, the human species suffers disadvantages from several points of view: it takes a (relatively) long time for the human infant to be able to fend for itself; its physiology is not suited for living unaided under extreme climatic and weather conditions; it has no natural prey; and so on. Such a species—if it is to survive at all—will have to place an enormous premium on its ability to make the environment(s) habitable, that is to say, learning is extremely crucial to its survival.

Evolutionary theory further tells us that the sexual act is an inefficient way of guaranteeing progeny (Ridley 1993). One of the functions of sex amongst human beings is to facilitate pair bonding, and, to some extent, group formation. Coping with groups has been as important as coping with nature for the survival of our species. Thus, human groups constitute the second environment of the human infant.

When we look at human beings and their learning processes from the point of view of these two environments, we see that the activity of making a habitat is complex: one has to learn to live with the group; one has to learn to live in the bigger environment.

All human beings are socialized within the framework of groups. I am using 'socialization' in the broadest sense possible, that is, living with others. Who these others are, what it means to live with them, are things that an organism learns when it is socialized. Largely, what the human organism learns depends on what is transmitted to it. The resources of a group—its customs, traditions, institutions—constitute the reservoir from which the organism learns.

The same reservoir puts constraints on both what is transmitted and the mechanisms of transmission. Child-rearing, formal and informal schooling, family life, group interactions—these are the mechanisms of transmission from one generation to another. These mechanisms themselves have evolved, either through deliberation or unintended discovery processes, constrained by the nature of that which requires transmission. Further, what is actually a learning process—when looked at from the point of view of the organism that is socialized—is also a teaching process if looked at from the vantage point of those who socialize this organism. These people also draw upon the resources of the group to which they belong.

Methods and ways of teaching an organism will teach if, and only if, they dovetail into the processes of learning. Now, the question is this: Are we genetically compelled to learn in any one particular way? Evolutionarily speaking, I believe that the answer will have to be in the negative because of the great diversity of environments: not only have human beings structured their groups differently during the course of history, but they have also occupied different regions on earth. It is important to note that the argument from the point of view of diversity does not establish conclusively that we are not 'programmed' to learn in any one specific way. It could still be the case that there is one learning process (unidentified at the moment), which is flexible enough to be applied in a variety of ways. Nevertheless, given the variety of human achievements, at this moment, it is more attractive to speak of different kinds of learning processes.

Configurations of Learning

For human infants born into a group, learning involves going-about in the wider environment and going-about in the social environment. What they learn from their group are the goings-about which are transmitted to them. Mostly, the broader environment is accessible to them through the social environment, and it is the latter which forms the goings-about in the world.

One of the differences between human groups is the way they are structured. That is, human beings have created different kinds of social environments. Because learning involves going-about in the world, it is plausible to suggest that cultural differences will have 'something' to do with differences in the learning processes.

Present across different groups are several kinds of learning processes: the kind required to build societies and groups; the kind that creates poetry, music and dance; the kind required to develop theories and speculations. These different kinds of learning processes are the common adaptive strategies developed by each human group which has survived as a group. Groups transmit these learning processes to their members. The latter, in their turn, learn them to a different degree and in different combinations.

Since the processes of learning also involve meta-learning, namely, learning to learn, the individual learns as the 'teachers' teach. That is, different kinds of learning processes are coordinated so that one kind of learning process subordinates other learning processes to itself. Cultural differences have to do with the differences in these *configurations of learning*.

An individual organism born into a human group is taught the use of the resources that socialize. That is, learning is not just the activity of making a habitat but also meta-learning in the use of the resources of socialization. In the process of learning (making a habitat) and meta-learning (using the resources of socialization), the organism builds its culturality.

That is to say, configurations of learning not only teach, but they also impart to the learners the ability to learn in particular ways. Culturization, on this account, is not only about *how* a specific configuration of learning teaches; it is also about *the how* of learning and meta-learning (learning to learn). The learning and the teaching processes make use of the same resources—the mechanisms of socialization—in both learning and teaching. Ranging from family interactions, friendships, peer-group interactions through stories, rituals and religious ceremonies, to schools, factories, clubs, associations—the variety of mechanisms is both wide and immense. Consequently, the extent to which individuals are able to acquire meta-learning is the extent to, and the manner in which, they are able to draw upon the resources of socialization to build, sustain, and modify the structures of their experience. An individual does not merely draw upon these resources. The more important point is that such use takes place in particular ways. That is to say, *the how* of an individual's meta-learning helps that individual in learning.

Dimensions of Culturality

If, as said above, individual culturality has two dimensions—the experiential and the teachable—and culturization involves talking about how a configuration of learning teaches, then, one is suggesting that a configuration of learning generates these two dimensions in an individual. Because the experiential dimension is unique, there is only one instantiation of that dimension. Because it is *sui generis*, it is not possible to compare the experiential dimension of individual culturality and speak of an exemplary 'Westerner', or 'Indian', or 'African'. Consequent to this, one can also say that there is no 'perfect' or 'imperfect' example of individual culturality. That is to say, being a culturized individual implies that there is no end to being culturized, but only a way of speaking about 'being more proficient' and 'being less proficient'.

Even if experience is unique to the individuals in question, it does not of course mean that the structure of their experiences is unique, too. These structures are learnt and built up by individuals. Because of this, at one level, we are justified in speaking about the relation between an individual and a configuration of learning by looking at the extent to which such an individual has acquired meta-learning.

By deploying the notions of individual culturality, the how of socialization, and the use of its resources, we can avoid issues of having to identify 'cultures' either spatially or temporally. Further, where there is no possibility of talking about an exemplary 'Turk', 'Indian', or 'Westerner', there is also no danger of speaking about either the monolithic nature or the diversity of one culture or another.

What we have is individual culturality (with a unique dimension and a teachable dimension to their culturality) using some resources of socialization in particular ways.

Can individuals be multicultural the way they can be multilingual? For instance, would it be sufficient if someone were to say that it is difficult to define language—because the boundaries between dialects, between periods, between speech and gesture, are hard to define— and that, therefore, we should merely talk of linguistic difference? I believe that it is a category mistake to speak of an individual as a 'multicultural' being. Such an individual's culturality would fuse different ways of using the resources of socialization but the individual would still have a 'single' culturality, like a single 'personality'. 'Multiculturality' is a concept that is applicable to a situation where different (that is, multi-) culturality is present. Furthermore, to speak of a 'multicultural' individual is to presuppose what is rejected in anthropology: the presence of clear and fixed boundaries between 'cultures'. The analogy with language, too, fails because, while it might be difficult to draw boundaries within a language (between dialects and periods, say) there is no problem in drawing a boundary between the Thai language and English, for instance.

What is a Cultural Difference?

Let us now return to Moore's question and Leach's claim. 'What makes the Sinhalese and the French Canadians culturally different?' admits of an answer, capable of empirical and theoretical confirmation and/or refutation: the *way* in which individuals from these groups go-about with each other, make use of stories, social associations, family relations, tells us what makes them culturally different. We can also answer our reformulation of Moore's question: What makes a difference, any difference, into a *cultural* difference and not a social, psychological or biological difference? Some difference (between individuals) is a cultural difference if it *entails a specific way of using the resources of socialization*.

Leach can now be refuted, while pointing out something intriguing even in his mistake. Cultural differences are not fiction, whether temporary or permanent; they are real, observable and empirically describable. Anthropological accounts are derivative of individual culturality, that is, such accounts are both sui generis and patterned. Consequently, they are both 'subjective' and 'objective' at the same time. The first is true because there is a unique dimension to the experiences of anthropologists and thus to their accounts. The second, too, is true because, in the example of Leach, they tell us how a Westerner has described these cultures. That is to say, a Western culturality is also expressed in these anthropological accounts. In this sense, we can also study and understand the nature of 'Western culture' by studying the way Western people have described the other peoples of the world. Since Edward Said, it has become commonplace to note that 'Orientalism' has a pattern and a structure: we can make sense of this pattern as a cultural pattern without 'reifying' either 'the West' or 'the Orient'.

We are in a better position to understand the practitioners' dissatisfaction with the existing notions of culture. There is a need to make good the theoretical sense of the adjectival use of the 'cultural'. Against the background of this proposal—which has attempted to elucidate one possible way of understanding such an adjectival use— we can better appreciate their desire to reject the notion of 'culture': one should not draw indefensible kinds of spatial and temporal boundaries between human groups. However, as I have shown, we need not reject the notion of 'culture' in order to elucidate the notion of the 'cultural'. Nor do we need woolly ideas like 'hybridity' (Ohnuki-Tierney 2005), or take philosophical stances about the existence of essences in the world. We can continue with theory formation and fieldwork, provided, however, that we take care to develop interesting theories and hypotheses about the world.

CHAPTER 2

The Future of the Present
Rethinking the Post-colonial Project*

In the previous chapter, I spoke of an alternate way of conceptualizing cultural differences. I identified that it was different from the existing anthropological theories not merely by introducing terms like 'culturality' and 'configurations of learning', but also by embedding them in a hypothesis developed within an evolving research programme, which I call 'comparative science of cultures'. In a sense, this programme is new; in another sense, which I will explore in this chapter, it is not. It is important to emphasize the latter because, as I shall indicate in the next chapter, every generation's effort to develop new theories and novel research programmes is crucially dependent upon the contributions of the earlier generations. In this chapter, I will show how my research programme can be related to the earlier attempts.

I believe that there is a line of thinking in Edward Said's *Orientalism* which, if pursued consistently, leads us in the direction of a

* Some parts of this chapter were previously published in 1998 as 'The Future of the Present', *Cultural Dynamics*, 10(2), pp. 101–21, London: Sage Publications; and (with Marianne Keppens) in 2009 as 'Reconceptualizing the Postcolonial Project: Beyond the Strictures and Structures of Orientalism', *Interventions*, 11(1), pp. 50–68, London: Taylor and Francis.

comparative science of cultures. Many have rejected the message of his book; others have pursued its arguments in different ways. I will probe the phenomenon of 'post-Orientalism' without intending to map its contours either historically or conceptually. Instead, I focus on the questions: What is next after *Orientalism*? Does Said's work hint in the direction of an answer?

Let us begin by noticing the current status of post-colonial thinking. First, there are mounting criticisms of the merits of the project and its shrill defence. Second, there is an increasing disagreement among the post-colonial thinkers themselves, ranging from the identity of the field (what is post-colonial thinking?) to its finality (what is its goal?). Third, important questions have become obfuscated under an impenetrable jargon. Fourth, a narcissistic self-reflection is paralysing the practitioners in this domain.

Given these facts, this chapter attempts to refocus the discussion on a dormant thread in Said that has hardly been elaborated upon. Its explication will provide a much-needed *telos* or goal to post-colonial thinking. Such a refocusing is necessary not only for those who identify themselves as post-colonial thinkers but even for those who want to throw the baby out along with the bathwater. In this sense, this chapter will outline the challenges facing post-colonial thought (as a genre), and show exactly why facing up to this challenge is important for all of us today, and not just for post-colonial thinkers.

Said and *Orientalism*

It cannot be said of all books that they change our perception of the world. In a very literal sense, such a predicate applies to Said's *Orientalism*. Until this book arrived on the scene, all one saw was pieces and fragments. After 360-odd pages one saw—or, at least, one thought one saw—patterns, structures, consistencies, a *Zusammenhang*, instead of seeing blurred images, and feeling vague dissatisfactions. One of the most interesting intellectuals on the current Indian scene captures this experience beautifully:

I will long remember the day I read *Orientalism*. It must have been in November or December of 1980. In India, this season is classically called Hemanta and assigned a slot between autumn and winter. In Calcutta, where nothing classical remains untarnished, all that this means is a few weeks of uncertain temperature when the rains have gone, the fans have been switched off, and people wait expectantly to take out their sweaters and shawls. I remember the day because the house was being repainted and everything was topsy-turvy. I sat on the floor of the room in which I usually work, now emptied of its furniture, reading Edward Said whom I had never read before. I read right through the day and, after the workmen had left in the evening, well into the night. Now whenever I think of *Orientalism*, the image comes back to me of an empty room with a red floor and bare white walls, a familiar room suddenly made unfamiliar. (Chatterjee 1992: 194)

The bare room, the study with which he was familiar, had suddenly become different. Not alien, not new, not even just unfamiliar. It became intimately unfamiliar—the India that many of us saw as well.

However, without the shelves and their books, this table and that chair, and that particular sofa by the window, the room is not a study. It is a study, because of other reference points, too: this particular copy of Hegel's *Phenomenology*; that dog-eared version of Kautsky's *The Agrarian Question*; that heavily underlined, cheaply priced, Progress Publishers' edition of the third volume of *Capital*. This familiar paraphernalia—the European intellectual tradition—had transformed the bare room into a study and had us believe that we knew the latter as well as the proverbial back of our hands. Until that day then, when the painters arrived and one read *Orientalism* with the room made bare, and then the realization dawned: we know India through the reference points of Western intellectual tradition. If we know India through the organization effected by Western intellectual tradition, how would it look if organized otherwise?

Said's book raised these thoughts in the minds of many of us. It succeeded in provoking us into looking in particular directions by depicting the consistent manner in which the West had described the Orient over the centuries. The book suggested that these descriptions enjoyed stability, possessed durability and had a peculiar kind of objectivity. The entire story, as told by Said, held out a promise as well: thinking through the issues raised by the phenomenon of Orientalism would/could lead to the coalescing of a very interesting research programme. How did Said's book promise this?

'The Orient': A Place and an Idea

When Said uses the word 'Orient', it refers to a physical space in the world: 'The Orient is not only *adjacent* to Europe; it is also the *place* of Europe's greatest and richest *colonies* ...' (Said 1978: 1; italics added). Thus, it became a part of the material civilization of Europe: 'The Orient is an integral *part* of the European *material* civilization ...' (ibid. 2; italics in the original; emphasis mine).

In the Orientalist discourse, the word 'Orient' acquires meanings within a way of talking about a part of the world. That is, an entity in the world is talked about (or represented) in some particular way (as a mode of discourse).[1] Such a theoretical term is an 'idea' with a history; other ideas surround it to the extent that it is part of a theory.

Therefore as much as the West itself, the Orient is an idea that has a history and a tradition of thought, imagery, and vocabulary that have given it reality and presence *in and for* the West. The two *geographical entities* thus support and to an extent reflect each other. (Ibid. 5; italics added)

The 'it' in the first sentence above refers to the 'idea of the Orient'. In the second sentence, the reference is to the physical spaces that the Orient and the West occupy. Without Orientalism, the word 'Orient' would have no reference to the Orient (in the world). However, the Orient *cannot* be physically present in the West. Nor is Oriental culture a subset of western culture. Instead, it is present *for* the West as a reality, that is, both as a culture and as a geographical entity; it is present *in* Western culture as an idea ('the Orient'). This is how we must understand Said's claim that 'the Orient is an integral *part of the European ... culture*. Orientalism expresses and represents *that part ... as a mode of discourse*' (ibid. 2; italics added). The claim is not only that Western culture spoke about the Orient but also that both are constructed entities.[2]

'The Orient' as an Experiential Entity

I shall be calling *Orientalism* a way of coming to terms with the Orient that is based on the Orient's *special place* in European western experience. (Ibid. 1; italics added; emphasis in the original)

Three things are of importance here: (a) The Orient has a special place *in* the European Western experience, that is, there is an Orient, which is *an experiential entity* to Europeans. One can speak of the special place of this experiential entity only when we relate it to other such entities located within the experiential world of Europe; (b) This experiential entity allows Westerners to come to terms with the Orient in the world; (c) As a consequence, the word 'Orient' now *also* refers to an *entity-in-experience*.

This 'experiential entity' appears analogous to the Kantian '*Welt-für-uns*', except that the '*us*' here picks out the Western world. This Kantian distinction returns elsewhere in the book: 'Islam became an image ... whose function was not so much to represent Islam *in itself* as to represent it *for the medieval Christian*' (ibid. 60; italics added). In fact, one of the underlying themes in his book is some kind of a Kantian claim about the 'unknowability' of the things '*an sich*': the 'Orient', 'Islam', the 'Orientals', and such like.[3] At the same time, Said does not want to subscribe to its epistemological consequence: 'To believe that the Orient was created—or, as I call it, "Orientalized"—and *to believe that such things happen simply as a necessity of the imagination, is to be disingenuous*' (ibid. 5; italics added). This unresolved tension in Said expresses itself in many ways throughout his book. Many criticisms of Said arise from this fact, the most obvious of which is his inability to say what *falsity* in the Orientalist image means. Is there some way of making sense of his work without trashing it for being philosophically incoherent?

Yes, there is. That would involve taking the notion of *cultural difference* seriously without trivializing it. As I have argued in the previous chapter, such a difference cannot be understood only as a difference in beliefs or as difference in practices between cultures. This way of plotting cultural differences is Western: it is merely the dominant way of talking about the differences between cultures the way in which one culture, namely, Western culture, experiences them. In this sense, Orientalism does not express the Kantian epistemic distinction. Instead, it becomes *a culturally specific way of expressing the difference between the 'Orient' and the 'Occident'*. And that lies in the manner in which discourse about the 'Orient' expresses the specificity of Western culture. In short, Orientalism becomes *a cultural project* of Western culture.

There are two senses in which the Western way of talking about the East is a cultural project. The first sense is an obvious one: 'To speak of Orientalism therefore is to speak mainly, although not exclusively, of a British and French *cultural enterprise*, a project whose dimensions take in ... disparate realms ...' (ibid. 4; italics added). However, in what sense is it a cultural project, and not just a military or a political project? Said hints at another sense, a more profound one: 'Orientalism ... has less to do with the Orient than it does with "our" world' (ibid. 12); 'That Orientalism makes sense at all depends *more on the West than on the Orient* ... Orientalism responded *more to the culture* that produced it than to its putative object ...' (ibid. 22; italics added).

Thus, how the East was made into the Orient, the way a discourse 'Orientalizes' the Orient, expresses something specific to Western culture. Orientalism speaks about the culture that produced it, namely, Western culture. To study Orientalism, then, is also to study Western culture.

The Orientalist Discourse

As Said says repeatedly, 'racist', 'sexist', and 'imperialist' vocabulary does not transform something into an 'Orientalist' discourse, any more than the use of 'dichotomizing essentialism' does. These are not the constituent properties of the discourse but merely its *imageries*. Such a discourse is not exhausted by a set of stereotypical images of people from elsewhere and the value of their cultures. Said's characterization of Orientalism occurs almost *en passant*. 'Orientalism ... *is*, rather than expresses, a certain *will* or *intention* to understand, in some case control, manipulate, even to incorporate, what is manifestly a different (or alternative and novel) world' (Said 1978: 12). Therefore, '*Orientalism is better grasped as a set of constraints upon and limitations of thought than it is simply as a positive doctrine*' (ibid. 42; italics added). This means that 'limited vocabulary and imagery ... impose themselves as a consequence' (ibid. 60). These are the consequences of constraints imposed upon Western thinking for understanding a world different from its own.

It is trivially true that all human thought is subject to constraints. Such constraining is a *conditio sine qua non* for human thought: it is constrained by language and by the conceptual resources available to it. That is, human thinking is always a particular way of thinking. To draw an analogy: it is not that 'human language' is subject to arbitrary constraints like 'English', 'French' or 'Sanskrit' that vary in time and place. Only when we learn these languages do we speak human languages. In the same way, thinking in some particular way makes for human thinking. For the sake of convenience, one might want to identify the notion of 'some particular way' with the notion of 'constraints'. However, this epistemic *trivium* should not be confused with that set of constraints which brings forth Orientalism. While Orientalist thinking is *also* human thinking (because it, too, is subject to constraints), it is not Orientalist because it is human. Orientalist thought, as a particular way of *thinking*, is 'Orientalist' because it is a *particular way* of thinking. What constitutes this particular way of thinking? What *kind* of constraints transforms human thinking into Orientalist thinking? Said's remarks are en passant here as well:

[T]he Orient and the Oriental, Arab, Islamic, Indian, Chinese, or whatever, become repetitious pseudo-incarnations of some great original (Christ, Europe, the West) they were supposed to have been imitating. (Ibid. 62)

To the Westerner, however, the Oriental was always *like* some aspect of the West; to some of the German Romantics, for example, Indian religion was essentially an Oriental version of Germano-Christian pantheism. (Ibid. 67)

In Western descriptions of other cultures, the 'otherness' of the latter has disappeared: the West is the great original; others are but its pale imitations. Orientalism describes non-Western cultures in a way that effaces differences; a limited vocabulary and imagery are the consequences of this constraint.

Constraints and Their Consequences

Such a circumscription of Orientalism is not merely of hermeneutic value. It also has a heuristic potential in two distinct ways. On the one hand, it prevents us from raising sterile issues; on the other, it enables us to think through and identify genuine issues and challenges. However, these thoughts are about what this constraint does. Is it possible to specify the *nature* of this constraint?

On Constructing the Orient

When Europeans came to the East (say, India or Egypt) and wrote down their experiences, they were not hallucinating. They did not write about their dreams or compose stories. The reports had some structure, whether authored by a merchant, a missionary or a bureaucrat. Reflections about such reports at second remove, or reflections on experiences at a later stage or in a distant way, led to the finding of a structure in these experiences. That structure is the Orient and the discourse about it is the Orientalist discourse.

The previous sentence is not a description of how the pattern or the structure was found. It is not as though any one person pored over these reports (though many did), trying out one inductive hypothesis after another (even though a few were formulated), until a satisfactory pattern emerged. These reports lent structure to what the Europeans saw. At the same time, such reports filtered out phenomena that could not be structured in this fashion. Thus, these reports contributed to structuring a European *way* of seeing and describing phenomena in other cultures. Such texts—which embodied an explanatory structuring of European experiences—would end up becoming the 'ethnological data' or the 'anthropological fieldwork' that theories would later try to explain.[4]

'Orientalism' is *how* Western culture came to terms with the reality of the East. Thus, 'Orientalism' refers not only to the discourse about experience, but also to the way of reflecting about and structuring this experience. In this sense, even though Orientalism is a discourse about Western *cultural experience,* it is not direct but *oblique.* It is oblique because it *appears to be about other cultures.* It is also oblique because the experience is not directly reflected upon. It is *Western* in the sense that it refers to the experiences of the members of a particular culture. Orientalism is the Western way of thinking about its experience of non-Western cultures.[5] However, *it takes the form of an apparent discourse about the Orient.*[6]

Elsewhere, Said puts it this way: 'Psychologically, Orientalism is a form of paranoia, *knowledge of another kind,* say, from ordinary historical knowledge' (ibid. 72; italics added). Let us look at this contrast between the 'knowledge' that paranoia is and historical knowledge. In fact, this contrast is more to the point than might appear at first sight: the distinction is drawn between 'ordinary historical knowledge' (that is, factual knowledge of other peoples and places) and 'paranoid knowledge' (where the person confuses his experiences of other people with the knowledge about them). The paranoid thinks that his beliefs about other people are true descriptions and does not see them as reports about his experience. Not only that, but he also stubbornly refuses to accept that his beliefs about other people are merely reports of his experiences and that they are not descriptions of other people. This is also the case with Orientalism. The Orientalist stubbornly refuses to believe that he is talking about his experiences; instead, he maintains that he is reporting about other people as they are in the world. If this Saidian analogy is accepted, we can make sense of one of the extraordinary epistemological properties of Orientalism.

This information (about the Orient) seemed to be morally neutral and objectively valid; it seemed to have an epistemological status equal to that of historical chronology or geographical location. In its most basic form, then, Oriental material could not really be violated by anyone's discoveries, nor did it seem ever to be revaluated completely. (Ibid. 205)

It is obvious why Orientalism possesses this property. Because it is a report of a cultural experience, and because no 'fact' or 'discovery' can ever refute experience, Orientalist knowledge cannot be refuted. Nevertheless, it appears 'objectively valid' and 'morally neutral' because one *assumes* that it is a set of claims about the world instead of seeing it as a report of experience.

The fact that it is a discourse about the Western experience of the Orient *implies* that people from other cultures cannot directly participate in disputes concerning the nature and place of the 'others' within the Western experience. One could reproduce Western discussions in Indian journals and periodicals, but it would not contribute to the debate because it would still be about the Western experience of the other, an experience that non-Western people *cannot access.*

Yet, many Indians speak of 'an imaginative construction of the Orient' with incredible ease. What is *their* relationship to this Orient? How could they access this object? After all, Orientalist writings make claims about the entity that they, the Orientalists, saw. *How can Indians see what the Orientalists saw?* Actually, the problems are even more acute. How can Indians vigorously participate in the debate? How can they discuss Europe's cultural experience of the East with European intellectuals, as though they, the post-colonial intellectuals from the East, were privy to such an experience? How can they even make *sense* of the claims that the Orientalists make?

In the form of cognitive questions, *how do the imagined and imaginary constructions appear to those whose imaginative products they are not?*

How does the 'Orient' appear to those from the East? If Orientalism is culturally constrained, does the reception of this discourse in the East make it something other than what it is in the West? I propose assigning to these questions the *status* of a litmus test.

The Litmus Test

Like all massive and significant social processes (revolutions, fascism, war), colonization, too, is complex. It has involved not only the colonizing of land and resources, subjugating peoples and their traditions, but also colonizing their experience and imagination. When modern Orientalism provided descriptions of other peoples and traditions, the colonized took such portrayals *as descriptions of themselves*.

The colonial powers described the colonized, and the latter accepted these as true descriptions. 'Colonial experience' refers to this conjunction. Correspondingly, if it is not mere hot air, 'post-colonial experience' indicates at least two things: (a) 'our' experience occurs *after* (the chronological sense of 'post') such a colonial experience; (b) 'our' experience is 'beyond' (the logical sense of 'post') the colonial experience in that this experience *includes* reflections about the experiences of the colonizer and the colonized. Then, modern Orientalism *cannot* appear to 'us' as descriptions of '*ourselves*'—because that is how they appeared in the *colonial experience*. Consequently, *to dispute the truth status of such descriptions*, or to decorate them *ad nauseam, is to remain a colonial subject and stay within the framework of the colonial experience*.

The rationale for this suggestion must be obvious. First, modern Orientalism is *how* Western culture spoke about other cultures. It is also about *how* such a way of talking enabled them to go about with people from other cultures: modern Orientalism enabled the West to colonize people from other cultures. Second, to both the colonized and the colonizers, Orientalism appeared as a veridical discourse about the world: it was a description of the colonized and their culture. Third, colonial experience refers to the experiential world of both the colonizer and the colonized. Fourth, both the colonizer and the colonized lived according to these descriptions: the colonized as the Oriental, and the colonizer as the Occidental. That is how Orientalism 'orientalizes'. Fifth, this discourse defines the parameters of how the colonizer and the colonized engage with it: challenging the 'truth' of descriptions and negotiating a 'better place' for the Orient within the Western experiential world. This is a *colonial contestation*.

The 'post-colonial predicament' refers to the *continuity* between the colonial experience and the experience of those living in today's world. It is the predicament not only of Edward Said, but also of most post-colonial thinkers: *they, too, continue to share the colonial experience*. They naïvely believe that the experiential entity of another culture is accessible to them; they contest the 'construction' of the Orient, as though this entity or the discourse about it makes sense to them. They attempt to provide or negotiate a 'better place' for the Orient within the experiential world of the West. In this sense, the post-colonial predicament refers to the *persistence of a colonial consciousness* after direct colonization has ended.

The difference between the colonial and the post-colonial intellectual would have to lie in the type of questions asked and the kind of answers sought. When the post-colonial intellectual engages himself with Orientalist writings, he must not do what Raja Ram Mohan Roy or Dayananda Saraswati did. He should not contest the truth of the Orientalist discourse or its imagery, because that is what Frantz Fanon or Aimé Césaire did. Instead, he has to look at Orientalism in a way that his predecessors did not. Orientalism is the raw material from which he has to construct an understanding of how Orientalism was at all possible. Simply put, Orientalism should tell us more about the West than about the Orient.

The Nature of the Constraints

As indicated earlier on, Said was the first to alert us to the existence of the phenomenon of Orientalism. While he was unsure whether Western 'constructions' of other cultures followed the *logic* of the Orientalist discourse, we need entertain no such doubts. Our certitude is both factual and theoretical. It is factual because of the sheer size of empirical research conducted since *Orientalism*; it is theoretical because the constrained thinking of Western culture must also manifest itself in its descriptions of other cultures.

Given this certitude, what should our research do? Surely, it should answer questions like these: *Why* develop a critique of Orientalist discourse? What forms should such a critique take? What is its function? However, most of the research conducted after Said's book is an ad nauseam repetition of the following claims: *that* Orientalism exists; *that* 'knowledge' is related to 'power'; *that* 'essentialism' is a sin; *that* one should not think in 'dichotomies' or 'binary oppositions'. In short, it is all but clear *why* one should provide a critique of Orientalism except for purposes of self-edification.

As I have said, 'Orientalism' refers not only to how Europe experienced the Orient, but also to how it gave expression to that experience. In doing this, Western culture built and elaborated on conceptual frameworks, using resources available from its own culture. Those descriptions also generated Europe's description and understanding of itself and the world. That is, Europe's descriptions of other cultures have been fundamentally entwined in many untold ways with the way it has experienced the world. To understand the way in which the West has described itself, the world and others, is to begin to understand the West itself. The challenge of Orientalism, thus, is a challenge to understanding Western culture.

It is an epistemic truism to claim that descriptions of the world are framed using the concepts of the describer. Consequently, such a description does two things. First, it provides a partial description of the world. Second, being framed this way and not that or another way, the description tells us something about the framer of such a description. This epistemic truism has immensely profound consequences on the subject matter. If constancy, consistency, and durability are present in the descriptions by the West of itself and others, then such descriptions tell us much about the culture that has produced them.

In this sense, the Western description of the Orient and its self-description are like two faces of the same coin. The constraint imposed upon the way the West experiences other cultures has partly to do with its self-image. What it thinks of itself, in turn, is parasitic upon what it thinks of other cultures. In other words, it looks as though two sets of constraints are operative here. One set of constraints, namely, its self-image, constrains what the West says of other cultures. The second set, its image of others, appears to constrain how it views itself.

What kind of constraints could they be? They cannot dictate the content. After all, this content is determined by empirical and theoretical research. But, these constraints do define the questions asked and the answers sought. Thus, they function as limits: they limit the kind of inquiries, and they are also the limits of Western imagination. What kind of limits are they?

It is obvious that every generation of thinkers is constrained or limited by the cognitive resources available to it. Indeed, while one cannot predict how these resources will be used by a particular generation, one can identify the cognitive limits of their use. Consider the possibility of Albert Einstein's being born as a contemporary of Thomas Aquinas's. Would he have been able to formulate his theories of relativity? Given what we know about human knowledge today, our answer can only be in the negative: he would not have had access to the experimental data and the theoretical concepts required to frame his theories. In this sense, even a genius is limited by his time. Although this fact does not tell us *what* such limits are, it does suggest that there *are* limits. While it is true that the limits of a genius are not those of an average scientist, each generation of thinkers is limited by the cognitive resources available to it.

The above argument merely tells us that all human thinking is constrained thinking. For this to become interesting, we need more. We need to show that successive generations of thinkers are subject to the same limits ('latent Orientalism') even where there is a break between their different descriptions ('manifest Orientalism'). Because earlier generations of intellectuals were limited by the same constraint as the contemporary generation, it should be possible for us to identify the *nature of the limits* as well. In other words, for a critique of Orientalism to have any bite, it is not sufficient to say that there are limits; one has to say what those limits are and provide empirical evidence for their existence. What are the limits on how Western culture thinks of itself, and how does it affect its image of other cultures?

Critics of Orientalism—from Edward Said to Ronald Inden—provide the following answer: the West thinks that it is a scientific, entrepreneurial, rational culture, contrasted with which stand the Western conceptions of the Orient. If one is satisfied by this answer, there are but two kinds of research possible. The first kind—the most dominant one—tries to explain the emergence of these images. Depending upon one's philosophical proclivities, one could identify the causes in some ontology or metaphysics; or in imperialism; or in the mantra, 'knowledge is related to power', or whatever. Or, it plays upon the fact that these self-images privilege the West above other cultures and that all cultures are prone to self-edification. One could then begin the endless journey of pseudo-philosophical despair over the nature and notion of representation. The second kind of research—though hardly influenced by Said—takes off in the opposite direction: it wants to show that some cultures are as rational and scientific as the West itself (Sen 2005).

Since Said, we have known that Western representations of other cultures have taken specific forms: Orientalism is an academic domain, a set of institutional structures, a discourse. That is, one is able to answer questions about the *forms* taken by Western conceptions of other cultures. Surely, the next logical step would be to formulate a similar question regarding the 'self-image' of the West as well. What *form* has the 'self-image' of the West taken? Enough has been said to enable a sharp, short answer: *the form of the social sciences*. We can now identify the two constraints more precisely: *the social sciences constrain Orientalist discourse; Orientalism constrains social sciences*.

If Orientalism entails thinking under a particular set of constraints, and if this set *is* the set called 'the social sciences', then it follows that using the latter is to reproduce Orientalism. When Indian intellectuals use existing theories about religion and its history—for example, to analyse 'Hindu–Muslim' strife—they reproduce, both directly and indirectly, what the West has been saying so far. Directly, in the sense that the 'secularist' discourse about this issue can hardly be distinguished—both in terms of the content or the vocabulary—from Orientalist writings of the nineteenth and the twentieth centuries. Instead of talking about 'Indians' or 'Hindus', one now talks about the Sangh Parivar or 'Hindu fundamentalists'.

It is an indirect reproduction of Orientalism in the sense that its constraints are reproduced when we 'study' Indian culture. To the extent that the most interesting writings in India today are also criticisms of Orientalism, *Orientalism is reproduced in the name of a critique of Orientalism*. It is completely irrelevant whether one uses a Marx, a Weber, or a Max Müller to do so. Equally irrelevant is the fact that one borrows the vocabulary from a Derrida or from 'post-modern', post-colonial writers in Paris or California, instead. In both cases, the result is the same: uninteresting trivia, as far as the growth of human knowledge is concerned; but pernicious in effect as far as Indian intellectuals are concerned.

Orientalism and Cultures

When the West looks at other cultures, the social sciences—
being 'constraints upon and limitations of thought'—constrain
Orientalism. If we were to look at social sciences *in isolation*
from Orientalism, we could say that they teach us about Western
culture. However, these 'social sciences' are many: not just in
terms of domains or fields of study, but also in terms of domain-
theories. How do we read *these* as expressions of a particular
type of culture? Are the changing theories and their assumptions
symptomatic of the changing nature of the West? Or, is there an
underlying continuity to these changes? There are many theories
about 'religion' and 'ethics'. Which notion or theory among them,
about either of the two, 'expresses Western culture'? How could
one justify such a selection *without* having a prior theory about
Western culture?

We need to note that these questions arise if we look at the
social sciences independently of Orientalism. They also appear with
respect to Orientalism, if we look at it as an isolated discourse about
'other cultures'. After all, Orientalist discourse is neither monolithic
nor homogenous. Over the centuries, many things have been said,
retracted and modified. There have been changing claims about
'other cultures'; the philosophy underlying these claims has changed;
the nature of theories that embed these claims has changed, and so
on. Therefore, I suggest looking at the one as providing answers to
the other. It means that *Orientalism and the social sciences clarify each
other's questions*. The former constrains the latter to ask particular
questions; these tell us about the kind of culture that asks *these,* and
no other, questions.

If this claim is true, we can begin to appreciate the signal achievement
of Said's *Orientalism*. He has provided us with the 'Archimedean point'
to move the world. It can now be shown *why* a critique of Orientalism
is required. Such a critique does not help us affirm our 'dignity', or
recover our pride, or saddle the current and the future generations
in the West with guilt complexes. In a true and fundamental sense,
it enables us to contribute to the growth of human knowledge. We
do that when, through a critique of Orientalism, we attempt to
understand a particular culture's way of understanding itself, other
cultures and the world. Such a task will force us to provide alternate

descriptions of the world that are richer and fuller than those we have today. If this is not a quest for knowledge, what is?

The Ethical Domain: An Example

Up to now, the mutual relationship between Orientalism and the social sciences has been formulated in the abstract. Two relatively concrete illustrations may go some way towards making this claim more credible. With this in mind, I would like to touch upon the conceptualization and description of the nature of the ethical domain in India, to begin with.

Most of us are familiar with the modern Orientalist descriptions of Indian people. The immorality of Indians is very much a part of this picture, as the following randomly chosen citation illustrates:

... [C]ould I transplant my reader to the purely native circle by which I am surrounded and could he understand the bold and fluent hindostanee which the Hindoo soldier speaks, he would soon distinguish the sources of oriental licentiousness, and how unprincipled is the Hindoo in conduct and character. In nothing is the general want of principle more evident, than in the total disregard to truth which they show; no rank or order among them can be exempted from the implication. The religious teachers set the example, and they are scrupulously followed by all classes. Perjury and fraud are as common as is a suit of law; with protestations of equal sincerity will a witness stand forth who knows the falsehood of his testimony, and he who is ignorant of what he professes to testify. No oath can secure the truth; the water of the Ganges, as they cannot wash away the filth of lying and deceit, so they cannot preserve the court of law from being the scene of gross and impious contradiction. No task is so difficult as is he [sic] who would elicit truth from the mouth of a witness. Venality and corruption are universal; they are remarkable, too, for their ingratitude. (Massie, 1985, Vol. 1: 466–7)

If the Orientalist discourse transformed Indians into immoral beings, what are we to make of a 'scientific' discourse that transforms Indians into moral cretins? For, that is the result of the cultural psychologist Richard Shweder's research (Shweder et al., 1987), where he tries to relate culture to moral development. In the course of conducting a cross-cultural research into the growth of moral awareness, Shweder and his co-workers developed a questionnaire supposed to test the presence of moral notions among their subjects. The contrasting cultures are the Indian and the American; the interviewees are both children and adults. From the list of cases that Shweder uses, here are the first five, in order of perceived 'seriousness of breach', as judged by eight-year-old Brahmin children:

1. The day after his father's death, the eldest son had a haircut and ate chicken.
2. One of your family members eats beef regularly.
3. One of your family members eats a dog regularly for dinner.
4. A widow in your community eats fish two or three times a week.
5. Six months after the death of her husband, the widow wore jewelry and bright-colored clothes. (Ibid. 40)

It is important to note that, in India, there was a consensus between the children and the adults regarding the first two cases (ibid. 63), but there was no consensus among children regarding the last three cases.

What are we to make of this research? First, the facts cannot be disputed regarding their veracity. It is almost certain that the Indian informants would consider the above cases as *paap* or even as *maha paap*. Second, this concept has been translated as immoral ('sin') by Shweder and his co-workers. Third, as a consequence, immorality has been interpreted as violation of ethical *norms*. None of these appears problematic until one reads through the rest of the cases. Keeping in mind that they are *ordered* in terms of the 'perceived seriousness of the breach', we further come across (ibid. 40):

8. After defecation (making a bowel movement) a woman did not change her clothes before cooking.
13. In a family, a twenty-five-year-old son addresses his father by his first name.

And as the fifteenth,

15. A poor man went to the hospital after being seriously hurt in an accident. At the hospital they refused to treat him because he could not afford to pay.

Now is the time to take stock. Consider the first case again: 'The day after his father's death, the eldest son had a haircut and ate chicken'. This 'moral transgression' consists of two actions: eating chicken and having a haircut. The same informants would not think of eating chicken as an unconditional 'moral violation'. Certainly, none would say that going to the barber was a 'sin' either. It now *follows* (as a matter of logic) that the conjunction of these two actions cannot be a 'moral transgression'. It is important to note here that the context of an action cannot transform the action into a moral action, if some or another norm is violated. The act remains immoral, even where we plead attenuating circumstances. Even a context-sensitive norm has to appeal to unconditional foundations, if it is to be considered as an ethical norm. In this sense, assuming that one is talking about the violation of ethical norms, we can draw only one conclusion. Indians cannot think logically and do not appreciate deontological consequences in ethical matters. This is Orientalist imagery. If we do not use it, however, we have a serious explanatory problem.

This problem gets compounded by the fact that what one would normally consider a moral breach is ranked fifteenth. If this were the moral domain in India, there would be no India to talk of. No culture could survive if its members thought that 'eating chicken and going to a barber', or a 'widow wearing jewellery', or 'addressing the father by his first name', were more immoral than not treating a poor man for his sickness. Indians might be moral cretins; if they were that, there would be no Indian culture today.

One supposes that Shweder is vaguely aware of the absurdity of the situation, especially when Americans do not see 'eating chicken' or 'not changing clothes after defecation' as moral transgressions. Instead of trying to figure out what has gone wrong with his research that 'cretinizes' an entire culture, Shweder tries to figure out an 'ideal' argument structure, which can provide a 'reasoned defense of family life and social practice'. How does it look? Here is how: 'The body is a temple with a spirit dwelling in it. Therefore the sanctity of the temple must be preserved. Therefore, impure things must be kept out of and away from the body' (ibid. 76–7). As I said before, the facts are almost certainly true. The problem lies not in the translation of the Indian 'paap' into the English 'immorality'. It lies in the very notion of the *ethical domain*. This notion comes from the field of moral thought and no matter who uses it—whether an Orientalist or a moral philosopher—it transforms Indians into moral idiots. What we see here is the meeting point between the modern discourse of a Shweder and the Orientalist discourse from colonial times.

Religions in India: Another Example

Consider this statement: Hinduism, Buddhism, Jainism are religions of India. Post-colonial intellectuals would probably add a few qualifications to this claim. They may say that it is not possible to speak of *one* Hinduism, *one* Buddhism, *one* Jainism. Instead, one should speak about *many* 'Hinduisms', *many* 'Buddhisms', *many* 'Jainisms', and so on. Second, they would also raise questions about who could speak for and about these religions. Third, they are likely to add that the British 'created' or 'constructed' these religions in India. The first two qualifications are cognitively uninteresting because one could accept that 'Hinduism', 'Buddhism', 'Jainism' do not name unitary phenomena but pick out varied sets of practices and beliefs. One could dispose off of the second qualification by suggesting that we are not after 'canonical' descriptions of these phenomena. By far, the most interesting qualification is the third one.

During the colonial period, the British created many things: an education system; a legal system; a bureaucracy; roads and railways. They did not exist in these forms before the British colonized India. Were religions like 'Hinduism' also created in this way? Some post-colonial thinkers are inclined to answer in the positive: the British created Hinduism as a religion, the way they created the Indian Civil Service. If so, there is nothing fundamentally wrong with the Orientalist writings on Hinduism. Some may be wrong, but we can correct them as more accurate information accumulates. The contemporary writings on Hinduism—whether from Indology or Religious Studies—would remain continuous with the Orientalist writings on the subject. That is, the 'facts' provided by the Orientalists become the point of departure for the writings in the social sciences. The latter either add to, or explain, these facts. This is also the status of the field today: the writings in the humanities and the social sciences maintain an unbroken line of continuity with the Orientalist writings on these 'religions' in India.

If that is the case, one can hardly understand what the excitement is about. If other items are added to this creation-story, one can blame the West as the 'big bad wolf': the British created 'sati', the 'dowry system', 'the caste system', and anything else one feels like. This exercise in apportioning blame is uninteresting. Post-colonial thinkers also say that such a story deprives the colonial subjects of their agency.

There is, however, another way of looking at the claim of creating these religions in India. Despite its limitations, drawing an analogy could make it more perspicuous. Imagine an extraterrestrial coming to earth and noticing the following phenomena: the grass is green;

milk turns sour; birds fly; and some flowers give out a fragrant smell. He is convinced that these phenomena are related to each other and sees (let us say) *hipkapi* in them. The presence of hipkapi not only explains but also shows that they are related to each other. To those who doubt the existence of hipkapi, he draws their attention to its visible manifestation: the tigers eating the gazelle; dogs chasing the cats; and the massive size of the elephants. Each is a fact, as everyone can see. However, neither severally nor individually do they tell us anything about hipkapi. When more like him come to earth and reiterate the presence of hipkapi—other conditions permitting—hipkapi not only becomes a synonym for these phenomena but also turns out to be their explanation. Thereafter, to ask what hipkapi is, or how it explains, is an expression of one's idiocy: does not everyone see hipkapi, this self-explanatory thing? In this analogy, the extraterrestrial visitor has 'constructed' the hipkapi. To him, it is an experiential entity. He talks—as his fellow-beings do—about this experiential entity in a systematic way.

That is what the Europeans did. The puja in the temples; the *sandhyavandanam* of the Brahmins; the *sahasranamams*—these became organic parts of the Indian religion. *Purushasukta* was the cosmogony of the caste system, and 'untouchability' its outward manifestation. Dharma and *adharma* were Sanskrit terms for 'good' and 'evil', and the Indian deities were much like their Greek counterparts. To the missionaries, Indians were idolaters; to contemporary liberals, they are mere polytheists. In terms of my analogy, they construct a hipkapi. To them, it is an experiential entity about which they talk systematically.

This would entail suggesting that the *Europeans created 'Hinduism' and the other 'religions of India' as their experiential entities.* The Orientalists, under this construal, did not describe what existed in the Indian culture. They created a hipkapi, constructed a pattern and a structure that lent coherence to their *cultural experience*. Then, claims about Hinduism become somewhat akin to claims about having visions of Mary at Lourdes. Only 'somewhat', because such a vision could be characterized as a hallucination, whereas one cannot say that the West has been 'hallucinating' about Indian religions. All writings on 'Hinduism', 'Buddhism', 'Jainism', whether their authors are Indian or Western, become suspect because they maintain an unbroken line of continuity between Orientalism and their own writings.

Can one tell such a story? It has been told. I not only argue (1994) that the West 'imaginatively' created Hinduism, but also explain why it was compelled to do so. This *compulsion* is rooted in the nature of religion, and I advance a hypothesis about religion that explains this compulsion. Thus, the hypothesis emerges as an alternative—a competitor theory—to those already in the marketplace about what religion is. It breaks the 'structural unity' that Orientalism has constructed. 'Hinduism', 'Buddhism', and the others become hipkapis. Consequently, it is possible to investigate which of the 'facts' that went into constructing the hipkapi belong together, which do not, and how. One can probe deeper into one's own culture, because one's experience is accessible for reflection. 'What is Hinduism? What is Buddhism?' translate themselves as tasks, which require one to account for the facts that appear to lend credibility to the existence of the hipkapi.

This point suggests that the West created 'Hinduism', 'Buddhism', *as religions*. It is not that they created a monolithic religion instead of recognizing the multiplicity of theories and practices that go under the label, 'Hinduism'. (For such a post-colonial perspective, see Sugirtharajah [2003].) Instead, I suggest that 'Hinduism', as a concept, provided the Westerners with *a coherent experience*. To the extent that it is a concept, it is a construct. It is also that because, *as an experiential entity*, it unifies the Western experience. However, this concept has no reference in the world, that is, there is no 'Hinduism' (whether as a religion, or as a multiplicity of religions) in Indian culture. As a result, the double qualification of Said makes sense: 'Hinduism' is both a false description of the Indian reality, and imaginary. It is false, not because the West gave a false description of the reality, but because it falsely assumed that the experiential entity was a real entity in the world. It is imaginary in the sense that it does not have an existence outside the experience of Western culture.

The same consideration applies to what Dirks (2001) talks about. The notion of the 'caste system' unified the British experience of India; they implemented certain political and economic policies based on their experience. But, this experience was *not of the caste system*. In fact, this experience was of no particular object, but it constituted the basis of their goings-about with Indians. By creating such a 'system', the British lent stability and coherence to their cultural experience. Both the caste system and the Indian religions are constructs in this specific sense.

It is not as though colonialism brought 'Hinduism' and 'the caste system' into existence. The Europeans spoke about these entities as though they existed. They acted as though these entities were real. *However, neither before nor after colonialism do such entities or phenomena exist.* They are hipkapis. These entities merely lend structure and stability to the European experience. In other words, the Orientalist discourse assumes that 'the caste system' or 'Hinduism' exist in Indian culture. Present-day social sciences also assume the same. Consequently, a critique of Orientalism becomes coterminous with the task of creating alternative theories in the domain of the humanities and the social sciences. The process of developing a critique of Orientalism also outlines the nature of its *grand telos*: *decolonizing the social sciences*.

Now, we can fully appreciate that Said's book opens up the perspective of an interesting research programme. Not only does it help us identify the fact that Orientalist discourse constrains the current social sciences, and the other way round, but it also helps us define the goal of post-colonial intellectuals: we need to decolonize the social sciences as well. That is what a critique of Orientalism entails.

Grand Telos or Fractured Goals?

Some contemporary post-colonial thinkers refuse to recognize the unity of this genre of thinking. They seem to believe that one cannot speak of 'the' post-colonial thought, either in terms of a unity of purpose or in terms of a unifying set of concerns and questions. One way of making sense of their refusal is to appreciate that there is, indeed, a disjunction in 'the Orient' of Orientalist thinking.

There is, first, the experiential entity, namely, 'the Orient'. This does not appear to be a singular object; it varies according to the experience of the individual. In such cases, criticism of the Orientalist discourse seems oriented towards providing such an experiential entity with a place other than the one someone else has accorded to it. Contestations about this entity are disputes over the place which this entity should occupy within one's experiential world.

Second, there is also a discourse about non-Western cultures. Because Orientalism presents itself as a veridical discourse about the peoples of the Orient, a critique of this discourse is coterminous with developing an alternate set of theories in many domains. That is the task of intellectuals from the erstwhile colonies. After all, they have difficulty in making sense of 'the Orient', the experiential entity of Western culture. They have difficulty in recognizing both themselves and their social world in the descriptions provided by Orientalism and the social sciences. Consequently, the onus is on them.

In other words, the issues are these: does the discourse about the Orient retain the same character in both the East and the West? Are there two sets of post-colonial projects—one for intellectuals from the West and the other for those from the East? Or, is it that the telos of post-colonial thinking—that of decolonizing the social sciences—unites the intellectuals from both the East and the West?

On Our Goal

What should Indian intellectuals do today, if their present is to have a future? What is the future for what they are doing at present? I have hinted that what they are doing at present has no future. There is no future to a parrot-like reproduction of Western theories, whether Marxian, feminist, or post-modern. There is, however, a future for their present if they think through the issues to which Orientalism has given birth.

I began with a citation from Partha Chatterjee. Let me also end with citations, both of which come from his books. The first is originally Gandhi's; the second is Partha Chatterjee's own conviction.
First, Gandhi:

Let us not be obsessed with catchwords and seductive slogans imported from the West. Have we not our own distinct Eastern traditions? Are we not capable of finding our own solutions to the question of capital and labour? ... Let us study our Eastern institutions in that spirit of scientific inquiry and we shall evolve a truer socialism and a truer communism than the world has yet dreamed of. It is surely wrong to presume that western socialism or communism is the last word on the question of mass poverty. (Cited in Chatterjee 1996: 112)

Now, Partha Chatterjee (1993: 169):

Now that there is a much greater eagerness to face up to ... historical material, its very richness forces us to throw up our hands and declare that it is much too complex.... [T]he feeling of unmanageable complexity is, if we care to think of it, nothing other than the result of the inadequacy of the theoretical apparatus with which we work. Those analytical instruments were fashioned primarily out of the process of understanding historical developments in Europe. When those instruments now meet with the resistance of an intractable complex material, the fault surely is not of the Indian material but of the imported instruments. If the day comes when the vast storehouse of Indian social history will become comprehensible to the scientific consciousness, we will have achieved along the way a fundamental restructuring of the edifice of European social philosophy as it exists today.

The distance between these two figures is obvious; but their nearness is equally striking: both anticipate the possibility of a reflection of the Indian cultural experience, and feel that such a reflection could lead to a reconfiguration of the intellectual landscape. In the course of subsequent chapters, I will think through this issue in a systematic fashion and explore what it means. For now, let us realize that these thoughts might not be idle dreams; instead, as I will argue further, they constitute the goal and a challenge for the generations to come.

Notes

1. 'What interests me most ... is not the gross political verity but the detail, as indeed, what interests us in someone like Lane or Flaubert or Renan is not the (to him) indisputable truth that Occidentals are superior to Orientals, but the profoundly worked over and modulated evidence of his detailed work within the very wide space opened up by that truth' (Said 1978: 15). Here, 'worked over' refers to how the details express both the gross truth of racial superiority (a theoretical claim) and the facts about the world. That is, these facts are 'theory-laden'. 'Worked-over' categories, then, are categories within a theory, and facts are worked over to the extent that they are theory-laden.

2. In Said's reflections in the 'afterword to the 1995 printing' of his book, we read the following: 'Actually ... very early in the book, I say that words such as "Orient" and "Occident" correspond to no stable reality that exists as a natural fact. Moreover, all such geographical designations are an odd combination of the empirical and the imaginative' (Said 1995: 331). The claim is not that the word 'Orient' does not refer, but that it does not have the kind of reference that 'leg', or 'rain', or 'mountain' has. In this sense, the 'Orient' refers to a man-made entity: like 'house' or 'movie theatre', or 'Dutch' or 'English'. As far as the 'odd combination' is concerned, one could say that historical and social geography, too, work with man-made 'realities': cities, jails, parks. None of these is 'stable': cities, parks, jails, change, shift, expand, contract, disintegrate, and so on. What is odd about this? Even if

one's representation of New York as 'the city that never sleeps' is part of a discourse about the USA, this does not imply that 'New York' does not refer to a place in the United States. See also p. 63.

3. However, Said does not keep track of the distinctions he implicitly introduces, and, at times, even mixes them up, as the following citation testifies. '[T]he third meaning of Orientalism ... (deals) with the Orient—dealing with it by making statements about it, authorizing views of it, describing it, by teaching it, *settling it, ruling over it*: in short Orientalism as a western style for *dominating*, restructuring, and having authority over the Orient' (Said 1978: 3; italics added). This citation exhibits the kind of problems Said needlessly creates. The pronoun, 'it', has two distinct references within the same sentence: it refers to *both* the concept of the Orient and to the Orient in the world. One teaches concepts (teaching 'it' clearly means teaching the 'concept of the Orient'), whereas one settles physical places (settling 'it' means settling the physical Orient), and rules over peoples in particular places (ruling over 'it'). 'Dominating and restructuring' refers primarily to physical and/or social entities, whereas, depending on the notion of 'authority', 'having authority' is applicable to either concepts or physical entities.

4. 'In two important and urgent ways, therefore, Lane gains scholarly credibility and legitimacy. First, by interfering with the ordinary narrative course of human life: his is the function of his colossal detail, in which the observing intelligence of a foreigner can introduce and then piece together massive information. The Egyptians are disembowelled for exposition, so to speak, then put together admonishingly by Lane' (Said 1978: 162–4). The construction of the Orient is possible only because all these reports exhibit a similar structuring of experience. '(The doctrine about the Orient) was fashioned out of the experience of many Europeans, all of them converging upon such essential aspects of the Orient as the Oriental character, Oriental despotism ...' (ibid. 203).

5. 'In a sense Orientalism was a library or archive of information ... What bound the archive together was a family of ideas ... proven in various ways to be effective. These ideas explained the behavior of Orientals ... most important, they allowed Europeans to deal with and even see Orientals as a phenomenon possessing regular characteristics' (Said 1978: 41–2). Here is one answer why Orientalism continues to exist in the European culture: it enables the European to deal with people from the East. Orientalism constructs the 'Oriental' in the sense that it describes people from the East as 'a phenomenon possessing regular characteristics'. This description, which appears to be about these people, enables the Europeans to go-about with people from other cultures. Modern Orientalism went about with people from other cultures through the process of colonization. Further, these descriptions also enable the Europeans to 'see' order instead of chaos.

6. 'The eccentricities of Oriental life, with its odd calendars, its exotic spatial configurations, its hopelessly strange languages, its seemingly perverse morality, were reduced considerably when they appeared as a series of detailed items presented in a normative European prose style' (Said 1978: 166–7). The strangeness or the otherness of cultures is first described in colossal detail and then it is comprehended by classifying it under a category from one's own culture that functions normatively.

CHAPTER 3

Comparative Science of Cultures
A Methodological Reflection*

To speak about the challenges and goals of the future generations is not only to speak about a research programme, but also to write programmatically. In that sense, this is a *programmatic chapter*, focused on the methodology of a comparative science of cultures. Despite this—partly because the research programme of comparative science of cultures is already undergoing development—I shall focus on some of the methodological questions and insights that have emerged in the course of its construction. Doing so will hopefully make the programme more attractive.

There are, and have been, many kinds of comparative studies: from comparative anthropology (Holy [ed.] 1987), through comparative history (Yengoyan [ed.] 2006), comparative political theory (Jenco 2007; Gebhardt 2008), and comparative theology (Clooney 2010)

* Some parts of this chapter were previously published in 1998 as 'The Future of the Present', *Cultural Dynamics*, 10(2), pp. 101–21, London: Sage Publications; and (with Marianne Keppens) in 2009 as 'Reconceptualizing the Postcolonial Project: Beyond the Strictures and Structures of Orientalism', *Interventions*, 11(1), pp. 50–68, 2009, London: Taylor and Francis.

to comparative analysis in multiple social sciences (Mahoney and Rueschmeyer [eds] 2003). I will not speak about any of them in the present chapter; instead, I will add to the existing diversity. Despite this, I hope the chapter is unorthodox enough to provoke a far more serious thinking about the methodologies of comparative studies than has been done so far.

I propose to carry out the task in distinct conceptual steps that constitute the different sections of the chapter. In 'The Profile of an Enterprise', an argument is built to show how one can profile the nature of a comparative enterprise by continuing the line of thinking initiated in the previous chapter about the problematic relationship between Orientalism and the social sciences. However, one does not have to endorse the Saidian critique of the Orientalist discourse in order to appreciate the existence of a problem, even though it may be convenient to use Said's ideas to introduce it. In this sense, the arguments I develop in this section should be acceptable even to those who disagree with the constraints I had identified in the previous chapter.

'A Cultural Asymmetry' develops, this problem in such a way that it can be formulated independently of whether one endorses Said or not. During this process, I point out a peculiar kind of *cultural asymmetry* that pervades the intellectual discourse in some domains of the social sciences today.

In the 'Three Dimensions', three important aspects of the kind of comparative enterprise that follow from the earlier arguments are isolated. At the same time, I hint both at the importance of post-colonial scholarship and identify some of its limitations. In the same section, some methodological generalizations are formulated.

I notice, in 'A Limitation Overcome', the limitations of these methodological generalizations and seek interesting ways to find solutions for them.

The sections 'Understanding the Asymmetry' and 'The Idea of "Critique"' relate one aspect of this methodology to a trend in Western philosophy that also establishes why, for this endeavour to succeed, the *cognitive condition* is that the *work of earlier generations* of thinkers be *adequately appreciated*. It also makes clear of what that adequacy consists. If the chapter succeeds in its aim, it must provide a new twist to the very notion of comparison itself.

The Profile of an Enterprise

Orientalism and Social Sciences Again

Let me begin by addressing those who are not persuaded by my interpretation of Said in the previous chapter. No matter how critically we do it, if we accept Edward Said's insights into the nature of Western discourses on non-Western societies, we also have to accept that Orientalism is about how the West experienced the East and gave expression to that experience. In the course of this process, the West built and elaborated conceptual frameworks using resources mostly available from its own culture.

While generating descriptions of other cultures—whether framed in positive or negative evaluative or axiological terms—Orientalism made use of a vast conceptual reservoir. It consisted of ideas and theories about human beings; the nature of languages; the structure of societies; the character of cultures; the importance of religion; the value of history; and the problem of politics. In turn, such a constructed discourse had its impact on the evolution of subsequent theorizing about Man and Society. In other words, Orientalist discourse did not evolve in splendid isolation but in continuous interaction with, and as a part of, the growth of the social sciences. It is not an extraneous and alien growth on the otherwise splendid corpus of social sciences. Instead, it is an inextricable part of the social-scientific discourse.

However, one of the problems with the Saidian terminology is the difficulty in making sense of the social sciences. If '... Weber's studies of Protestantism, Judaism, and Buddhism blew him (perhaps unwittingly) into the very territory originally charted and claimed by Orientalism' (Said 1978: 259), what can we say about his theories on the development of capitalism, the relationship between economies and societies, and the nature of political authority? If the European writings on 'Hinduism' are Orientalist (King 1999a; Sugirtharaja 2003), what about their histories of Christianity? If we assume that Marx's claims in *The Grundrisse* about India are squarely in the Orientalist camp, where do his theses about commodities, money and capital belong? Is Freudian psychoanalysis itself Orientalist because, using that theory entails that a non-Western culture, say the Indian culture, is populated by pathological beings afflicted by secondary narcissism and other assorted ills (Carstairs 1957; Moussaief-Masson 1980; Courtright 1985; Kripal 1998)?

To these questions, neither Said provides an answer, nor do those inspired by him. Inden (1986, 1990) criticizes the 'Orientalist constructions of India' by using Collingwood's notion of history. Are we to assume that using Collingwood's concept of history to understand India is non-Orientalist, whereas using the Marxist or the Weberian notion of history to study India is Orientalist? Or, should we assume that Western historiography about the West itself is 'Orientalist' insofar as historians do not make use of Collingwood?

In Said's case, it seems as though the existing social sciences are alternatives to Orientalism. This stance has to do with the 'humanistic' orientation that Said entertains. He believes that knowledge about human beings must be both general and specific: 'general' in the sense that it tells us about 'human beings as such' and does not divide them up in arbitrary ways; 'specific' in the sense that it must not lose itself in abstractions or 'collectives' but give us knowledge of 'flesh-and-blood' individuals.

However, there is also his critique of Orientalist discourse. Orientalism, as a field of study, stands on its own. It studies the 'Oriental': a type, an abstraction, a fictitious creature with some 'essential properties' who populates the domain of discourse. This 'Oriental' is a bi-dimensional figure: he is not the 'flesh-and-blood' individual of our world.

Said notices that Orientalist discourse has wittingly or unwittingly borrowed ideas from many social scientific theories:

Orientalism borrowed and was frequently informed by 'strong' ideas, doctrines, and trends ruling the culture. Thus there was (and is) a linguistic Orient, a Freudian Orient, a Spenglerian Orient, a Darwinian Orient, a racist Orient—and so on. (Said 1978: 22)

He is also certain from where alternatives to Orientalism are likely to come:[1]

... enough is being done today in human sciences to provide the contemporary scholar with insights, methods, and ideas that could dispense with racial, ideological, and imperialist stereotypes of the sort provided during the historical ascendancy by Orientalism. (Ibid. 328)

On the one hand, if we follow Said, Orientalism is a massive *cultural project*, which has had a huge impact on Western culture, people and their imagination. People produce and reproduce Orientalist discourse without realizing they are doing so, and even without wanting to do so. Furthermore, the Orientalist discourse also appears to create and reinforce Western 'self-conception' and 'self-representation'.

Yet, on the other hand, if we are to believe Said, such a discourse has no impact on the growth and development of the social sciences. This enterprise—which is *also* a cultural project of the West—is completely unaffected by, even oblivious to, the other cultural project. One cultural enterprise, Orientalism, appears to borrow continuously from the other cultural enterprise, the social scientific discourse. Social sciences, on their part, do not appear to borrow anything from the Orientalist discourse or from the concomitant cultural images about man and society. Not only that, but they are also alternatives to the Orientalist discourse. Surely, this suggestion is implausible.

Why is it implausible? The answer is obvious. The existing social sciences—which are primarily Western initiatives—make claims about human beings and their societies in both the West and the East. Orientalism does not merely put across claims about non-Western cultures but also creates and reinforces certain ideas about Western man and his society. Therefore, we have two sets of claims about the social and the cultural world: one set of claims formulated by Orientalism and the other formulated by the social sciences. Because of their subject matter, these claims cannot be irrelevant to each other; either they are compatible or they are not. Because Orientalism borrows from the social sciences, their claims must be compatible. From this, it follows that the claims of Orientalism must also be compatible with the claims of the social sciences. If this is the case, the existing social sciences cannot provide us with alternatives to Orientalism; instead they, too, must continue the legacy of Orientalist writings. The images of man and society that the existing social sciences either reinforce or take for granted must be continuous with Orientalism. In other words, thinking through one of the critical strands in Said's thinking seems to carry some disturbing implications with respect to the social sciences that we practise today.

A Paradox?

Perhaps, this is what Dipesh Chakrabarty is signalling at when he formulates the *aporia* confronting the intellectuals from non-Western cultures in his 'Post-Coloniality and the Artifice of History':

For generations now, philosophers and thinkers have produced theories embracing the entirety of humanity. As we well know, these statements have been produced in relative, and sometimes, absolute ignorance of the majority of humankind, i.e., those living in non-Western cultures. This in itself is not paradoxical, for the more self-conscious of European philosophers have always sought theoretically to justify this stance. The everyday paradox of the third-world social science is that we find these theories, in spite of their inherent ignorance of 'us', eminently useful in understanding our societies. What allowed the modern European sages to develop such clairvoyance with regard to societies of which they were empirically ignorant? Why cannot we, once again, return the gaze? (Chakrabarty 1997: 3; emphasis removed)

Prima facie, there is something very peculiar about his claim and questions. There is supposed to be a paradox but it is not clear where it is located. Let me try to provide a reasonable reconstruction of this paradox.

Social science—if it is any kind of science—is knowledge. Its objects are human beings, society and culture. To the extent that it is knowledge, social science cannot claim ignorance about its objects. All these are facts, under the assumption that 'knowledge' and 'ignorance' have different meanings. In the way we normally use the words, of course, 'knowledge' and 'ignorance' share neither the same extension nor the same meaning. That is, they do not range over the same objects in the same way.

Here are the two facts noticed by Dipesh Chakrabarty: (1) some social sciences which study human beings and their societies, are ignorant about aspects of non-Western cultures and societies. This statement implies that these social sciences, therefore, cannot be knowledge of those aspects of cultures and societies with which they deal. If knowledge is useful in understanding those cultures and societies, it further follows that these social sciences cannot be useful in that venture. (2) We (from non-Western cultures) find the very same social sciences useful in understanding all aspects of our societies and cultures. From this statement, it follows that these sciences do embody knowledge.

The first sentence notes the fact that the social sciences are 'inherently' ignorant about aspects of non-Western societies and cultures and, therefore, they cannot be useful for understanding non-Western cultures and societies. The second notices the fact that they are useful in understanding all aspects of these societies and implies that social sciences do embody knowledge. The first statement is true. The second statement, too, is true. It is also true that, under the assumption about knowledge and understanding, the implication of the first statement is the negation of the second. Severally taken, both statements merely describe a situation. Jointly, however, they cannot both be true and yet they are. The conditions under which these facts are true require that 'knowledge' and 'ignorance' share the same extension. That is, knowledge is ignorance if—and only if—knowledge is not ignorance.

Dipesh Chakrabarty suggests that this claim is not only paradoxical but also true. It is true because the claim is a (partial) description of the situation of Third World intellectuals, and because they realize this to be the case as well. In other words, not only are they committed to the truth of this paradox, but they also realize that the situation forces them to affirm this truth as their own. Thus, these intellectuals live not merely paradoxically, but also in the awareness of the paradox. Their experience, then, involves these two dimensions and both have to do with the social sciences.

Similar thoughts have been expressed as challenges elsewhere, too. For instance, the Sri Lankan-born anthropologist Valentine Daniel said even earlier: 'Enough of Weberizing and Durkheimizing Indian ethnological data. How about Manuizing and Paninizing Western culture, including the science of culture, for a change?' (Daniel 1984: 53; see also, Mariott 1976: 195.)[2]

Bending the Stick the Other Way

Let me now try to capture this sense of unease in more general terms. To do this, I will formulate the issue in an *exaggerated form*, which will get corrected later on. For now, let us accept that the intuition which guides such thoughts as the above is the realization that, whatever their explanatory power or problem-solving capacity, the existing social sciences are not adequate for the task of making the non-Western world intelligible. There is a feeling of dissatisfaction with the conceptual apparatus that obtains today; the disquiet arises from the fact that interesting and important issues are not even being formulated as questions for an inquiry. One of the tentative explanations often put across to account for this unsatisfactory state of affairs is that the social sciences of today are 'Western'. That is, the social sciences embody assumptions (whether all its assumptions, or only some of them, are 'Western', needs to be looked into) which blind them to recognizing issues that are very important to an understanding of non-Western cultures (for example, Claes 1996; Van Den Bouwhuijsen, Derde and Claes 1995).

However correct it might prove to be later, this intuition is not sufficient for the task of assessing theories from the field of social sciences. It would be a folly to reject the existing conceptual frameworks merely because we feel that they do not quite manage to do what theories are supposed to. There is no way of assessing theories, unless it is by comparing them with rival theories. We could sensibly begin with theory appraisal if, and only if, we have two or more theories which are competitors to each other with respect to the phenomenon that they explain (Lakatos 1980; Laudan 1977).

In one sense, it could be said that there are rival theories in the field of the social sciences: structural as against cognitive anthropology; the Austrian school of economics against Keynesian economics; Marxian economics against micro- and macroeconomics; Parsonian as against Weberian sociology ... Therefore, it may seem that the problems are solved, even before their formulation. It becomes merely a question of ascertaining which of these competitor theories are best suited for the job.

But, this is not what these authors have in mind. To explicate that thought better, let us look at the issue this way. Without the least bit of exaggeration, it could be held that the study of societies and cultures is a project that the Western world has initiated. Over the centuries, Western intellectuals have studied both themselves and other cultures and, in this process, have developed sets of theories and methodologies to understand our social and cultural worlds. What we call the 'social sciences' today are the result of, a gigantic labour performed by brilliant and not-so-brilliant men and women from all over the world over a long period of time.

Let us formulate a hypothetical question in order to express a problem: *would the results have been the same, or even approximately similar if, say, Indians, instead of Europeans, had undertaken the task?* That is, let us suppose that, in the imaginary world of which we are talking, it was the effort of Indian intellectuals reflecting about themselves and European culture, as they saw them both, which eventuated in the social sciences. *Would the results have looked like contemporary social sciences?*

The most natural answer to this question is: 'We do not know'. It would be worth our while to reflect on this answer. The inability to answer the question does not arise from the impossibility of answering questions about hypothetical situations. All our scientific laws describe hypothetical situations and we can say what would happen in those situations. (If I *were* to drop a stone from the top of a building, what would happen? The stone *would* fall downwards.)

The ignorance in our case has to do with the specific kind of hypothetical situation which the question picks out, and with the feeling that there is no way of checking the veracity of the answers given. That is because we have no model of such an attempt, we have no way of deciding how to go about answering the question. Worse still, because we have no models where the answers can come out either true or false, we feel that all answers to this question are meaningless and, therefore, that the question itself is meaningless. The question has not violated any syntactic or semantic rule; it has not committed any category mistake; yet, *we do not know how to make sense of this question.*

There is a peculiar air about this state of affairs. One is unable to make sense of a question which asks Indians, literally, how they appear to themselves and how the West appears to them. Yet, they have been studying both the West and India for quite some time now. As a result, if you allow a mild hyperbole, I will assert that the problem of neither 'incommensurability of cultures' nor of 'indeterminacy of translation' arises. They might become problems if the background assumptions and theories which underlie a study were different. The background assumptions and theories which guide a Western anthropologist studying Asian culture are the same as those that guide an Asian anthropologist studying his own. If one of them should face problems, so would the other. Both study the same phenomenon (the 'inscrutability of reference' notwithstanding) with the same tools embodying the same assumptions. The nature and the relative importance of a problem are not different for the two, and these are so organized by their background assumptions.

With the background assumptions peculiar to it, Western culture has problematized phenomena which, for many of us, have taken on the status of facts. One talks endlessly about the problem of 'underdevelopment'; the 'question of human rights in India'; 'the amorphous nature of Hinduism' and, in the same breath, 'Hindu fundamentalism'; 'the problem of modernity and nationhood'; 'the women's question in India'. The same is also true for one's perspectives on the West.

But, there is a problem here. If Indian culture differs from that of the West, and if, perforce, its background theories and assumptions are other than those of the West, one cannot possibly either formulate questions or assign weights to them—whether India or the West—in exactly the same way that the West does. Yet, one does so, invariably and as a matter of fact. How can Indians make sense of questions routinely copied from Western social research, and go on to answer them by means of empirical studies? Yet they do, and they act as though these questions did make sense to them.

We, from other cultures, know the West the way the West looks at itself. We study the East the way the West studies the East. We look at the world the way the West looks at it. *We do not even know whether the world would look different, if we looked at it our way*. Today, we are not in a position to make sense of the previous statement. When Indian anthropologists, psychologists, or sociologists do their anthropology, psychology, or sociology, it is really the West talking to itself.

Thus, it appears as though the problem is not about the presence or absence of rival theories in the domain of the social sciences; instead, it sucks the entire domain of the social sciences into its scope. The challenge that intellectuals from non-Western cultures face is nothing short of breath-taking: they must attempt to *decolonize the social sciences, no less!*

On the Novelty of the Task

I do believe that, whether realistic or not, whether pretentious or not, this is the *historical task* that intellectuals from non-Western cultures will face over the coming generations. The emergence of countries and cultures like India and China into world prominence is going to confront their intellectuals with this objective: they, too, will have to do what Europe and the United States have done so far. And that involves a *striving for intellectual hegemony*. The increasingly important economic and political role which these countries are going to play on a world level is also going to translate itself in cultural and intellectual realms. About a full two thousand years ago, the pagan cultures of Greece and Rome met an emerging Christianity, which triumphed. Today, the circle has come a full turn: two other ancient pagan cultures (non-White and non-Christian in nature) will meet the reigning intellectual and cultural hegemony of a predominantly Christian culture. The challenge of intellectual hegemony is going to express itself as the afore-mentioned historical task. Of course, this is inter-generational in nature; no generation, leave alone some individual thinker, is capable of bringing such a task to fruition. This qualification, obviously, does not make the task any less daunting than it is.

How does this task present itself to intellectuals from non-Western cultures? Does the execution of this, too, involve postulating the age-old opposition between the 'us' and 'them'? Or, do the historical achievements of Western culture change the way the problem is formulated today? Let me first give a short answer on which the rest of this chapter will elaborate. I believe that the task is going to present itself as a *comparative* enterprise. No matter how combative the initial formulations are going to be, one will be *compelled* to take the hard-won insights and theories of the earlier generations into account, if the task is to be completed. That is to say, the 'decolonization' of the social sciences (or 'provincializing Europe'—to make use of Chakrabarty's pregnant if provocative formulation) *cannot* take the form of a total rejection of the social sciences of today, or of the intellectual labour of people from the past centuries. In fact, what makes the coming century exciting is the fact that the task of 'decolonizing' the social sciences will either be a collective global effort of intellectuals across the world, or it simply will not take place. The intellectual hegemony that non-Western intellectuals will be forced to seek can only be *achieved* through negotiation with intellectuals of the Western world and with their cooperation. In this sense, the hegemony of non-Western intellectuals will not be 'their' hegemony. It cannot, and will not, take the form of the 'us' and 'them' opposition. This opposition will have to be transcended and that will be possible *only* because of the fact that, today, such an opposition does exist which constitutes our *point of departure* as well. In the rest of this chapter, I shall show how and why that is the case, and *why it is a cognitive condition* and not a prophetic rant.

A Cultural Asymmetry

Let us begin with the following question: how should we look at the Orientalist discourse? One view—let us call it *the received view*—sees it as a description of the Orient, whether veridical or flawed. In defence of the received view, one could say that such descriptions are flawed in so far as they are wrong or false, and they are so only due to insufficient knowledge of the Orient. Here, the wrongness or falsity picks out an (almost) inevitable phase through which all academic disciplines pass. As more accurate knowledge accumulates, the Orientalist discourse will simply 'improve' and become coterminous with the knowledge of human beings, whether in the West or the Orient. While this received view on Orientalism has its merits, it is not of much use because the notion used here of 'wrongness' and 'falsity' has almost no teeth. In exactly the same sense, one could say that the Greek or the Egyptian astrology was flawed or wrong, and that it became the Copernican astronomy as accurate knowledge accumulated. Our astrophysics will then be seen to supersede Copernican astronomy simply by being 'more accurate'. In other words, such a defence of Orientalism makes discussions about its 'truth' and 'falsity' only *marginally interesting* from a cognitive point of view. They are only marginally interesting because they do not allow us to come to grips with the growth of scientific theories (Dilworth 2008), the nature of scientific change, and the partially incommensurable character of scientific progress (Hoyningen-Huene and Sankey [eds], 2010).

To understand any of these, one has to discuss the difference between Greek astronomy and Copernican astronomy in terms of their concepts, axioms, and theories. To do that, we cannot look back from our vantage point and suggest that one theory is more accurate than the other (Westman [ed.], 1975). We need to understand them the way in which they confronted each other historically: *as rival and competing theories*. As such, they were not trying to propose different solutions to a common and shared problem; in fact, the problems themselves were *different*. That is to say, one has to differentiate between theories, not only in terms of proposed solutions to common problems but also in terms of how each of these theories formulates the problem. For scientists involved in research, the general claim that all theories (including those from their domain) simply become 'more accurate' as 'more knowledge' accumulates is quite useless: they need to know the specific problems confronted by a theory and the range of proposed possible answers. In this sense, the received view on Orientalism merely suggests that a 'more accurate' description of non-Western cultures is an alternative to 'Orientalism'. This is just about as useful and illuminating as suggesting that a 'more accurate' description of the natural world would provide us with an alternative to the paradoxes of quantum physics.

The second way of describing the Orientalist discourse—let us call this a *comparative view*—appreciates this state of affairs and provides a context for situating a possible dialogue between Western and non-Western cultures. This context is the fact that all these cultures are different forms of life and, due to globalization, they meet each other as alternatives to each other. In appreciating this historical fact, the comparative view on Orientalism either downplays the alleged Westernization of non-Western *cultures* or sees it as a process of adaptation by non-Western cultures. Consequently, *Orientalism is seen as a description of the Western experience of the Orient.* As I argued in the previous chapter, Orientalism becomes *the Western way of thinking about its experience of non-Western cultures.* This 'Western way' has to do with the *form* that such reflections on experience take: *they take the form of an apparent discourse about the Orient.*

Hopefully, we can now see why these two views on Orientalism need not be at loggerheads with each other, even though they have been so ever since Edward Said published his book. The first is pitched at such a level of abstraction that what it says about Orientalism is applicable to all domains of human knowledge; the second attempts to conceptualize a historical situation, where Western culture (and the discourses emanating from that culture) confronts non-Western cultures *as an alternative.* Rightly or wrongly, ever since modern colonialism, Western culture has presented itself as an alternate and desirable form of life to peoples from non-Western cultures. But, there is an *asymmetry* here: while the Western form of life is proposed as an alternative to non-Western forms of life, non-Western cultures are never seen as alternatives (at a macrolevel) to the Western form of life, even where many intellectuals from the West look admiringly at various aspects of non-Western cultures. In this sense, the kind of alternative that the West is to other cultures does not fall in with the notion of 'alternative' that we know from our logics and linguistics. 'Being an alternative to' is a *symmetrical relation*: if X is an alternative to Y then Y is also an alternative to X.

In this globalized world of ours, it makes perfect sense to suggest that India, Iraq, or Pakistan should try to emulate Europe or the US, whereas it seems both obscene and ridiculous to suggest that Europe and the US should try to emulate India or Iraq. This *signals* that Western culture is seen as the 'endpoint' for non-Western cultures and that only as such does it meet the others in the world arena. However, not many intellectuals openly want to take such a stance. Not only does it smack of the now-rejected developmental ordering of human history, but it also does not allow for an appreciation of how these cultures are meeting each other today: *as alternate forms of life*. However, acknowledging this fact implies that there should be symmetry between these alternate forms of life, which is implicitly dismissed by the dominant intellectual discourses in the field of the social sciences. We need to keep in mind that the rejection is merely implicit, a hidden premise in the argumentation, as it were: no intellectual domain has done the kind of research that would show why Western culture is the only alternative to non-Western cultures.[3] The current understanding of non-Western cultures in the Western world is too thin to allow the generation of this implicit stance as an explicit conclusion. In this sense, this is a *cultural asymmetry*, where Western culture is seen as the only alternative to all other cultures, whereas there are no extant alternatives to this culture. In the first place, comparative research addresses itself to this problem and attempts to restore symmetry (whether crowned with success or not). Taking the rejection of a developmental ordering of human history very seriously, the comparative enterprise attempts to make sense of the current state of affairs and to restore cognitive consistency to the intellectual parlance of today. The only way of doing that is to try to look at non-Western cultures (or, at least the intellectual productions of such cultures) as possible alternatives to the Western form of life. That is to say, comparative studies want to restore an imbalance that exists today between cultures, and to allow us to make sense of the fact that the different cultures in today's world are different forms of life, and that they confront each other as alternatives to one another.

Three Dimensions

In the process of generating descriptions of non-Western cultures, the Western culture built and elaborated on many conceptual frameworks. These frameworks also helped Europe in its description and understanding of both itself and the world. That is, in the first place, Europe's description of other cultures is entwined in many untold ways with the way it has experienced and, thereby, described the world. If we keep to the post-Saidian distinctions, we could say that Western descriptions of non-Western cultures ('Orientalism') are deeply and indissolubly connected with the ways in which Western culture has described the social world ('social sciences'). When modern sociology describes the Indian caste system, or when modern anthropology studies Hindu practices in some part of India, both presuppose the 'facts' dredged up by the earlier generations of Orientalists. Facts—as we all know today—are mostly theory-laden and, hence, they are facts of some theory or another (Feyerabend 2010). Thus, for instance, when Mancur Olson, Jr (1984), accounts for the Indian caste system by 'explaining' the facts that Nehru (in his *Discovery of India*) puts across, he is presupposing the truth of those theories and frameworks which Nehru used. Nehru used Orientalist descriptions of the Indian society of his day and made their facts his own. In this sense, Olson is not accounting for the Indian caste system by using the notion of fossilized coalitions in India; he is trying to establish the truth of Nehru's observations (that is, the truth of the Orientalist descriptions of India) by developing a hypothesis that purports to explain Indian society. This suggests at least one manner of conceiving the relationship between Orientalism and the social sciences: *where uncontested, there, the latter presupposes the truth of the Orientalist descriptions of non-Western cultures*. Thus, even if we are not enamoured of the field of post-colonial studies, we can appreciate the rationale for its existence and popularity: these studies contest the truth of the colonial descriptions of non-Western cultures. In doing so, they underscore *the need for comparative research* to exist as a distinct way of studying cultures and societies. This is the *first dimension* that we should keep in mind: there is a need for comparative research of the type just talked about.

In order to see why this need arises, we need to understand *the second dimension* by considering the *'what'* of the post-colonial contestation. Let us use India as an example of a non-Western culture. India has been independent for more than sixty years. Therefore, it would be reasonable to expect that there are no lines of continuity between the way the British described India and the way post-Independence generations look at India (both in India and in the West within the same time frame). Of course, we are not talking about descriptions of all kinds of facts about the people, the country or its weather, where the absence of continuities would, indeed, be astonishing. Instead, we are talking about the continuities in fundamental and structural descriptions: *India is corrupt, caste-ridden, immoral, and so on.* As any student of contemporary India knows, such continuities are seen as being present. Surely, there is something wrong with this situation.

Many argue that, if something is wrong with this situation, it has to do with Indian society itself. That is, they ask whether there would be such lines of continuity, if there were no 'truth' to the British portrayal of Indian history, traditions, and culture. This stance makes use of the 'fact' of continuity to suggest that the British descriptions are true. The contemporary experience of Indian culture and society appears to lend truth-value to the colonial descriptions of India.

However, the above stance assumes that the contemporary experience is itself unproblematic. What happens *if that is not the case*? Do the lines of continuity indicate that these experiences themselves are still colonial in nature (Breckenridge and van der Veer [eds], 1993)? Such questions would throw doubt upon the 'factual nature' of the British descriptions of India, and suggest that these descriptions *could be untrue*. Consequently, they would also challenge the 'truth' of some of the contemporary descriptions of India. The lines of continuity do not function as evidences for the 'truth' of the colonial descriptions; instead, they raise questions about *the problematic nature of contemporary experience*.

In what way is the contemporary experience problematic? Let me answer this question by focusing on colonialism. To describe the problematic nature of colonial experience, the commonly adopted approach has been to interrogate the intellectuals of India (Gandhi, Tagore, Sri Aurobindo) on the issues they faced when confronting colonialism as a living system. Whether adequate or not, these interrogations are carried out with the explicit understanding that the current theories of colonialism do not succeed in making the phenomenon intelligible to us today. In this sense, speaking in the abstract, the attempt to build an alternative theory can, indeed, be accommodated within the mainstream social science scholarship. However, what makes such an accommodation difficult (if not impossible) is the fact that the existing theories do not question contemporary experiences, but presuppose them as true. That is to say, should an alternative theory of colonialism ever come into existence due to this interrogation, there would be rivalry between this theory and the current theories. Their rivalry would reside not merely in the fact that they give different explanations for the phenomenon of colonialism; it would also be constituted by fact that their presuppositions are antithetical in nature. Hence, the very way they formulate problems would be opposed to each other. In this sense, such is the nature of disputes today that there is a need to distinguish between these two kinds of theories by chalking out a domain of comparative research.

More generally put, here is the difficulty: while the multiple theories of colonialism that exist today are rival theories because they formulate different solutions to a common problem, their differences from a theory about colonialism which might emerge through comparative research lie in the fact that the latter conceptualizes the problem of colonialism itself differently. If that is the case, the issue becomes: which way of conceptualizing the problem is cognitively more adequate? However, before we settle the issue one way or another, we need to keep the difference between these two endeavours in mind. The existence of a domain of comparative research marks the beginning of such recognition. This, then, is the *second dimension*.

There is also a *third dimension*: the kind of 'comparison' involved. Even though the first phase in such a comparison would consist of drawing parallels between thinkers from Western and non-Western cultures (say, between Gandhi and Rawls), this, in itself, does not make it 'comparative'. Something more is required.

To elucidate this point adequately, let us return to what was said earlier about the relationship between the social sciences and Orientalism. I suggested there that, according to the comparative view, the Orientalist discourse is an oblique reflection on Western cultural experience, even though it appears as a description of other cultures. That is, to understand the description of the social world as given by the West and the way it has described other cultures is to begin the process of understanding Western culture itself.

In one sense, this stance is congruent with the insight we have about human beings: when a person describes another human being, the resulting description also tells us 'something' about the describer himself. However, like all such insights, it is also ambiguous: what exactly is that 'something'? Does it tell us of the psychology of the describer, or his ideology, or his cognitive assumptions, or his world view, or his prejudices? In other words, what exactly should we focus on in that description that would allow us to say 'something' interesting about the describer? Furthermore, how can we know whether what we identify in such a description is true, or, at least, not false?

Before attempting to answer the last two questions, we need to note their nature. The first question tells us that, when we study some description also *as a self-description,* multiple things could be studied. That means we have to specify very clearly how we approach such self-descriptions in order to study them. The second question is more generic in nature in the sense that it confronts every hypothesis we make about the world: how do we know whether our hypothesis about some object is true or that, at least, it is not false? Therefore, I will ignore the second question in the rest of what follows and focus mainly on the first. What kind of answers would be permitted in the context of comparative studies in this regard?

Consider what a natural scientist does: he provides (or at least attempts to provide) a partial description of the natural world. Assuming such a description to be true, we can study his description of the natural world as saying 'something' about himself. Depending on how we study this description of the world, we can formulate some hypotheses about the psychology of the scientist (which would give us 'psychology of the scientist'), or the social forces operating on him (which would give us 'sociology of the scientist'), and so on. We could also study the same description as a cognitive product, that is, *as a hypothesis that has specific cognitive properties.* In other words, we study the hypothesis of a scientist about the world as 'something' that gives us clues about what science is. So, when we study many such scientists and study their descriptions of the world as though such a study gives us some clues about the cognitive nature of such descriptions, then we are empirically developing a hypothesis about what science is. To put it even more simply: if we are to understand what 'science' is, then we have to study the cognitive properties of the descriptions that scientists provide about the natural world. In fact, this is how we have been studying sciences for centuries, and that is also the reason why we know more about sciences today than, say, a few hundred years ago. Of course, it is surely the case that 'science' is much more than the cognitive properties of the theories that the natural scientists have produced (Franklin 1986). This claim is not denied here: all that is being said is that the cognitive nature of scientific theories (that is, the descriptions of the world provided by scientists) can be studied as 'self-descriptions', and that such a study gives us at least a partial understanding of what sciences are. Needless to say, one could also study these descriptions in terms of psychological conditions (this would give us the 'psychology of science'); or sociological conditions (this would give us the 'sociology of science'); or epistemic conditions (this would give us an 'epistemology of science'); or historical presuppositions (which would give us a 'history of science'), under which such theories are produced.

The same consideration holds good at the level of individual descriptions provided by members of a particular culture. If many members from a particular culture (say, the Western culture) have produced descriptions of another culture (say, some specific non-Western culture) in such a way that all such descriptions exhibit some shared pattern or another,[4] then we can *also study the cultural conditions* under which such patterned descriptions are generated. Studying such cultural conditions as though they constrain creative human thought, or as though they produce the pattern in such descriptions is to study *the culture of the describer through the medium of his descriptions*. Simply put: if all (or even most) individual descriptions of some non-Western culture exhibit a common structure or a shared pattern, then this structure or pattern allows us to formulate questions for research that reveal the nature of *Western culture*.

A Limitation Overcome

We now need to focus on a single culture in order to explicate the heuristic power of this methodology and, once again, I shall choose Indian culture. Consider the following 'facts', which enjoy a quasi-universal consensus due to centuries of ethnographic work:

(a) India has many indigenous religions (Hinduism, Buddhism, Jainism, Sikhism), and the Brahmins are the priests of Hinduism; (b) native to Indian society is a hierarchical social structure called 'the caste system', which is sanctioned by religion. To these, let us add another 'fact'—accepted till the beginning of the twentieth century, but one which, due to 'political correctness', has disappeared as an explicit claim; (c) Indians are immoral. Leaving aside the theoretical nature of these 'facts' for the moment, let us merely note that these facts constitute the common structure or a shared pattern of works written on India from at least the sixteenth century onwards (traced by Gelders [2009] to an even earlier period).

As already indicated, there are two ways of looking at this pattern. The *received view* would take it as veridical: such a pattern is present in Indian culture.[5] In fact, the disappearance of the third fact—as an explicit claim about the morality of the Indians—could be used to suggest that, because intellectuals maintained a distance from the 'imperialist' and 'racist' attitudes of the earlier generations, such gross generalizations have lost the place they had once had. However, the received view makes an assumption which is equivalent to saying that *whenever* natural scientists put across hypotheses, the latter *always* describe patterns in the natural world. What creates problems for this assumption is that many such hypotheses have been shown to be wrong or false. That is, before we accept any hypothesis as a true description of the world, we need to submit it to cognitive tests. The fact that many people (or even all people) repeat and endorse such a description is no evidence for the truth of the hypothesis: after all, for centuries, people believed and endorsed the claim that the sun revolved around the earth. In an exactly analogous way, although centuries of work repeat and endorse the presence of a pattern in Indian culture, it does not tell us that such a pattern is, indeed, present there.

The second way of looking at the issue—*the comparative view*—transforms the presence of the pattern into questions for research with a 'how' and a 'what': (a) how did Europeans discover the existence of indigenous religions in India? What enabled them to discover these religions and make them conclude that Brahmins were the priests of Hinduism? What evidence is there for either of the two? (b) How did Europeans discover the existence of a hierarchical social structure, when neither its principles nor its mechanism is known to Indians or Europeans? What evidence is there for the claim? (c) How do we explain the conviction of generations of intellectuals in the West that Indians are immoral, when it is simply impossible to convict all these thinkers as 'racists' and 'imperialists'? What evidence does our generation possess that they did not?

Note that there is an additional reason why these issues cannot be settled by pointing out either to the current consensus or to contemporary experience: in the comparative perspective, the lines of continuity between the Orientalist discourse and the current social sciences is a problem to be investigated; the nature of contemporary experience is precisely what is being interrogated for its truth.[6] In exactly the same way that Galileo interrogated our experience of the sun's movement for its truth, comparative research interrogates the contemporary experience for its *truth*.

How should we go about answering the above questions? How can we begin our research into any or all of these questions? If we consider the received view on Orientalism, we are not greatly benefited; either it dismisses the questions, or gives an answer like the following: 'Through empirical observations, people have discovered that this is what Indian culture is like'. ('Why do we see the sun revolving round the earth?' 'Because it is the case that the sun revolves round the earth, and that is something people have always empirically observed.') In one sense, the received view takes a commendable stance: empirical observations or experiences cannot be dismissed. However, in merely assuming such a stance without much ado, it also short-circuits the process. While it is true that scientific explanations need to 'save the phenomena' and not deny them, we have to realize that only explanations do so: Galileo's theory saved the phenomenon of the movement of the sun. He denied that our experiences provided us with the truth, but also explained why we needed to experience the movement of the sun on the horizon. In an analogous way, we need to retain the facts that people have reported about India: that it appears to have religions, a hierarchical social order, and so on. One cannot claim that entire generations over many centuries have been hallucinating. However, these facts do not speak for themselves; we need a theory to explain these facts and experiences. That is what the comparative view does in transforming the presence of patterns into questions for research.

An Example from Religion

In doing so, the *first step* in answering these questions consists of recognizing the following: we are studying descriptions of India in order to understand the cultural conditions under which such descriptions have been produced. That is to say, *in the first step*, we bracket the truth-value of Western descriptions of India[7] and look at them in terms of the cultural experiences of the members of Western culture. As proposed earlier, these experiences are the constraints exercised by Western culture on human observation and thought. Thus, we have to reformulate our questions with respect to the Orientalist descriptions of India. Is there something in the nature of Western culture that makes its members believe in: (a) the existence of religions; (b) the presence of a hierarchical social order; (c) the absence of morality in Indian society and culture? In order to answer these questions, we need to undertake research into the history of Western culture with respect to these themes. What are the assumptions that guide the study of religion in Western cultural history? Note what has happened in this process: we begin the process of understanding Western culture by studying its description of religions in India (Balagangadhara 1994). This point can be generalized: *to understand Western culture, we need to study how the West has described other cultures*.

In the *second step*, we formulate a hypothesis that accounts for why Western culture has found religions in India. When Western intellectuals routinely 'discover' the constitutive presence of indigenous religions (for instance, Hinduism, Buddhism, Jainism) in India, we can suggest that Western culture considers such a presence important in constituting the identity of a culture.

This suggestion (or hypothesis) can be further tested and strengthened by investigating how religion has been studied by multiple domains, ranging from religious studies through sociology to different theologies, in Western culture. This provides us with a hypothesis about the relationship between Western culture on one hand, and religion on the other. This is the *third step*. The last two steps provide us with a second generalization: *to understand Western culture, we also need to study what the West says about the cultural world*.

We need to combine the above two generalizations in order to take the *fourth step. Western culture is what it says about other cultures and what it says about the cultural world.*[8] The (partial) hypothesis about the relation between Western culture and religion can be further tested in two ways: (a) by studying how Western culture has described cultures other than Indian; (b) what the self-description and self-representation of the West is. If, indeed, the predictions made in the third step are confirmed, then one can put across a hypothesis about the relationship between Western culture and religion.

It is only at this stage that we can assess the truth-value of Western claims about Indian culture. That is to say, depending upon what our hypothesis about the relation between Western culture and religion is, we can decide whether the claims about Indian religions are true or false.

An Example from Ethics

For a very long period of time, ethics in Western intellectual tradition has been coextensive with religious beliefs and practices. The contributions of the Greco-Roman world (Aristotelian through the Stoic and the sceptical traditions) have been absorbed, reinterpreted and refracted through the lens of a religious tradition. Secular ethics is of relatively recent origin, and the relation between religious and secular ethics is a subject of controversy (Stout 1988). The fragmentary nature of our ethical theories has led major philosophers to deny the possibility of a systematic ethics (for example, MacIntyre 1984; Williams 1985); others to try and construct one (for example, Arkes 1986); and still others to champion casuistry (Jonsen and Toulmin 1988).

One of the long-standing ideas regarding ethical differences between cultures has been that the rules of moral behaviour vary from one culture to another. What is considered moral in one culture need not be seen as such by the others. There is alleged to be a factual diversity of moral rules. For example, 'going to a barber for a haircut and eating chicken after one's father dies' is considered a profoundly immoral (!) behaviour by all caste groups in Orissa, India, whereas it is seen as totally non-moral by Americans (see, Shweder *et al.* 1987). This factual variety does not damage our normative belief that it is in the nature of moral rules to hold universally. The requirement of universalizability is an integral part of our very idea of ethics. The norm, for example, that people ought not to be tortured for their religious or political beliefs, does not allow exceptions on grounds of race, time or culture.

My hypothesis is that the fundamental difference will be at the level of the moral domain itself. It is not that Indians have a set of moral norms which are different from Western culture; the ethical domain itself is constructed *differently* in these two cultures.

Different in what way? Consider the following claim: in an Asian culture, not only is there an absence of the concept of 'morals' but also of the very cluster of concepts required to speak about the phenomenon.

Consider as a specific example the classical Chinese language in which the early Confucians wrote. Not merely does that language contain no lexical item for 'moral', it also does not have terms corresponding to 'freedom', 'liberty', 'autonomy', 'individual', 'utility', 'rationality', 'objective', 'subjective', 'choice', 'dilemma', 'duty', 'rights', and [what is] probably most eerie of all for a moralist, classical Chinese has no lexical item corresponding to 'ought'—prudential or obligatory. (Rosemont, Jr 1988: 61)

This claim is as puzzling as it is startling: in classical Chinese, it is not possible to speak of 'moral duty' or 'moral dilemmas' or 'moral choices'. It is not even possible to formulate a rule which uses the notion of 'ought'—either obligatorily ('All ought to do X'), or prudentially ('If one desires X, then one ought to do Y'). In Western intellectual tradition, we believe the 'essence' of a moral principle or norm lies in its being formulated by using 'ought', either prudential or obligatory. Without it, there would be no difference of any kind between factual and evaluative statements, and the 'ought' and 'is' statements. Yet, it is precisely that which is impossible to do in Confucianism. The philosophical significance is immense: 'Speakers (writers) of languages that have no term (or concept clusters) corresponding to 'moral' cannot logically have any moral principles' (ibid. 60).

But, rightly enough, we take Confucianism at least as an example of a moral system. What is the upshot of the above remark? Rosemont, Jr, formulates the issue as follows:

If one grants that in contemporary western moral philosophy 'morals' is intimately linked with the concept cluster elaborated above, and if none of that concept cluster can be found in the Confucian lexicon, then the Confucians not only cannot be moral philosophers, they cannot be ethical philosophers either. But this contention is absurd; by any account of the Confucians, they were clearly concerned about the human conduct, and what constituted the good life. If these are not ethical considerations, what are? (Ibid. 64)

This problem is not limited to classical Chinese and Confucianism alone. In India (Balagangadhara 1988), exactly the same problem confronts us. The 'ethical' domain itself is constructed differently: ethical language is not a normative language; ethical relations are factual relations; people act ethically without needing norms of ethical behaviour.

The intriguing question—apart from the truth-value of these claims—is about their intelligibility: what is identified as the moral domain in Asia? How do they formulate ethical judgements? How do they criticize behaviours ethically? How do they settle ethical disputes? How do they learn to be ethical? Above all, how can we recognize it as an ethical domain?

Making one culture intelligible by using the language of another is merely one face of the coin. The other has implications within the West itself. Unlike the received view (for example, Parfit 1984), I would like to argue that the quandaries faced by Western ethical theories have little to do with its age but with its original: religion. What virtues and vices are; why they are that; why norms must hold universally; and what constitutes a moral life—these are parts of a theological vocabulary. Should it be possible to demonstrate the truth of this hypothesis, the consequences would be immense. Neither the Greek nor the Roman intellectuals can be pressed into the service of 'secular' ethics. Plato and Aristotle must become radically unintelligible to a culture which calls itself heir to their civilization. The distance between Athens and Jerusalem will then be at least as great as that between Bombay and New York.

An attempt to specify differences along these lines should help start building a different kind of bridge between cultures. Cognitively speaking, such an attempt might even explain why we have not had a science of ethics so far. Universalizing the provincial experience of a culture does not give us a science of any sort, but merely strengthens the illusion of being a universal culture.

The same applies to other domains, whether it is about the presence of hierarchical social structures or the nature of politics. When we study the West this way, we notice that our problems about how to study Western culture are answered in an objective, non-arbitrary and scientific way. *Western culture itself is studied in a comparative way.* Western culture is what it says about the others and what it says about the cultural world. We *compare* what it says about the others with what it says about the world in order to understand *what Western culture is.* Any hypothesis about Western culture has to account for Western descriptions, both of other cultures and of the world. To condense it: *only a hypothesis that accounts simultaneously for both Orientalism and the social sciences can tell us what Western culture is.* From this it follows that, before we get 'one grand theory' about Western culture, we need to have multiple partial theories about all those domains straddled by Orientalism and the social sciences. Needless to say, we are far, far removed from being at that stage today.

It is here that we see the limitations of current post-colonial studies. Lacking insight into the kind of comparative research that is required, they short-circuit the process: *they wrongly believe that self-representation of Western culture is derivable as the antonym of Western descriptions of other cultures.* If India is considered 'feminine', 'irrational' and 'superstitious' by the West, then they argue that the West has constructed itself as the opposite: 'masculine', 'rational' and 'scientific'. Not only are these adjectives useless in helping us understand Western culture, but they are also empty; in fact, one can argue just the opposite: because of a particular self-understanding, Western culture has described other cultures as its antipodes. Surely, it matters what one says here: self-representation is a derived conclusion or it is the original premise; the choice we make here has its impact on what we say about Western culture or non-Western cultures. In contrast to this, there stands a method of comparative research which claims that understanding the 'self-representation' of Western culture is the end-point of a process; to understand that process, one needs a hypothesis about comparative research.

Understanding the Asymmetry

At first sight, it looks as though this methodology can be generalized, and that it should also work when we study Indian culture: this culture, too, is what it says about others and what it says about the cultural world. However, if we dig into Indian intellectual traditions with this expectation in mind, we are bound to come out puzzled:

(a) 'native' Indian traditions have produced very little about 'others' and even less about 'the cultural world'; (b) modern Indian intelligentsia appears merely to reproduce Western descriptions of India (when they talk about India) and Western self-descriptions (when they talk about the West). How are we to understand or explain these facts, and what do they say about a comparative study of Indian culture?

Let us look at these questions separately, and let us do so by beginning with the issue about the absence of 'native' Indian descriptions about the others and the cultural world. What exactly is absent in Indian culture? I will confine myself to the topics already chosen: religion and God; ethics; social structure.

The standard textbook trivia which we teach our students routinely assure us that not only are there multiple 'native' religions in India (Hinduism, Buddhism, Jainism; different forms of Saivism; multiple varieties of Vaisnavism; the Bhakti movement, Sikhism, and many other kinds of 'popular' religions), but also that they rose in conflict with the ruling 'orthodoxies'. For instance, the pure Vedic religion is supposed to have given birth to a degenerate Brahminism. The Sramana traditions (exemplified by both Jainism and Buddhism) are alleged to have fought Brahminism. The latter itself is said to have mutated into Hinduism, partially strengthened by the Advaitic religion that later fought Buddhism, and so on. In such a case, one would expect a huge volume of literature regarding religion (what religion is, what these individual religions are), and even more, literature in theology. Yet, there is hardly any theology in India (if we look at Christianity as an example of what it means to write theological tracts), and there is hardly any explicit reflection on the nature of religion. (All one needs is an acquaintance with the history of Christianity to notice how staggering this absence is.) To this day, neither the scholar nor the layperson can answer the question about what makes, say, Hinduism a religion; or what that Brahminism is which Buddhism fought. Are we seriously to believe that, for centuries on end, Buddhism—as a religion—fought another religion, Brahminism, without even being able to say what made Brahminism a religion?

Similar considerations hold good elsewhere. Other than the voluminous *Subhashita* and *Dharmashastra* literature, India has produced hardly any noticeable tracts and sustained reflections on 'ethics' (Van Den Bossche and Mortier 1997). There is no equivalent of an *Ethica Nichomachea*, let alone a *Summa Theologica* in Indian intellectual traditions. This does not mean that there is no evidence for intellectual reflections; on the contrary. Yet, certain kinds of reflections are noticeable by their absence.

One such is the famous 'Indian caste system'. All and sundry assure us that the Indian social structure is synonymous with 'the caste system', but all we have by way of an explanation (or even justification) of this system is a few verses: in the Purusha sukta, in the Gita and in some of the Dharmashastras. No Indian could tell you the 'principles' of this system, even though quite a few modern 'theories' about it are floating around. Indologists (Dumont 1972), sociologists (Bouglé 1971), anthropologists (Van Den Berghe 1981), political theorists (Olson, Jr 1984) have provided all kinds of descriptions without being sure what kind of system 'the caste system' is supposed to be.

In this sense, we notice two kinds of facts when we try to study Indian culture. First, there is a noticeable absence of intellectual reflections on these, and allied, phenomena; second, in the course of the last three hundred years or so, Indian intellectuals have merely reproduced Western descriptions of Indian culture and its traditions. When we study India, our question should be: why is there such a vacuum?

Let me make the above general point in a more concrete way as well. Consider the questions that people in the West routinely ask today: Why do Hindus wear a bindi? Why do Indians not eat beef? Is it true that most Indians worship the phallus? What do Indians think about the caste system? Do they still practise sati in India? Why do Indian gods have six and eight arms? What is the symbol of the Hindu religions? Do most Indians worship statues in temples? Do Buddhists really not believe in God? In that case, why are there temples for the Buddha? Are the Hindus religious? And so on, and so forth. Consider now the fact that most Indians do not ask these questions in the process of their socialization. Why are these questions not raised there? I mean to say, why do they not go around asking questions about eating beef, wearing a bindi, worshipping the *Shiva linga*, and so on in India? Why have people not found it important to write huge tracts about such practices? Surely, it is not because they know the answers to these questions; if they did, they would have no problems in providing the same answers to Western interlocutors.

Here is a simple but very important answer: it does not occur to most Indians to raise these questions about their traditions. It does not occur to them not because they are any less curious or intelligent than people in Western culture, but because such questions do not make sense in their cultural milieu. That is, they learn not to ask such questions about their traditions, and this learning is a part of learning to become a member of Indian traditions. Of course, when we say that they do not ask such questions, it does not mean that they have never raised these questions at any point in their lives: for instance, as children, they, too, would have raised many such questions, and been satisfied by the answers.

When Indians confront such questions in the West, two things happen: (a) they feel compelled to provide an answer; (b) the answers they give very closely track the answers already provided by Western culture. That is to say, when such questions are asked about Indian traditions, one should not assume that those questions are intelligible to those Indians; they are not. It is in the nature of Western culture to raise such questions. Furthermore, such questions also outline the kind of admissible answers.

One of the most important consequences of this claim is this: when Western culture quizzes Indians about the nature of their traditions, the former culture is telling us about itself. To provide answers to Western interlocutors about Indian traditions, one needs to understand the nature of Western culture. Simply put: to understand, let alone answer, such questions about Indian traditions, one has to understand Western culture.

In other words, we face an asymmetry. To study and understand Western culture, we need to study what it says about the others and the world. However, we need to do exactly the same thing even when we want to study Indian culture. Alternately put, we compare Western descriptions (of the others and the world) to understand the West; if we want to understand India, we have to begin by saying why (and in what sense) India is not like the West. Our desire to study India by looking at what it says about the others and the world is not met with.

Why is there such an asymmetry? It has to do with colonialism that established frameworks of inquiry into the nature of human beings and societies through the use of power and violence. Once established and generalized, such frameworks continued to draw their legitimacy through sources other than those that were cognitive in nature. Today, this legitimizing process has reached its apotheosis in the guise of an attitude which suggests that a science of culture and sciences of the social are simply impossible because of human and epistemic limitations. Needless to say, a persistent 'anti-scientific' attitude adds fodder to such an attitude.

Why do we have to indulge in this kind of comparison when we study other cultures? Does it mean that Western culture is the 'norm' and that we have to explain other cultures as 'deviations' from this norm? Why can we not, in the process of studying other cultures, study them directly? Why compare? For instance, to study India, could we not simply continue with 'empirical' and/or 'textual' studies produced in India to understand Indian culture?

I would like to answer these questions in two ways. The first is to draw attention to the fact that the only framework that we could possibly use today to study Indian culture would come either from Orientalism, or from the social sciences, or both. If we use these frameworks, we will merely add to the existing Western descriptions of India, and these would not advance our understanding of Indian culture. Of course, one might have no problems with either, and, in so far as such frameworks allow us to find 'the truth', we should go ahead. This is the received view on Orientalism and the social sciences, whose legitimacy requires endorsements until the emergence of alternate and rival theories that challenge the current understanding. That, in fact, has been my argument so far. However, I am not interested in criticizing this view, but in elaborating on the answers given by comparative research.

In elaborating on the comparative view, I would like to return to the Indian case and to the observation made about Indian intelligentsia: this layer reproduces Western descriptions of both India and the West. This observation is not meant as a criticism; it is merely what we say it is: an observation. However, I would now like to add a nuance to this statement in a way that would help us methodologically.

Even when Indian intelligentsia reproduces Western descriptions, by virtue of the fact that it is Indians who do this, we can say that they speak both about others and the cultural world. However, in reproducing these Western descriptions about India and the others, something additional intervenes: the Indian intelligentsia, too, is *constrained* by Indian culture. This means, they do not simply parrot Western descriptions of India but *transform* them in the process. Indians reproduce Western descriptions *as Indians understand them*. This is the nuance that requires addition. This addition opens up a way for us to study, too, in a comparative way. There is a pattern and systematicity to the Indian transformation of Western descriptions of other cultures, the cultural world and themselves. This pattern provides us with clues about Indian culture. The insight here can be summarized in the following way: to understand India, we need to study how they transform Western descriptions of India and the world. This, too, can be generalized: *to understand non-Western cultures, we need to study the way they transform Western descriptions of the world and themselves*. Such a study will provide us with insights into the *mechanisms* of transformation. These mechanisms, in their turn, will provide us with knowledge about the cultural conditions that constrain their thinking.

Underlying comparative research is the realization that both Orientalism and the current social sciences are flawed in some respects. However, this recognition takes a form that is different from a mere criticism of them. Their mistakes become problems requiring explanation, and, therefore, the labour of earlier generations of intellectuals becomes our point of departure. Instead of rejecting their claims and efforts as wrong, misguided, or whatever else, we need to take their results utterly seriously. Where they are wrong, we can improve upon them provided we understand that we need to explain their mistakes, too, from within the framework of theories that we try to build. The dynamic exhibited in such a process is analogous to the dynamic of scientific progress: the earlier theories are both incorporated and transcended by newer theories. In other words, the labour of previous generations of intellectuals (whether from the West or from other cultures) is a constraint on any theory formation that we might undertake, in the same way as they are in the natural sciences.

The Idea of a 'Critique'

Beginning with Immanuel Kant, a new concept made its home in German philosophy: the concept of a 'critique'. Kant claimed that David Hume woke him up from a 'dogmatic slumber' (even though it is very likely that Kant never read Hume) and that, as a result, he wrote *The Critique of Pure Reason*. Hegel developed critiques of Kant.

However, it was left to Karl Marx to make the notion more widely known than either Kant or Hegel did. He wrote not only critiques of Hegel, but also a critique of political economy: his 'economic' theory was seen as a critique of the political economy of his day. Since then, this notion has either meant a 'rejection' of science (as in the case of the Frankfurt School), or is conflated with the more mundane and all too familiar word, 'criticism'. Of course, in the modern intellectual world, one announces one's radical intention not by saying that one 'criticizes'; instead, one always 'critiques'.

One of the reasons why the notion of critique lost its original significance has to do with the lack of clarity about the meaning of the word, and the alleged 'troubled' relation between the notions of 'science' and 'critique': after all, Marx developed a critique of the 'science' of political economy. In Marxist intellectual traditions— especially in what has been called 'western Marxism'—this gave birth to questions of the following sort: is *Das Kapital* a 'science' (as Marx claimed) or a 'critique' of a science (as Marx suggests in the sub-title of his work)? How could Marx claim that his work was 'scientific', when he explicitly and emphatically rejected the 'science' of political economy of his day and developed a theory in opposition to those of David Ricardo and Adam Smith, for example? How could the 'science' of political economy be both 'scientific' and a 'critique' of that science at the same time? And so on.

Though it is fascinating, I do not intend to narrate this century-long discussion here. Suffice it to note that these discussions assume that 'science' and 'critique' refer to the cognitive or epistemic status of the texts (or, in modern parlance, 'discourses') in question: Marx's text (or 'discourse') is either a 'science', or it exemplifies a 'critique' of a science. I would like to suggest that the relationship between a science and a critique should be looked at differently, so that it allows us to appreciate their difference properly.

Immanuel Kant and Karl Marx did two different things: (a) they pointed out mistakes in the work of their predecessors; and (b) they developed a theory that explained how and why those mistakes were necessary. Kant, for instance, outlined the antinomies of pure reason and explained how these come into being. This explanation is a part of Kant's philosophical theory about knowledge. In the same way, Marx explained why, of necessity, Ricardo committed the mistakes he did and this, too, is a part of Marx's theory. In other words, the notion of a 'critique' picks out a relationship between two succeeding theories: it is a relational predicate that applies to a predecessor theory and a succeeding theory. The latter includes an explanation of the mistakes (including an account of their necessity) of the former within its purview. Because it is a relational predicate, one can also speak about it as a property of the succeeding theory: the theories of Kant and Marx are 'critiques'. However, we need to note that this predicate is relative in nature. It is relative to two theories, of which one is a predecessor and the other, a successor. In this sense, Marx criticized the earlier science of political economy, and also explained its mistakes; by virtue of this, his theory is a 'critique' of the science of political economy. However, to the extent that one believes that Marx's theory is also scientific, then, to that extent, the relationship between Ricardo and Marx is the same kind of relationship as between, say, a Copernicus and a Galileo.

A critique is a relational predicate that is applicable to theories, whether they are scientific or philosophical in nature. It tells us that a later theory exhibits and explains the mistakes of the earlier theories as a part of its own explanatory hypotheses about some relevant part of the world. At a generic level, such a cognitive movement expresses the dynamic of the growth of scientific theories: the mistakes and the successes of the earlier theories (for the most part) are explained in the later theories. A comparative science is such a critique: it is a critique of Orientalism and contemporary social sciences that are influenced by Orientalist theorizing. On one hand, without the presence of Orientalism or contemporary social sciences, such a comparative science would fail even to exist. Thus, it presupposes the work of preceding theorists and their theories. On the other hand, such a science also explains the mistakes of earlier works and incorporates their explanatory successes as well.

In this sense, not all scientific theories are critiques, only some are. The appellation signals that one or the other theory builds on the work of earlier generations in some domain. It suggests, too, that the new theory argues that the earlier theories were wrong, but that their mistakes were, in some sense, inevitable. It hints, furthermore, that the new theory is a break of some sort when compared to its predecessor theories. In doing so, it also sketches out an objective starting point for research. Thus, it answers the question that has preoccupied centuries of philosophical discussions: with what must a science begin? Today, this question is not considered as an important problem in the philosophy of sciences, but that does not mean that it has lost its significance.

Consider a simple way of formulating the problem. How could a comparative science succeed in theorizing about the West and India when generations before us have failed to carry out the task adequately? From where should such a process begin? This beginning itself presupposes some implicit theory, and it appears as though there are good reasons to begin an investigation the way this chapter has outlined such a research. Thus, it is not a research that begins without presuppositions, but one which accepts the fact that all research has multiple contexts: linguistic, historical and conceptual. Together, these contexts have provided us with a set of problems: why were the earlier generations wrong? How can we explain their mistakes without appealing to *ad hoc* hypotheses except by incorporating their failures in the process of developing a hypothesis about some part of the world?

To make it more concrete, consider how these questions emerge in some of the sub-domains about which I have already spoken. Why did earlier generations think that Indians were immoral? One could come up with many ad hoc hypotheses as answers: they were racist, imperialist and xenophobes. While many such answers are given, they are both ad hoc and implausible. They are implausible because they transform entire generations into unauthentic bigots in the process of answering the question. A comparative solution to this problem is compelled to answer the same question differently. The answer has to be sought in what ethics is, in the nature of Western ethical thought and Indian ethics. In other words, any such answer emerges as an alternative theory of ethics. At the moment, it is of no consequence how and in what sense it is a competitor to Western ethical thinking. The point is that it accounts for the perception of the Western world about Indian morality by appealing to the nature of ethical thinking. The same considerations hold good in the other two domains about which I have talked: religion and the caste system.

In other words, there is a criterion to judge whether or not one or another theory is a critique and, as such, is a part of comparative science. Does the theory explain the failures and the mistakes of earlier generations of intellectuals as necessary mistakes, given the nature of the phenomenon under question? Does the theory under consideration explain the earlier mistakes as part of a theory about the phenomenon that is being investigated? In answering these two questions, the question of where to begin also gets answered. It provides a non-arbitrary and objective point to begin investigating the social and cultural phenomena. In doing so, it also suggests why comparative science could succeed when earlier generations had failed. In this sense, the subsequent chapters (and this entire book) should be seen as making contributions to such a critique. In the full sense of the word, my effort is 'a contribution to a critique' that succeeding generations are most likely to develop.

Notes

1. '... interesting work is most likely to be produced by scholars whose allegiance is to a discipline defined intellectually and not to a "field" like Orientalism defined either canonically, imperially and geographically. An excellent recent instance is the anthropology of Clifford Geertz ...' (Said 1978: 328)

2. Analogous ideas can also be found in Larson and Deutsch, (eds, 1988); Loy (1988); Roland (1988); Hall and Ames (1987); Shweder and Bourne (1984).

3. Note that showing the superiority of Western forms of democracy when compared to, say, the form of governance that Saddam Hussein practised is not an answer to the question. If—and only if—one can show that these forms of governance are particular products of these two cultures (the Western and the Iraqi cultures), only then will the answer have teeth. I suggest that no intellectual field has come up with this kind of research.

4. In fact, one of the achievements of Said's *Orientalism* is to draw our attention to the presence of such patterns in the descriptions provided by members of Western culture, when such individuals are separated from each other in time and space and are ignorant of each other's work. He called such a pattern 'latent orientalism'.

5. One could argue: Would all people over centuries have repeated and endorsed the presence of such a pattern in Indian culture, if it had not been present there? We shall soon see that this is not the best way to argue.

6. Nor will it do to say that we accept that all cultures are equally 'valuable'; we need good reasons to accept such an axiological claim.

7. Because this is what we have to determine: Are they true?

8. This generalization will turn out later to be surprisingly non-trivial and heuristically productive, as I will later argue in the chapter.

CHAPTER 4

Colonialism and Colonial Consciousness*

If we look at the drift of the arguments developed so far, one question forces itself upon us. We have discovered that there is no reason to give up the concept of 'culture', and that the research programme I discuss could also develop independent of the considerations elaborated in Said's *Orientalism*. In this sense, the comparative science of cultures, as a programme, could have come into existence any time in the course of the last hundred years or so. Why did this not happen before? The answers to this question are many, but one fundamental reason is this: the persistence of what I call 'colonial consciousness'. I would like to suggest that this phenomenon has not only retarded desirable cognitive developments but also continues to offer the greatest resistance to the project I have discussed so far. In the course of the following chapters, I add flesh and blood to this notion by approaching it from different angles. However, in order to understand colonial consciousness adequately, we need to grasp properly the event of colonialism itself. Therefore, it is with colonialism that I shall begin.

* An earlier version of this chapter (with Esther Bloch and Jakob De Roover) was published in 2008 as 'Rethinking Colonialism and Colonial Consciousness: The Case of Modern India' in S. Raval (ed.), *Rethinking Forms of Knowledge in India*, Delhi: Pencraft International, pp. 179–212.

Theorizing Colonialism

Colonialism has been one of the most significant phenomena in the history of humankind in the last three hundred years or so. Its importance can hardly be overstated. Yet, as many have said, it has not been adequately theorized (see Horvath 1972; Osterhammel 1997; and the preface in Page and Sonnenburg [eds], 2003). There is, of course, a great deal of material on the histories and the effects of, and the political resistances to, colonialism. Reading them, however, merely increases the puzzlement about colonialism: though it seems to be the root of all ills of the modern world, it is not clear how or why that should be the case. Perhaps, this has to do with an *implicit consensus* shared by many: everyone appears to know what it is, and most agree about its immoral nature. Colonialism emerges as a self-clarifying and a self-explaining phenomenon. If it is self-luminescent and so manifest an evil, why have many people in the 'Metropolis' argued for centuries on end, both about the nature of the phenomenon and its moral status?

This question becomes even more complex if we look at the participants in this debate. Liberal theorists like John Locke (Arneil 1994), John Stuart Mill, and revolutionaries like Karl Marx (Avineri [ed.], 1969) found colonialism a positive event in world history; among those who opposed it, there were conservative political thinkers like Edmund Burke. Today, however, there is a reconfiguration of this constellation: liberals, leftists, and radicals are unanimous in condemning colonialism; those who dare speak about its 'positive' aspects are the conservatives and those from the extreme Right. One cannot explain this state of affairs by drawing attention to the shifting nature of political labels like the 'Left' and the 'Right'. If a political theory that has criticized Fascism does a volte-face a century later to celebrate it as a 'liberation movement', such a situation questions our understanding of Fascism rather than say much about the shifting nature of political labels.

Consequently, on what grounds can one determine whether the ethical and the political stance one assumes with respect to colonialism is adequate? I believe that both the refusal of Marxist theories to assume an ethical position and the nature of moral criticism that exists today are symptomatic of our lack of clarity about the nature of the phenomenon. Often, criticisms of a colonizer's specific action replace an ethical criticism of colonialism. Ethical objections to both the role of the British Crown and the activities of the British East India Company do not allow for an automatic extension. That is, such arguments are not criticisms of the project of colonialism in general or of the colonization of India, unless one can show what is unethical about the project itself. What can be *unethical* about a project that—among other things—industrialized the colonies, established courts of law, laid railroads, and introduced scientific education, modern medicine and parliamentary democracy? As long as we do not address this issue properly, there are no obvious reasons to assume that the earlier generations of thinkers were wrong. Today, it is not clear how or why colonialism is an evil or from where it draws its evil strength. In other words, we lack an adequate understanding of colonialism. At least, that is partly what I want to suggest in this chapter.

How does one show that something—in our case, substantial knowledge about colonialism—is absent? Based on what we know about colonialism, if we could reasonably expect the absence of a phenomenon and yet notice evidence of its presence, we would be justified in claiming that we do not know much about colonialism. I believe we do have such a candidate: *colonial consciousness*.

In both the 'Metropolis' and the colonies, colonialism generated a particular way of looking at the world. Using the word 'colonial consciousness' to indicate this particular way of looking at the world for now, I would like to suggest the following: if colonialism were to belong to the past, then we would expect colonial consciousness to be absent from the descriptions of the modern world. If we find indications of its presence, we clearly need to rethink the claim that colonialism is a phenomenon of the past.

Such questioning is possible only if one assumes that the way people describe the world depends non-trivially upon the structure of their world. A colonial Indian subject is likely to describe his world differently as compared to an intellectual born after the event. This assumption is a part of our understanding of colonialism. Should there be no difference between the colonial and the modern-day descriptions of India, it could only mean one of two things, *both of which* show the inadequacy of our understanding of colonialism. Either there is nothing 'colonial' about British descriptions of India or, if there is, the colonial ways of describing the world persist even after 'colonialism' has allegedly ended. In both cases, our notions of the relation between colonialism and colonial consciousness—and, consequently, our understanding of colonialism itself—are due for a revision. Is colonial consciousness absent from the descriptions of modern India? If present, what are its implications for our understanding of colonialism?

The Colonizers versus the Colonized

One of the striking things about British rule in India is its *success* in developing certain ways of talking about Indian culture and society. The British criticized Indian religions; the Indian caste system (Dirks 2001); the Indian education system (Pennycook 1998); practices like sati (Mani 1998); the dowry system (Oldenburg 2002), untouchability, and so on. They *retold* Indian intellectual history by describing it as indigenous responses to some of the ills that they, the British, saw in Indian society and culture: for example, Buddhism, as it emerged out of their reconstruction, was a revolt against Brahminism and the caste system (Almond 1988) even if, as a revolt against the caste system, it did not prove very successful. Many Indian intellectuals made British criticisms their own: the Arya Samaj, the Brahmo Samaj, and many other Hindu reform movements exemplify this trend. This way of talking has been a success because it has continued to define contemporary discussions about India. They have not transcended the terms of the debate as set by the British.

To demonstrate the truth of the above statement, let me begin by saying that one looks at colonization *as though* it were a contest between the colonizer and the colonized about their respective strengths. The colonization of India by the British expresses British superiority and, by the same token, uncovers the weakness of Indian society.

This appears to be a thread running through the implicit consensus about colonialism because many explanations for this weakness are floating around: (a) India was never a nation before the British made her into one; (b) the weakness of Mughal rule in India; (c) the caste-ridden and divisive nature of Indian society; (d) the absence of a centralized state and the presence of many small kingdoms; (e) because of which the British policy of 'divide and rule' was successful. There are many more than these five, but this list should suffice. 'How could a few thousand have conquered a nation of millions, if we had not been weak?' That is how both Mahatma Gandhi and the Indian independence movement formulated the problem. Indian nationalist thought crystallized around the certainty that colonization expressed the weakness of Indian society and culture, and the strength of the British.

However, the above perception does not emerge from a scientific study of colonialism but from the *rhetorical force* of another question: 'If colonization is not an expression of weakness, what is it? An expression of strength?' Even though every historian routinely assures us that 'higher' civilizations can be conquered and overrun by 'barbarians', the studies of colonial history do not appear to have moved away from this rhetorical question. On the contrary, they try to provide 'insights' into Indian weakness, and tell us what they were. Of course, the strengths of the colonizer appear obvious. There was the emergence of natural sciences that pre-dated colonialism; and then there was the industrial revolution that post-dated colonialism. *Popular consciousness* has telescoped both these events into a single state of affairs: the scientific, technological and military might of the West. The consensus (more or less) is that colonialism expresses the 'weaknesses' of the colonized and the 'strengths' of the colonizer.

In such a case, colonialism becomes analogous to a contest between two *theories* like, say, the Aristotelian and the Galilean theories. One has won, thereby proving the other false or *passé*. In other words, *colonialism expresses the civilizational superiority of the West*. To what extent is this belief present in the implicit consensus about colonialism? I would like to argue that it is omnipresent. Even though most intellectuals would deny holding such an opinion, one can show why many are logically compelled to subscribe to it. Drawing on examples from different domains of study of modern India, I will show that the consensus is broader and has a deeper root than one imagines.

Some Dimensions of Corruption

The Politics of Corruption

According to Transparency International's *Corruption Perceptions Index* 2002, India ranked behind Colombia, Argentina, and Honduras and occupied the seventy-third place in the list of least corrupt countries (http://www.transparency.org; accessed 1 June 2012). In 2005, India slid to the ninety-second position. Colombia now occupies the fifty-sixth position, whereas Argentina (ninety-eighth) and Honduras (109th) have moved further down the scale. In 2010, India climbed back to the eighty-seventh position, but was still behind Colombia (seventy-eighth). Argentina (105th) and Honduras (134th) slid further down the scale. In India, the newspapers are full of stories about corruption (see the collection of articles in Grover and Arora [eds], 1997), and everybody knows somebody who is 'on the take'. It is almost axiomatic that every politician is corrupt (Halayya 1985; Bhatnagar and Sharma [eds], 1991). The same applies to almost everyone in government service—from the highest-ranking officer to the lowest door attendant (Das 2001; Srivastava 2001). All state-owned enterprises (from electricity to telephone) appear to suffer the same fate. Banking and insurance sectors owned by the state seem to join the queue as well.

That is what is visible in the media. Very little is written about business-to-business corruption where an entire hierarchy demands suitable homage from their suppliers, mostly small-scale businesses themselves. If we include 'greasing palms' to get seats in 'fully booked' theatres; beds in private hospitals; seats on trains and private airlines; or to gain entry into educational institutions, we are probably talking about the corruption of twenty per cent or more of the Indian population. If we also consider the black market, it is anybody's guess as to how many Indians are corrupt (Sardar 2001). In short, corruption is as ubiquitous in India as the air we breathe which, in most big cities is polluted, as we well know. The media does not stop clamouring, the citizens do not stop complaining, yet there is no solution in sight. Of course, many commissions have been set up to investigate corruption. The problem is that the commissions set up to punish the corrupt end up becoming corrupt themselves.

Gunnar Myrdal (1968), a developmental economist, was one of the first writers of international stature to raise the issue of corruption in the context of Asian economies. He identified corruption as one of their main obstacles to economic growth. Since then, we have had many proposals to understand corruption (Alatas 1990): from claims that it is a regrettable but inevitable phase in transitional economies (Huntington 1968), through its positive contribution to the growth of economies (Bayley 1978), to its debilitating effect on society. While some argue that corruption is a result of British colonization (Verma 1999), there is enough material to suggest that the British encountered corruption before they established their rule over India (Misra 1977). In fact, one of the typical lamentations in nineteenth-century Britain was the corrupting influence of the 'Orient' upon young and impressionable minds (Juneja 1992). Even if these analyses remain fragmented, in some sense at least, they remain tied to the larger issue of the relation between the development of societies and the nature of corruption.

In the last two decades or so, economic theories of political corruption have come to occupy centre stage (Hopkin 2002 and the articles in Williams and Doig [eds], 2000). With the growing realization that political corruption is not limited to countries in Asia, Africa and Latin America, but is also prevalent in Western democracies, the quest has been to find a suitable general 'theory' of political corruption. Though laudable, this quest has pushed the broader issues into the background without tackling them. It has done that by circumscribing the phenomenon narrowly as political corruption, namely, the corruption of public officials. Even here, the focus is on explaining how corruption could take hold among public officials (Tullock 1996). These explanations are adequate for our purposes in the same way that an explanation of homicide is adequate for understanding genocide. When we talk about corruption in India, we are not talking about the actions of some individuals, which might make sense on the assumption that they deviate from the standards upheld by the rest. Instead, we are talking about a widespread *social phenomenon* (Chaudhuri 1994; Vittal 2000) that differs from the talked-about political corruption the way a fight between two individuals differs from a war between two nations.

The analyses of corruption in India today do not progress beyond the repetition of 'platitudes' regarding both its origin and the ways of combating it (Braibanti 1962 identifies twelve such). What one hears on the streets; how the élite talk about it (Pavarala 1996); what scholars write about it (Das 2001; Rose-Ackerman 1999; and the articles in Williams and Doig [eds], 2000); and what villagers say about the local bureaucrat (Gupta 1995) are almost identical in nature: 'We need a strong moral entity to root out corruption'. In a situation where the entity itself is corrupt, the question, of course, is *Quis custodiet ipsos custodes* (Who will guard the guards themselves)?

If corruption has shown a *phenomenal growth* since Independence (Visvanathan and Sethi [eds], 1998), it can only mean that it is the social fabric or the social structure which enables such a rapid growth. The Indian soil, so to speak, must be very conducive to the growth of 'a cancer that eats into the innards of the country'. Indian society hosts this cancer, and its immunological mechanisms are ineffective in fighting it. If the people of India constitute the cells of the country and if 'corruption' is the disease, the only possible immunological mechanisms are, of course, the social and moral principles. In which circumstances would a person be a fool not to take bribes? The answer is obvious: in a situation where everyone else is corrupt. That is to say, corruption must be a *successful* social strategy: because everyone else is corrupt, it pays to be corrupt oneself. That is, in today's India, *it is rational to be corrupt*. If Indians have become corrupt so massively, so quickly and so easily, what does it tell us about their morals or society? Let us postpone the issue of morality for the moment and focus on the nature of society.

It is in social groups that one learns to be corrupt. If 'being on the take' is a successful social strategy, then it follows that the social group from which an individual learns it must itself *embody* this strategy. That is, the social group must itself be corrupt. However, corruption is not limited to any one particular social group in India, no matter how one defines the constitution of such a group. If 'corruption' cuts across all social groups present in Indian society, it follows that the nature of 'society-at-large' itself must be responsible for this situation: Indian society corrupts every one of these groups. The nature of this society must be such that it teaches the individual to *learn* to be corrupt in his goings-about with fellow human beings. That is, in some appropriate sense of the term, *the social structure must itself be corrupt*.

The Sociology of Corruption

If much of the Western description makes the caste system synonymous with the Indian social structure, caste itself appears as ubiquitous to Indians as the very air they breathe. From politicians to political pandits, from the pimps to the prime minister—all seem to belong to the caste system. Most intellectuals—ranging from the extreme Right to the extreme Left—have firm moral opinions on the subject. Quite a few theories float around as purported explanations of the caste system. Some see a deformed class-relation in it; others, a fossilized coalition of associations (Olson, Jr 1984). Some see hygienic principles operative in the caste system (Dumont 1972); still others, some transaction rules (Marriott 1990). Some call it racial segregation, whereas others see in it the propensity of human beings to maximize fitness through extended nepotism (Van Den Berghe 1981).

Whatever one's thoughts on the subject may be, most intellectuals appear to agree that the caste system is an obsolete form of social organization. The index of its obsolescence is the hindrance that it offers to everything that is desirable: progress, economic development, social equality, justice ... As many people believe, it is the bane of Indian society and culture. The caste system appears to epitomize everything that is bad and backward.

Why does it so stubbornly refuse to disappear? How can one eradicate this social and cultural impediment to progress? The existing answer—in both theory and practice—is surprisingly simple: the caste system persists because of 'prejudice' and that is what one should remove. About what kinds of prejudice is one talking? Let us run quickly through some of them: the prejudice of 'untouchability'; the prejudice which condemns one to servitude due to accident of birth; the prejudice that Brahmins belong to a superior 'caste' because of karma ... Not only is this a well-known list, so also are the anecdotes that accompany it. There are horror stories of discrimination practised by upper-caste groups: denial of basic human rights to some people; refusal to allow lower-caste groups to enter temples; refusal by upper-caste groups to partake of food and water with lower castes. As this anecdotal discourse progresses, it transpires that the caste system is virtually synonymous with untouchability, moral discrimination, the denial of human rights, and so on. That is, these (and allied) prejudices are instilled in people from their birth, and the caste system is kept alive by the practice of these prejudices. Very simply: *the caste system is a set of immoral practices*.

Let us get a grip on the *extent* of the immorality of the caste system by comparing it to other large-scale (immoral) phenomena that we know. For example, discrimination against the minorities in the US is not a social organization, even though it is a social phenomenon. The apartheid regime was both the policy of a government and a regime imposed on society, but it was not a social structure. Fascism was a political movement (and a state form), but it was unstable. The caste system is, in some sense, all of these and much more.

It appears to have managed to survive onslaughts from Buddhism, the Bhakti movement, colonialism, capitalism, the Indian reformers, current Indian legislation, and Western theorists. Clearly, in that case, we have a unique, sui generis phenomenon on our hands. It is more evil than colonialism and the concentration camps, more widespread than ethnic discrimination, and has a longer history than slavery.

While one might be willing to grant that practices like those indicated above are immoral, it might not be obvious why the caste system becomes an immoral *system*. The answer is simple: *'caste' is an ordered and structured system*. Every social organization is an ordered and structured entity, and the caste system is a social organization. The immorality of this social organization lies in the fact that it imposes immoral obligations in an ordered and systematic way. That is, the caste system is an immoral social order twice over: not only does the practice of caste discrimination violate certain moral norms but also, as a social order, *it makes immorality obligatory*.

When is someone—anyone—immoral? The answer is obvious: only when one willingly chooses to act in an immoral way. That is, the action has to be voluntary and must be the result of a choice in the presence of relevant alternatives. The caste system might impose immoral obligations, but an individual can choose not to obey them. Buddhism and the Bhakti movement illustrate this. From this, it follows that those who are within the caste system—and remain within it—are immoral in a systematic way. In this case, except for the individual heroes who have opted out, *all other Indians become immoral*. (After all, caste division is present even among Christians and lower-caste groups, and it is recognized in the schedules of the Indian Constitution.) If one takes the stance that the caste system is the embodiment of corruption, then one is arguing that Indians are either immoral or intellectually weak. It also suggests that Indian 'culture' and 'religions', too, are immoral. In this way, the talk of the 'masses' mimics the manner in which the intelligentsia talks about caste and corruption: Indians are immoral and corrupt. This tale carries a sting in its tail: if corruption and caste are rational and successful strategies of social survival, the 'norms' that generate such strategies must themselves be immoral. That is to say, the inescapable conclusion is that *Indian ethics itself must be corrupt*.

The Ethics of Corruption

In the journal, *Asian Philosophy*, an Indologist and a philosopher, Van Den Bossche and Mortier (1997) team up to tell us something about Indian ethics by analysing a Jain text (the *Vajjalaggam*, *VL* for short). It was composed anywhere between 750 and 1337 CE by a Jain poet, Jayavallabha by name. This 'ethical' text, Van Den Bossche and Mortier tell us, belongs to the *Subhashita* literature and is a challenge of sorts: 'One problem with the study of Indian ethics is that the ancient Indians themselves did not make a clear-cut distinction between the "moral" and other spheres. They did not have a word for our term "ethics" at all' (Van Den Bossche and Mortier 1997: 85). The ancient Greeks introduced not only the word *ethica*, but also gave us many substantial treatises on that subject, including Aristotle's *Ethica Nicomachea*. If this Indian text—composed around 650–1,200 years ago—does not even have a word for the phenomenon called 'ethics', then how could it be an ethical tract at all? After all, the 'text does not contain one single general rule stated in the prescriptive mode. General rule of conduct may easily be derived from various statements, but it is significant that the rules are not formulated as such ... The statements are written in the evaluative rather than the normative mode' (ibid. 95). If there are no normative rules in this particular text, it is not a deficiency of this text alone. As noted already, Sanskrit, the language of this text, does not even have a word for the domain, namely, the ethical. Consequently, the authors do not study it as an ethical text but 'as a socio-ethical document', which gives a 'mosaic-like picture of feelings, attitudes and thoughts of different authors of *ancient India*' (ibid. 87; emphasis mine).

A question arises, though: how can one speak about 'ancient' India when talking about a text composed during the 'Middle Ages'? Here, the reader has to assume that 'antiquity' is *civilizational*: compared to the 'ancient Greeks' (of about 2,500 years ago), the Indian civilization of about 700 years ago is more 'ancient' (that is, more primitive). Of course, this claim is not explicit but, especially in light of their eloquent conclusions, it is the only possible interpretation.

Although VL exemplifies reflective ethical thinking, it contains no explicit propositions that argue for or against one type of virtue theory or another and it even sometimes lacks the terms necessary to formulate them. In this respect, the writings of the Greek and Roman virtue theorists are undoubtedly *more reflective* than what is found in the VL. Yet, *this is a difference of degree, not of kind.* The writings of the Greeks and the Romans in turn contain little reasoning about ethical language when compared to modern and contemporary moral philosophy. (Ibid. 96–7; emphasis mine)

Contrary to what our authors claim, however, there is *both* a difference in degree and differences in kind: the former, when one compares Greek and Roman ethics with contemporary moral philosophy; the latter, when one compares Indian writings on the subject with those of either of the two.

Even though *VL* 'embodies' ethical thinking, it does not argue for any kind of ethical theory. In fact, it lacks the words necessary for conducting an ethical discussion. The lack of terminology to talk *about* ethics differentiates Indian traditions from Greek culture. That is to say, there is a difference *in kind* between Greek ethics and Indian ethics: the former had the words to talk about it, whereas the other does not. Further, this difference has some significance regarding the 'reflective' thinking that *VL* is supposed to exemplify. How is it possible to reason and think about ethics, when one does not even have the words with which to do so? Obviously, one cannot. That is, there is a *second kind* of difference, too, a consequence of the first: Indian culture did not have the ability to reason and think *about* ethics. (That is why *VL* provides 'a mosaic-like picture of feelings, attitudes and thoughts'.)

There is also a *third kind* of difference. We can understand that better if we understand the *degree* of difference between the ancient Greeks and contemporary moral philosophy: the latter is 'more' reflective than the former. If 'ancient' Indian culture did not have the terms in which to think about ethics, why did its intellectuals not feel the need to *create* such terms (as late as in the thirteenth or fourteenth century)? One presumes that Indian thinkers did not feel the need to create such terms simply because there was no need for it. This, then, is the third kind of difference. Why would there be no need to think about ethics? The choices are not many: there is no ethics in India to think about. Here is a *fourth kind* of difference: Indian 'ethics' is non-existent.

If these *differences* separate Indians from their Greek (or Roman) counterparts, Indian thinkers are on the lower rung of the moral ladder even if they come after the Greeks by almost a thousand years.

Such a civilizational ladder has to look thus: the Indians (of about 1,000 years ago) at the bottom; the ancient Greeks (of more than 2,500 years ago) above them; and contemporary moral philosophy occupying the top. From the point of view of contemporary virtue ethics, if we are to believe our authors, Indians are either intellectual imbeciles or immoral or both.

Indians are intellectually weak and fundamentally immoral. These have been the colonial descriptions for the last couple of hundred years, as the following randomly chosen voices from the past testify. In 1790, Dr Claudius Buchanan, a missionary attached to the British East India Company, arrived in Bengal. Not long after his arrival, the good doctor stated, 'Neither truth, nor honesty, honour, gratitude, nor charity, is to be found in the breast of a Hindoo.' In the words of Charles Grant (1746–1823), chairman of the East India Company: 'We cannot avoid recognizing in the people of Hindustan a race of men lamentably degenerate and base ... governed by malevolent and licentious passions ... and sunk in misery by their vices.' Upon his arrival in 1810, the Governor-general, the Marquis of Hastings, opined, 'the Hindoo appears a being merely limited to mere animal functions, and even in them indifferent ... with no higher intellect than a dog ...' In a review of *The Life of Robert Lord Clive* (Macaulay 1836) we find:

[Lord Clive] ... knew that the standard of morality among the natives of India differed widely from that established in England. He knew that he had to deal with men destitute of what in Europe is called honour, with men who would give any promise without hesitation, and break any promise without shame, with men who would unscrupulously employ corruption, perjury, forgery, to compass their ends. His letters show that the great difference between Asiatic and European morality was constantly in his thoughts.

Such thoughts *also* reappear in today's experience, whether of the caste system or of corruption or of Indian ethics. When contemporary academics pontificate or the intelligentsia moralizes, the voice may change but not the message: Indians are imbeciles and immoral.

Perverse Phenomena

This message does indeed belong to the realm of possibility. It is logically possible that Indian society and culture are immoral. It is also possible that Indians are intellectually deficient. However, paradoxically, these very same descriptions *also deny* this possibility, but they do so in a perverse way.

The notion of immorality could mean two things: either one violates some moral principle or one follows an immoral injunction. Keeping this in mind, and assuming that corruption is a socially successful strategy, let us note that, because Indians choose and pursue this strategy, they have to think and act rationally. This is an obvious conclusion since to pursue a socially successful strategy is to be rational. Because we are talking about corruption as a social phenomenon, and not as isolated cases of human weakness, we need to ask questions about the conditions of its possibility and the conditions of its reproduction. The minimal requirement for both is that those who take bribes must keep their word and deliver the goods. In the absence of legally enforceable contracts, corruption can flourish in a society only on condition that there is *impeccable integrity* among the corrupt. This integrity is of an 'impeccable' sort because: (a) there are no other 'witnesses' to the act of corruption outside the participants; and (b) there is no need or possibility for any kind of legal mechanism to enforce the 'agreement'. Corruption as a social phenomenon is possible if, and only if, both parties impeccably observe the ethical rule of keeping promises. That is, the so-called 'honour among thieves' (Husted 1994) is an indispensable condition for corruption to become a wide-spread *social phenomenon*. In other words, an 'ethical integrity' of a *perverse sort* (among members of a society) is a presupposition for a description that transforms an entire society into an association of immoral people.

What kind of perversity is involved? Such people choose to obey the immoral obligations imposed by the social order that the caste system is alleged to be. Again, obedience *to obligations* tells us that these people are ethical as well. Indians are immoral not because they violate moral obligations but because the obligations which they obey are immoral in nature. The *perversity* is obvious: Indians are immoral because they consistently *obey obligations*, even if they are immoral in nature.

Such descriptions as those we have seen, then, carry two messages. There is a surface message that transforms Indians into imbeciles and immoral people. There is a deeper message that presupposes their rationality and ethical ability. Alternatively put, the meta-message about the rationality and morality of a people contradicts the object-level message that says just the opposite. In other words, even though the message is that Indians are intellectually deficient and immoral, the meta-message affirms that the opposite is the case. The confluence of these two messages does not carry any plausibility whatsoever.

Nevertheless, these descriptions appear 'empirically true' to those who reiterate them endlessly. Both Indian and Western thinkers unhesitatingly, if unreflectingly, endorse them. In this sense, somehow, it must appear 'plausible' to them. How can we make sense of a situation where an *inherently implausible* message (because it carries two contradictory messages simultaneously) assumes the status of an empirical truth? To the students of history, the answer is obvious. It has to do with how these descriptions emerged in the first place and what happened to them subsequently.

Let us remember that the earliest descriptions of India were those that travellers and missionaries provided. They were framed within an explicit theological framework, namely that of Christianity. According to this framework, heathen religions dominated Indian culture. 'Heathendom' was the name of the sway that the devil held over people. Without the intervention and revelation of God, human beings were an easy prey to the machinations of the devil and his minions, and they were easily seduced away from worshipping the true God. In this process of seduction, the priests of the devil played a major role: they were accountable for the ills of the people just as Western culture is held accountable for the evils of the modern-day world. Indian religions were 'heathen' religions, the people worshipped the devil, and the Brahmin priests played a central role in the degeneration of religion. Because there is an intimate relation between 'being moral' and following the 'true religion', it was obvious that heathen religion implied the corruption of morals. Put succinctly, immorality always accompanied false religion.

Over a period of centuries, this theological framework used in the description of Indian society, her people and culture, solidified into a conviction that became a part of the common sense in the West (Balagangadhara 1994). The possibility of proselytizing Indians came from the same Bible: the corruption of a people not only expresses the need to do so, but also indicates the possibility for conversion. In worshipping the devil, human beings are expressing their hunger to worship the true God. Their straying from the true path indexes their ability to walk the same path. These theological conclusions were part of the 'ethnographic descriptions' of India for centuries on end.

For the following generations of intellectuals, these theological conclusions took the status of empirical truths and premises. The Indian culture and society of their day were obviously corrupt. However, this corruption also taught the truth that Indians were capable of learning. That is, they could be educated and civilized. The 'civilizing mission' of Western culture requires a literal interpretation (see also, Fischer-Tiné and Mann [eds], 2004), if we are to understand the liberal and the Marxist theorists of the earlier period. Centuries of such ethnographic descriptions of India had schooled these generations. Their point of departure and their theoretical frameworks were built upon the conclusions arrived at by the previous generations.

Consequently, the civilizational superiority of Western culture became their *premise*. In describing India, they appealed to Western notions of common sense. Centuries of descriptive straitjacket forced them to select and present 'facts' in some particular way. Over time, these became the facts of our political and the social sciences.

To the Christian missionary, it was obvious that the devil and his minions, or his 'priesthood' (namely, the Brahmins), misguided the Indians. If one was 'secular', one merely secularized these explanations and sought the cause in the 'evil conspiracy' of the Brahmins and/or in the civilizational inferiority of India. Consequently, it was the task of the Christian West to bring either the true religion or civilization or both to the shores of India. Both these 'explanations', whether religious or secular-religious, were the presuppositions and not the results of any 'scientific' or academic study of Indian civilization and culture. For Christians, the truth and the concomitant superiority of their religion were contained in the Bible; for those who secularized this belief, the truth was 'borne' out by the event of colonization. In short, its familiarity masks the inherent implausibility of the message. Further, the way the paradox is resolved is also very familiar: the very corruption of Indian ethics indexes the ability of Indians to learn, the same way that their seduction by the devil expresses their hunger to worship the true God.

When such presuppositions direct the framing of a description, the results are pre-determined. The story confirms what one already knows. This is what logicians call *petitio principii*: the fallacy of assuming the truth of what one wants to prove. In this sense, this 'truth' about the 'White Man's Burden' underpins, sustains, and confirms both the British descriptions of India and the contemporary discourses about India, both in India and in the West. Criticisms of the kind we read—whether on caste or on corruption—are moral in nature. Without exception, they make use of the Western normative ethics for their moral criticisms. However, doing so *necessarily* involves making *factual* claims about the absence of ethical thinking in Indian traditions. One cannot escape this necessity by any kind of protest because the kind of necessity involved is *logical* in nature. Anyone who formulates *moral* criticisms of caste and corruption is *logically compelled* to deny the presence of 'morality' in Indian traditions. This is what the British said about India. This is what Indians believe to be true. This is how Indians experience themselves and their culture.

Colonial Consciousness

This then is colonial consciousness. It is not merely the belief in the civilizational superiority of one particular civilization. It is a belief that functions both as a cognitive premise (whether as a suppressed premise or as an explicit one) and as a logical conclusion of the descriptions of the colonized and, as such, it is a massive exercise in *petitio principii*. *Colonialism involves creating and sustaining such a consciousness.*

The European culture mapped aspects of the Indian culture on to itself in order to understand and explain the latter. This is an anthropological *trivium*. However, to colonial consciousness, the theoretical explanations are integral parts of the framework of civilizational superiority.

In that case, colonialism is not merely a process of occupying lands and extracting revenues. It is not a question of encouraging the colonized to ape Western countries in trying to be like them. It is not even about colonizing the imaginations of a people by making them dream that they, too, will become 'modern', developed and sophisticated. It goes deeper. Colonialism denies the colonized peoples and cultures their own experiences; it makes them aliens to themselves; it actively prevents descriptions of their own experiences except in terms defined by the colonizers. This situation makes colonialism intrinsically immoral. Colonial consciousness is not only an expression, but also an integral part, of the phenomenon that colonialism is. In that case, colonial consciousness itself becomes immoral. Colonialism is also immoral because it creates an immoral consciousness.

Colonialism and Colonial Consciousness

Colonialism as an Educational Project

The above characterization of colonialism requires some qualification, lest it appear as a form of 'nativism', that is, a celebration and glorification of things native. Let me provide that by pointing out that many earlier writers looked at colonialism as an educational project. What did they see in colonialism which allowed them to perceive it as a pedagogical project or process?

Let me begin by specifying what education does. It modifies experience by introducing certain frameworks for description. These frameworks either form experiences or introduce modifications in such a way that the earlier experiences are no longer accessible to the subject that is experiencing. The early experience of a child, as shaped by naïve physics or naïve biology, is no longer accessible to it as it grows up and learns physics and biology in the classroom. This scientific knowledge shapes or forms its subsequent experiences of the world.

In a way similar to the educational process, colonialism comes between the colonized and his experience of the world. The colonizer's terms of description intervene and direct the reflections of the colonized about his experiences. In this sense, *structurally speaking*, colonialism *resembles* the process of education. Apart from the structural similarity between these two processes—education and colonialism—there is an additional reason why colonialism has been described as an educational project by many. As we have already seen, belief in civilizational superiority contains two messages: an object-level claim about the cretinism and immorality of the colonized and a meta-message that affirms their ability *to learn*. Consequently, it is understandable why many from the earlier generations saw colonialism as a pedagogical process that enabled natives to learn.

However, what distinguishes education from colonialism is the nature of the framework that intervenes between experience and its articulation. In the educational process, the framework is justified and justifiable on cognitive grounds alone. The criteria of rationality which evolve over time allow us to make the best choices at any given moment regarding education. In this sense, what makes colonialism immoral is not just the fact that it robs people of their experience of the world, but also that it does so using a framework that is unjustified and unjustifiable.

Furthermore, colonialism does not introduce such a framework explicitly. It creates such a framework over a period of time in many subtle and not-so-subtle ways. Unlike the education process, there are no criteria of rationality by using which one might modify the framework. Therefore, not only does the colonizer *impose* such a framework, he also needs to sustain it in a non-rational way. Consequently, the imposition and the sustenance of such cognitive intermediaries between the colonized and their experience of the world require resorting to *violence* on part of the colonizer. This tells us why colonialism is additionally immoral: it denies the colonized their experience of the world by imposing on them unjustifiable frameworks of description through violence. Robbing human beings of their own experiences of the world in this way is treating them as not being human beings. Such a phenomenon contravenes all notions of agency, whether moral or otherwise. This makes colonialism immoral. (See the next three chapters for different elaborations of this view.)

Discussions about the immorality of colonialism have not progressed much beyond an appeal to some form of utilitarian calculus: the positive as against the negative effects of colonialism upon the colonized (see D'Souza 2002; Césaire 2000, respectively). Such discussions are neither satisfying nor convincing given the absence of anything that remotely resembles an acceptable utilitarian calculus. In the characterization I have provided, we can see why colonialism is *intrinsically* immoral. *Through the use of force and violence, colonialism prevents the colonized from accessing their own experience of the world.*

Freedom from such a framework—the freedom to access one's own experience of the world—requires a displacement of the colonial framework. However, such a displacement cannot occur unless one becomes aware that it is preventing one from accessing one's experience. Such awareness comes through a pedagogical process; it requires education. One has to become critical of colonial consciousness, and this involves a rational scrutiny of the nature of the imposed framework. In doing so, one is forced, as it were, to examine the nature of the native framework critically as well. Such an educational process has two implications which are of some importance to our purposes.

First, one cannot combat colonialism through violence; only non-violent attempts to access one's experience can 'fight' colonialism. In this sense, the only appropriate resistance to colonialism can be a (non-violent) moral and pedagogical act. Second, one cannot make a naïve return and embrace the displaced native framework. The transformed nature of one's experience as well as the necessity to reflect critically both upon the nature of the native framework and the fact of its displacement, rule out a naïve return to a 'pre-colonial' world. It is thus that colonialism forever alters the social and cultural world of the colonized.

We can also appreciate the truth in the perception that colonialism expresses the 'strength' of the colonizer, if we keep the structural similarity between colonialism and education in mind. It is a contest between two frameworks which are used to access and describe experience: the colonial framework and that of the colonized. Even though one has not displaced the other because of cognitive superiority, the fact of displacement remains. If one abstracts the *process and the nature* of such a displacement from the event and, instead, merely looks at the result, the conclusion is anything but startling: colonialism has indeed dislodged the native frameworks. In a contest between 'theories', one has won, albeit not on cognitive grounds. However, if one only focuses on the victor and calls the other the vanquished then, indeed, colonialism indexes the 'weakness' of the native framework.

The Colonizer and the Colonized

Colonialism, however, requires *collusion* between two parties: the colonizer and the colonized. In that case, to the extent that it makes sense to speak of moral responsibilities for the event, it appears as though both are responsible. However, such a stance is likely to raise hackles. How can one suggest that the victim of a crime is morally culpable as well? Is the raped one guilty of the act or only its victim?

This is not a good analogy because I am suggesting something different. I would like to say that both the colonizer and the colonized are morally responsible, but *in two different ways*. The colonizer is responsible for *actively initiating* the process that prevents people from accessing their own experiences. The colonized is morally responsible for *propagating* and *perpetuating* the same process; but he does that in a different timeframe.

To students of political history, it is obvious how the colonizer is morally responsible: he imposes his assumptions on the colonized and, by actively inserting them between the colonized and their experiences, he prevents the latter from accessing their own experiences. It is an active insertion by the colonizer because he has to displace the native frameworks forcibly and, therefore, through violence. It is also active because the displacement of one framework by the other does not take place on cognitive grounds and merits, but occurs through force and coercion.

Colonial consciousness does not involve only subscribing to the truth of an isolated statement about civilizational superiority. Rather, it requires commitment to a theoretical framework that structures how one experiences the social and the cultural world. Such a framework intervenes between oneself and one's experience, and forms one's understanding and articulation of what one sees in the world. To get a flavour of the way this framework functions, consider *how* Sir Babington Macaulay defends the need for introducing the English education system in India.

It is, I believe, no exaggeration to say that all the historical information that has been collected to form all the books written in the Sanskrit language is less valuable than what may be found in the most paltry abridgements used at preparatory schools in England. In every branch of physical or moral philosophy the relative position of these two nations is nearly the same ...
The question before us is merely whether ... we shall teach languages [Sanskrit and Arabic] in which, by universal confession, there are no books on any subject which deserve to be compared to our own; whether, when we can teach European science, we shall teach systems which, by universal confession, whenever they differ from those of Europe, differ for the worse; and whether, when we can patronize true philosophy and sound history, we shall countenance, at the public expense, medical doctrines which would disgrace an English farrier ... astronomy, which would move laughter in girls at an English public school ... history, abounding with kings thirty feet high, and reigns thirty thousand years long ... and geography, made up of seas of treacle and butter. (Cited in Keay 1988)

Underlying this defence of a particular education system is a framework that weighs not just the relative merits of two educational systems but also the two civilizations in an absolute way. Colonial consciousness imbibes *this framework* about civilizational superiority. This framework then filters and articulates the experience of the world.

Consequently, the notion of 'internalization' of the colonizer by the colonized is crucial for getting a grasp on the cultural psychology of the colonized, but I will focus purely on the relevant cognitive aspects. The framework inserted by the colonizer generates a set of psychological attitudes and feelings (Memmi 2003), which are required to keep it in place—the feeling of shame about their own culture; the conviction that they are backward; the desire to learn from the colonizer—and which are fundamental in this regard. Equally important is the cognitive form in which the colonizer has described the colonized. It has the appearance of a 'scientific' theory, adorned with plausible-looking 'explanations' surrounded by the fact of colonization itself. Colonization functions as *evidence* for an explanation of the backwardness of these societies and cultures. The differences between the respective cultures are theorized as lacunae; the *differentia specifica* of Western society and culture become the *summum* of human achievement. The colonized take over these theories and their tropes (Spurr 1993) and adorn them endlessly with details.

Indian intellectuals and reformers enthusiastically embrace the criticism of the 'Brahmin' priesthood, which was a reformulation of the Protestant criticism of Catholic Christianity, as a 'scientific' criticism of the 'caste system'. How is it possible to have a firm moral opinion on the caste system, when no one understands what that system is? This question hardly troubled the British; it hardly troubles Indian intellectuals. While it made sense for Western theorists to speak of the need for a secular state because of their specific histories, how could one simply take over the terms of the debate and 'apply' them in India? Contemporary discussions on Indian 'secularism' miss their point and purpose, but that does not seem to distract the proponents in the debate. The most basic cognitive weakness in the venture is that the colonized have little or no understanding of the relation between Western theories and the culture of their origin. As indicated already, the Western cultural experience of India has assumed the status of a 'scientific framework' for describing Indian culture and society. The colonized are morally culpable because they propagate and sustain a framework which prevents them from accessing their own experiences.

In this process, one *accepts* that the *European cultural experience* of India is a 'scientific' framework for Indians to understand their own culture. However, this very acceptance prevents them from accessing their culture and experience. Consequently, they are unable either to articulate or to understand their own experiences. They deny their experiences while they futilely and busily try to make alien experiences their own.

The Hybridity of the Colonized

Sociologists and anthropologists have often spoken of 'syncretism'— the evolution of commingled cultures from two or more parent cultures—when referring to the phenomenon of mixed cultures. In post-colonial studies, however, one uses the term 'hybridity' while referring to 'the creation of new transcultural forms within the contact zone produced by colonization' (Ashcroft, Griffiths and Tiffin 2003: 118). Ashcroft suggests that 'hybridity and the power it releases may well be seen as the characteristic feature and contribution of the post-colonial, allowing a means of evading the replication of the binary categories of the past and developing new anti-monolithic models of cultural exchange and growth' (Ashcroft, Griffiths, and Tiffin [eds], 1995: 183).

The term 'hybridity' has been most recently associated with Homi Bhabha (1994). By emphasizing the interdependence of the colonizer and the colonized, he tries to disclose the contradictions inherent in the colonial discourse. This term also highlights the colonizer's *ambivalence* regarding his position towards the colonized 'Other'. Bhabha sees hybridity as a transgressive act which challenges the colonizer's authority, values and representations, and thereby constitutes an act of self-empowerment and defiance. This 'mimicry' disrupts colonial discourse by doubling it. Hybridity, Bhabha argues, subverts the narratives of colonial power and dominant cultures; it is an act of self-empowerment by the colonized within the framework of colonial power. The series of inclusions and exclusions on which a dominant culture is premised are deconstructed by the entry of the formerly excluded subjects into the mainstream discourse. The dominant culture is contaminated by the linguistic and racial differences of the native self. Hybridity can thus be seen, in Bhabha's interpretation, as a counter-narrative, a critique of the canon and its exclusion of other narratives. In other words, the 'resistance' of the colonized takes the form of 'mimicry'. The colonized imitates the colonizer and thus challenges the authority of the colonizer. However, Bhabha focuses his attention only on the impact of the mimicry of the colonized upon the colonizer. What additional things could we say if we were to look at the colonized assuming that he is a 'mimic-man'?

If the colonized is expressing his 'resistance' through imitation, it follows logically that this 'mimicry' is *not authentic*. Imitation is the 'camouflage' (Bhabha draws upon Lacan here) that hides his true intention, which is to express resistance. He needs to hide it, furthermore, because he is unable to express it openly. This inability, however, is *moral* in nature: he does not have the moral courage to express his resistance openly but needs the act of imitation as a subterfuge. He is, in short, *a moral coward* as well. In other words, there is duplicity, deceit and cowardice involved *even* in the process of imitation. Writing such a resistance into the heart of the colonized is to write *immorality into his core* and transform him into a fundamentally inauthentic and unethical being. Is this not what the colonizer also said? The native is not to be trusted under any circumstance, including, and especially, when he tries to imitate the master.

Such logic also provides us with a psychological profile for 'mimic-men'. How does inauthenticity and immorality constitute the core of the 'hybrid'? The 'camouflage' that Bhabha talks about is either 'natural' (the way the chameleon naturally disguises itself) or it covers up the 'something else' in the colonized. However, Bhabha conceives 'hybridity' as the contrast set for 'essentialism'. Consequently, there is nothing else (the 'true' or the 'essential' colonized) to contrast with the 'camouflage'. The hybrid functions by *disguising his intention*: it is 'natural' for the hybrid and the 'mimic-man' to be inauthentic and immoral. It is 'natural' not in the sense that it is a biologically acquired property through the mechanism of natural selection, but a socially learned one. The 'mimic-men' learn that it pays to indulge in 'mimicry'.

Following Homi Bhabha's logic, the 'hybrid' is not only inauthentic and immoral, but also a voyeur. That is to say, 'mimic-men' are not able to reflect on their experiences; typical of these hybrids and 'mimic-men' is their inability to access their own experience. When I say 'their own', I do not suggest anything more than the following: typical of the hybrid is his inability to access his experience. They continue with their mimicry and act as though they were still the colonized. Even when the hybrids become the 'dominant culture', they are unable to unlearn what they had learnt when being colonized. Instead, they continue with the same practice that had once paid dividends. In other words, he is a voyeur, someone who gets his kicks by trying, futilely and perversely, to make someone else's experience his own. That is, he simply assumes *as true* that the Western cultural experience is the only framework available for formulating the problems facing Indian culture; assumes as true that the Western cultural experience is also his experience of his culture. *When he 'looks' at his culture he merely sees a variant of Western culture.* Colonization creates *generations* of such hybrids. In their turn, the hybrids breed to bring forth their look-alikes.

This is what happens when 'mimic-men' breed and branch. They not only breed more hybrids but, in the process, also conjure forth their opponents. Such men, according to Bhabha's own logic, have inauthenticity and immorality inscribed on their hearts. They do indeed mimic the West: inanely, incessantly, thoughtlessly, and immorally.

These reflections tell us not to use 'hybridization' as a catchall phrase. It is trivially true that human cultures have evolved in mutual interaction. There is nothing gained by saying that all cultures in the world are 'hybrid' in nature. If we make such a statement, then we are required to distinguish between *different kinds of hybridity*: the hybridity of contemporary Western culture is different from the hybridity of post-Independence India. However, once we say this, we also say that boundaries are needed. One might want to 'wish away the boundaries' the way Nederveen Pieterse (2001) wants to. One can do so only if one does not realize that, if all boundaries are done away with, all we get is an amorphous whole.

Post-colonial thought, as a genre of thinking, becomes ethically suspect. It celebrates 'hybridity' by transforming the colonized into an immoral creature. 'Subversion' becomes a legitimate strategy because of the nature of the colonial principle of exclusion. Even if we assume that such a principle is immoral, what moral justification is there for using 'forgery' and 'mimicry' as 'subversive' strategies? The only justification I can think of is this: the colonized are justified in their immorality because the colonizers are immoral. That is to say, the immorality of the other becomes a justification for one's own immorality. Apart from implicitly defending this principle, post-colonial thinkers go further: while the immorality of the 'colonizer' lies in the principles and the nature of his regime, the immorality of the colonized becomes his 'ontological property'. Let me put this conclusion in the starkest of terms: *the colonized people are immoral creatures, whereas what is immoral about colonialism is its regime.* Post-colonial thought endorses what the colonizer said about the colonized; only it now tries to 'justify' this description. Both colonial and post-colonial thinkers agree that Indians are immoral and untrustworthy. One calls it 'immoral' and criticizes it; the other calls it 'subversive' and celebrates it. One criticizes immorality and the other justifies it. Both, however, accept the colonial descriptions of the colonized. This is precisely what colonial consciousness is all about. The post-colonial thinkers of today, it appears, are standing in for the masters of yesterday.

We can now appreciate what colonialism is, and how it generates and sustains colonial consciousness. The framework about the civilizational superiority comes between the colonized and his experience of the world, a framework shared by the colonizer. These characterizations help us grasp some of the attitudes of the thinkers from yesteryear, while appreciating where they went wrong. They also tell us that these attitudes have not disappeared but continue to guide theorizing in an implicit way.

In the following three chapters, I shall elaborate on the various manifestations and the several dimensions of colonial consciousness and the violence that goes into generating and sustaining it. We shall then discover just how deep and broad this phenomenon really is. In this process, we shall also find out why the project of decolonizing the social sciences is both necessary and urgent.

CHAPTER 5

India and Her Traditions
An Open Letter to Jeffrey Kripal

In 1995, Jeffrey Kripal, currently professor at the Rice University in the US, wrote a book, *Kali's Child: The Mystical and the Erotic in the Life and Teachings of Ramakrishna* (1995; second edition 1998), on Ramakrishna Paramahamsa, the Bengali guru of Swami Vivekananda. In this book, crowned as the best first book by the American Academy of Religion (AAR) in 1995, he uses his version of Freud's psychoanalysis to 'explain' the mysticism of Ramakrishna. Many Indians in the US were outraged by his portrayal of the Bengali guru. The academia in the US continues to see the negative reaction of Indians as an expression of 'Hindu fundamentalism'; some Indians teaching in the US universities agree with their Western colleagues.

I disagree. I do not believe that Indians who react to Kripal's description are blinded by prejudice; nor are they victims of the so-called 'Hindu fundamentalism'. In the next two chapters, I show why the 'Hindu' reactions make cognitive sense. In this chapter, I question Kripal's arguments in one particular way; in the next chapter, I address the same problem in an entirely different way.

For this chapter, instead of continuing in an academic vein, I have chosen the form of an open letter. The choice of this format has partly been determined by the need to express the sense of outrage that many Indians feel when they read Kripal. One can be outraged for cognitive reasons alone, something that many US academics do not appear to understand. I would like to show how and why such an expression of moral abhorrence is justifiable in this case. It is justifiable because, as I shall argue, people like Kripal inflict violence of the kind I have talked about in the previous chapter. I will now outline this process of violence and point to one of the most tragic dimensions of colonial consciousness.

★ ★ ★

Dear Jeffrey Kripal,

Many voices will have joined in this debate by the time I get to publish this. Mine is one of them. In the course of this communication, it is possible that I may raise my voice now and then to make some point or another. Let this only draw your attention to the fact that we are disputing some issues, not as disembodied minds but as human beings; *Menschliches, Allzumenschliches* (human, all too human), as Nietzsche put it so beautifully.

Before writing this letter, I went back and reread your book on Ramakrishna. I emerged puzzled and surprised. I achieved a better understanding as well—if not of his mysticism then at least of your efforts. There was also a degree of incomprehension: how was it possible that your doctoral adviser, renowned for her expertise on all matters Hindu, missed noticing the obvious? In this letter, I will not write everything I would like to, owing to constraints of size and readability. Therefore, let me tell you beforehand that this letter will merely express my perplexities: why you do not see what you do; why you say one thing and do the opposite; why, while seeking knowledge, you are so eager to embrace ignorance. The issues I want to tackle require this format of writing. So, please indulge me. In order to set out the problem, I will begin by sketching some relevant anecdotes.

1. As is the case with most Indians, I learnt English through the medium of an Indian language. I was taught that puja was worship, 'devas' meant 'gods' (in the lower case), and so on. It was not clear who exactly 'God' was, even though I was taught that one wrote 'God' with a 'big G', as we used to say. I guess I assumed that 'God' referred to the entity one 'chose': mine, for instance, was *Ishwara*. Somehow, I fell in love with this 'erotic ascetic' (as Wendy Doniger titles her book

on Shiva) with his abode in the cemeteries; with his tendency to be easily provoked to anger; his *veebhooti*, his snake, and, of course, his children Ganesha and Skanda. No doubt, it has also something to do with my own name and my short temper (as we say in India). One day—I must have been around fourteen then—I discovered that linga meant phallus (as it was explained to me) and that it was a symbol of male fertility. So, when my sisters and mother went to do puja in the nearby temple of Mallikarjuna (another name for Shiva), they actually went to worship a phallus. I was terribly, terribly embarrassed by this explanation, and also felt it was wrong, but did not know what to say about it. I still remember running to the temple to see whether the Shiva linga looked like a phallus. I must confess that it did not. However, my insistence on this fact generated jeering laughter from the person who had given me this information: 'How many have you seen? That is what the penis will look like when you grow old.' My sense of 'wrongness' persisted, the embarrassment never left me, but I did not know what to say.

2. Fast forward to nearly a decade later. I was twenty-four and on my first trip to Europe. I 'knew' about homosexuality in the abstract (that is, it had never occurred to me to visualize it concretely), and had 'no problems with it' (as I used to put it those days). However, I was quite unprepared for the sight of males French kissing each other openly and, therefore, was incredulously fascinated by the scene when I first came across it in Amsterdam. Anyway, I went back to India having learnt about some of the outward manifestations of homosexual love.

As you no doubt know, it is common practice in India for friends to walk on the street holding hands and moving them breezily. It is also not unusual to put your arm across the shoulders of your friend while walking or cycling. I had a friend who was in the habit of clasping my hand while walking along with me. After my return from Europe, I could no longer reciprocate: I knew what it could 'imply'. Even though I had had no problem doing the same before I went to Europe, after my return, I could not. It was embarrassing; but I could not share this feeling with my friend who had never been to Europe. I could not tell him to stop doing it either because it would have affected our friendship. So, I tried not to walk next to him when we were together in a group. When the two of us were alone and on the street, I solved this new problem by *constantly* holding a lighted cigarette in the hand he would want to clasp. Instinctively, as it happened many a time, he would move to the other side; then, so would my cigarette.

3. Fast forward again, to nearly a quarter century later. Today, I am able to reflect on the significance of embarrassments like the above. Now, I have begun to fashion the intellectual and conceptual tools needed to question these experiences: not mine alone but those of a culture. What was the nature of the wrongness and embarrassment I felt when I discovered that linga meant phallus? Why did I feel embarrassed to hold my friend's hand? What sense of wrongness prevented me from telling him what 'embarrassed' me about this simple act of affection between friends? Many readers in this debate, too, express a similar sense of wrongness. Probably, most of them do not belong to the Hindu Right or to the Hindutva movement. Nor are they expressing an ironed-out, prudish, 'neo-Vedantic' strain, as you put it. Instead, they are shocked and feel wronged by the way you have portrayed Ramakrishna. What are they trying to express, when they attempt to put this feeling into words? That is what this letter is mostly about.

4. According to you, Ramakrishna's religious life can be described in terms of a cluster of pathological symptoms. Under the terms of this description, the saint is pathological. *Does not such a description trivialize Ramakrishna, his religious life and his teachings?* One would be inclined to say 'yes', but you deny it. You say (a) you are not *reducing* religious life to the saint's pathology; (b) indeed, if anything, you do the opposite. You say that the uniqueness of Ramakrishna's religious life lay in the transformation of the 'dark natures' of psychic energies so that they 'began to glitter with the gold of the mystical' (p. 322). Therefore, you claim you are not trivializing. Does this claim withstand scrutiny?

Let us deal with the issue of *reduction* and get rid of it quickly because it is actually a red herring. As a preliminary to this task, we will agree on the following about your partial use of Sigmund Freud. Whether or not a particular reading of Freud (or psychoanalysis) is defensible is not the issue. Let us assume that it is a justifiable reading of Freud and/or psychoanalysis. Let us also further assume that one could use the Viennese master to understand the person from Dakshineshwar. Under these assumptions favourable to your project, let us examine what you do.

You provide interpretations: of the 'secret' passages in the biographies of Ramakrishna, of Kali's form, and of some physiological and psychic symptoms of Ramakrishna. However, you cannot merely 'interpret'; *you have to explain*. This move from interpretation to explanation is *logically necessary* because psychoanalysis is an explanation of the psyche. One does not have the freedom to choose *a psychoanalytical explanation* and deny that one is providing an explanation of a psyche. In that case, what are you explaining and what does your explanation do?

4.1. There is a logical relationship between the *explananda* (that which requires explaining) and the *explanans* (that which does the explaining). In this relationship, as in any non-circular explanation, the terms in the explananda do not occur in the explanans. For instance, I cannot explain gravitation by using the notion of gravitation. I need other terms to do the explaining: mass, electromagnetism, nuclear attraction and so on. Similarly, if the religious life of Ramakrishna is the *explanandum*, then the explanans has to appeal to other terms and concepts. If it did not, the explanation would be circular: one would be explaining the religious life of Ramakrishna by invoking the religious life of the saint. Consequently, your psychoanalytical explanation has to explain the religious life of Ramakrishna by appealing to the trauma of his sexual abuse.

When one phenomenon, Y, is explained by another phenomenon, X, then one is *reducing* the description of Y to the description of X. (This is one of the meanings of 'reduction'.) Such a reduction is total, even if the explanation is partial because the terms in the explanans *replace* the terms occurring in the explananda. If it has to be an explanation, however partial it might be, a reduction has to take place. Consequently, in the partial explanation that you provide, you *have to reduce* Ramakrishna's religious life to his sexual abuse. Yet you claim that you are not 'reducing' his religious life to that. All explanations reduce; you claim to provide us with an explanation; and yet, you say, you are not 'reducing'. How can one understand your protest? Either you are not explaining (in which case, you are not reducing) or you have a different notion of reduction in mind.

4.2. Consider another example which might illustrate this different notion of reduction. Let us suppose that we are able to psychoanalyse

Albert Einstein and come up with an explanation of his creativity. Could such an explanation of creativity ever predict the 'meaning' and 'content' of either the special theory of relativity or the general theory? It could not. The explanation of creativity would be a theory of the unconscious of Albert Einstein, whereas his theory of relativity is a theory in physics. At the stage where our knowledge is, we have no idea how we could go from a theory about the unconscious to a theory in physics. Therefore, one cannot derive his theories of relativity by reducing his creativity to his unconscious. Is this what you mean when you say that you are not reducing the 'meaning and content of Ramakrishna's religious experience' to his sexual abuse? Even here, one's fear of reduction is misplaced. The non-derivability of the 'meanings and content' in both these cases (Einstein's theory and Ramakrishna's religious experiences, respectively) has nothing to do with human creativity or the meaning of human freedom or the nature of reality. Rather, it has to do with what reduction is, and what it can and cannot do.

4.3. What conclusions can you draw from the foregoing? There are four logical possibilities. One possibility is that you explain but do not reduce. On conceptual grounds, we can rule this out. So also with the possibility that you neither explain nor reduce. This leaves us with two possibilities: either you explain and reduce, or you do not explain but reduce. If you explain and reduce, your apprehensions about reduction are misplaced. Reduction is not a problem in this case. However, if you do not explain but merely reduce Ramakrishna's religious life to sexual abuse, then there is a problem. In this case, your protests about not reducing cover up the fact that you are *reducing without explaining*. In both these cases, the issue of reduction is a red herring. In the first case, your explanation requires reduction; in the second case, your protests are not genuine. In other words, the real issue is the following: do you reduce Ramakrishna's religious life *without* providing an explanation or do you *explain* his religious life which requires reduction?

5. In order to tackle this issue, we need to see how you frame your explanandum. How do you describe what you want to explain? What *is striking* about your descriptions of this is their triviality. In describing the phenomena that you claim you want to explain, it seems as though you feel the need to trivialize them. I am not observing your psychology but noticing the results of its exercise. In your book, you

have covered umpteen pages trying to establish that Ramakrishna was a tantrik who had problems with Vedantic thought. Because this issue is central to the 'life and teachings of Ramakrishna' (a part of the subtitle of your book), let us see what you make of the Tantrik and the Vedantic traditions.

Let me begin with the 'boring Vedanta', as you put it. (Even if Ramakrishna used this phrase, do not presume to know what he meant.) According to your account, Vedanta claims that the *world is an illusion* and that only Brahman exists.

If the world is an illusion, Vedanta has to deny the existence of the world. To Vedanta, in the way you construe it, the world *is the empty set*. That is to say, all experiences are on a par because they are all illusions. One cannot distinguish between experiences unless one introduces the notion of a differentiated reality. From this, it follows that a vedantin should not be able to discriminate, say, between the following: the pain you experience by stubbing your toe; the pain you have when your arm is cut off without anaesthesia; and the pain you feel when a loved one dies. If he does draw a distinction between them, he is distinguishing between one illusion and another, and the only way of doing that is by ascribing the status of reality to these illusions: this is 'less illusory' than ... this is 'more real' than ... this hurts 'more than' ... this pain is 'different from' ... and so on. If he does not distinguish, and if he insists that there is no difference between falling into a lake and bumping his head against a tree, who will take him seriously? Surely, if Brahman is all there is to the world according to Vedanta, all vedantins must be perfect imbeciles. In that case, we do not need heavy-duty tantrik stuff to shoot them down; a simple dose of common sense will do.

Shankara was a vedantin, as you know. If you had even glanced at his writings—his *Maya Panchakam*, for example—you would have known that what you say does not make sense. In this poem, he describes the power of maya and ascribes agency to 'her'. He speaks about those whom she spellbinds: they are a plurality of creatures and include the learned, the human, the animal, and, of course, Brahman. How could he talk about the 'power' of maya, her incredible abilities to control creatures, if both maya and the plurality of these creatures and their experiences did not exist? Maya makes sense only if *the world and its richness exist*. Maya does not imply the absence of the experiential world; instead, it presupposes it. To say that maya is the nature of the world makes sense. It is, however, *linguistic nonsense* to say that illusion is the nature of existence. How could vedantins discuss with each other if they spouted semantic nonsense?

It is obvious where the problem is partially located. You translate 'maya' as 'illusion'. This translation does not work when you are talking about one of the central categories used by many Indian traditions. To understand why it cannot be a translation of maya, consider the following argument. After all, Vedanta claims that when one realizes the unity of 'oneself' and Brahman, one achieves enlightenment. If 'everyone'—except the enlightened—is under the sway of 'illusion', what causes it? Vedanta claims there are causes. If there are causes, they cannot be 'illusionary' entities. If causes exist, so do their effects. 'Illusion' is an effect. Therefore, illusion also exists. If we were to equate 'existence' with the 'real', Vedanta would become flatly nonsensical. Whatever else Vedanta might be, it is not semantic nonsense. Surely, before indulging in silly contrasts, one should understand what Vedanta denies and what it does not.

Indeed, you do draw silly contrasts. For example, you seem to suggest that there are two different Ramakrishnas: Vivekananda's Ramakrishna who is content with the undifferentiated Brahman; the other, your Ramakrishna, who needs the manifold world. If Ramakrishna was an enlightened person, then his attitude—both towards Brahman and towards the world—is part of such a person. By distinguishing these attitudes as 'vedantic' and 'tantrik', surely you are not claiming that you are in a position to differentiate between *an advaitic and a tantrik enlightenment*. Are you? You glibly talk about the two Ramakrishnas as though one could talk like this without it being nonsense. One could, but only if the notion of enlightenment were rendered into a trivial adjective, which qualifies nothing.

Instead of reflecting on these issues adequately, you moralize: the tantrik tradition challenges the mores of middle-class Bengalis (though, I must confess, they look more like middle-class Americans of today than the Bengalis of yesterday); hence, the defiance and the 'secrets' of the saint. What, if any, is the relationship between morality and the paths to enlightenment? In all Indian traditions, the quest for enlightenment begins when ethical questions and answers cease to satisfy. In most cases, a person's need for enlightenment is directly proportional to the degree to which his or her daily life becomes dissatisfying. Ethics directs the manner in which the person goes about in his or her daily life. Dissatisfaction with daily life also implies dissatisfaction with what ethics is and what it can do. In this sense, *all paths* to enlightenment 'challenge' the ethics of daily or worldly life. In fact, the most radical challenge to *ethics itself* comes from these paths to enlightenment. The tantrik tradition follows a path that is different from every other path, Jeffrey. (The same claim is applicable to each path.) Consequently, the tantriks, too, radically 'challenge' the ethics of daily life (and not just middle-class morality), but do so in a manner that is different from every other path. Are you really qualified to recognize enlightenment, differentiate between the states of enlightenment, and assess the quality of these paths independent of their value to the practitioners who followed them? If you cannot, what drives you (a layperson ignorant of all these matters) to take up cudgels against the assessment of a Vivekananda, who appears to be an enlightened pupil of Ramakrishna's?

You say you are trying to understand. I am with you on this. You further suggest that we need to 'dig' with the best tools we have to understand people like Ramakrishna, and states like enlightenment. I am with you here. We need not cease our inquiries for fear of uncovering unpleasant secrets, you hint. I could not agree more. However, we part company when *you trivialize in order to understand.* You trivialize the vedantins when you speak of their 'boring Brahman'; you trivialize the tantriks when you see in them an infringement of middle-class morality; you trivialize both when you try to contrast them with each other.

6. If you trivialize the phenomena that you want to explain, they will take their revenge. They will render your explanation trivial. That has happened to your 'explanation' of Ramakrishna's religious life.

Here is how you yourself put it: 'In effect, Ramakrishna *took* the "anxious energies" of his early sexual crisis for which he almost killed himself, and *"turned them* around the corner", where they revealed their essentially mystical natures ... he *took* what were regressive symptoms and, through Kali and her Tantric world, *converted* them into genuine experiences of a sacred, mystical realm' (p. 324; all emphases mine). There are, however, certain problems regarding consistency here. The first problem arises because you say Ramakrishna 'did things' with psychic energy. To *do* what he did, required him to have a grasp of the nature of his conflicts and some idea of how to 'turn them around the corner'. Yet—as you are at great pains to point out—his conflicts were a 'secret' to himself. He could not even know, according to your story of secrets, that he had a conflict. He was aware of doing certain things. There were things about his actions that he could not explain. Even if he was 'anxious' to explain them, or asked other people repeatedly for such explanations, these do not establish that he experienced a conflict. I am sure he did not know why milk turned sour or how birds fly, or why he lost hair; perhaps he even 'anxiously' asked his pupils to explain these and other sundry matters. None of them needs to generate a conflict. In other words, consistency requires you not to say that *Ramakrishna actively managed* his psychic energy.

There is a second consistency problem. You speak of 'the radical passivity' of Ramakrishna in the following terms: 'Ramakrishna's belief in the complete inability of the human being to initiate actions was total. Human agency is a pernicious illusion' (p. 68). You might think otherwise about human agency; but to keep the saint minimally consistent we should not ascribe agency to him.

A third consistency problem arises due to your use of psychoanalysis. When we talk about the unconscious, its conflict and its structure express themselves in a cluster of symptoms. An individual can 'sublimate' this conflict if he gains an insight into the nature of the conflicts. (Psychoanalytical practice tries to provide an individual with such an insight.) Ramakrishna did not have this insight, as far as your story is concerned. Consequently, if 'sublimation' occurred, then it would have to do with the manner in which this unconscious was *dynamic*: apart from expressing itself in certain symptoms, it also resolved its own conflict. This resolution took the form of Ramakrishna's religious life.

In fact, many other problems arise when you speak of Ramakrishna's managing his conflicting energies in the above citation: '... *he took* what were regressive symptoms and, through Kali and her Tantric world, *converted* them into progressive symbols, into genuine experiences of a sacred, mystical realm' (p. 324; italics added). I will not be able to speak of all the problems that such a stratagem engenders. Suffice it to note in the present context that, apart from facing consistency problems, you are also begging the question. Remember, you have to explain Ramakrishna's religious life. Kali and her world are a part of Ramakrishna's religious life. If you explain his religious life (visions of Kali, and ecstatic trances) by using his religious life (visions of Kali and ecstatic trances), you will have simply begged the question.

6.1. Therefore, we need to rewrite your explanation, if we are to keep *you* consistent. Either, Ramakrishna's trauma and his unconscious 'sublimated' themselves into his religious life or, Ramakrishna's unconscious 'sublimated' itself into his religious life. Very well. One can accept this 'explanation' if you explain *the how: how did such a transformation occur*? How did the unconscious resolve the conflicts and 'sublimate' them? What were the mechanisms? Here is how you answer these questions: '[F]or the homoerotic energies themselves, freed from the usual socialized routes by the "shameful" nature of their unacceptable objects, *were able to transform themselves, almost alchemically*, until their dark natures began to glitter with the gold of the mystical' (p. 322; italics added). These energies were 'able to transform themselves'. How? 'Almost alchemically'. In other words, *'somehow'*. Not only do these energies *'somehow'* transform themselves, but they also *'somehow'* continue with this transformation until they reach a certain stage, where they begin to 'glitter with the gold of the mystical'. 'Somehow'? 'Almost alchemically'?

You might want to say that we are not clear about the mechanisms. And that the 'somehow' and the 'almost alchemically' merely function as place- holders for a currently non-existent, but possible future, explanation. And that this is merely a hypothesis you are putting forward. However, do you realize the price you pay for giving these possible answers? You render your explanation both trivial and ad hoc. To appreciate the charge of triviality, consider the following: Ramakrishna's neural structure 'somehow' generated his religious life; Ramakrishna's genes 'somehow' interacted with his environment to enable his religious life ... and so on. Do such claims advance our knowledge of anything? They do not. *They are trivially true: all things happen 'somehow'*. Only knowledge tells us which things do not happen 'almost alchemically', as it were.

However, considered as explanations, they are ad hoc in the sense that you literally suck explanations out of your thumb to explain his 'symptoms'. Apart from the story you pen, here are a few more: Ramakrishna had a currently unidentified rare disease, which caused his religious trances; Ramakrishna had a currently unknown brain affliction (a tumour growth), which caused the symptoms from which he suffered; Ramakrishna exhibited a currently unidentified behavioural syndrome ... With just a little patience and a bit more inventiveness, one could conjure up many more explanations, which would satisfy the 'facts' you have gathered. Each is as bad as the other. The upshot of this is the following: unless you specify the mechanisms involved in the 'transformation', your explanation is both trivial and ad hoc.

6.2. Instead of recognizing what has happened, you go to great lengths to hide this 'trivialization process' (if I may thus term your attempt) from yourself and from your readers. From the many 'strategies' you employ, let me take two at random to illustrate my observation.

The first is your continuous use of the word 'secret'. The word plays multiple roles in your text: it signals a deliberate ploy to hide some truths as well as express some others. It suggests the 'unspeakable' and also symbolizes deeds. And so on. An uninitiated reader gets the impression that you are the 'digger' who uncovers not merely some secrets, but the very nature of secrecy itself. However, a careful perusal of your book suggests that you have very little understanding of what 'secrecy' could possibly mean in Indian traditions, or why Indians talk of secrets. For instance, did you know that the Mahavakyas (for example, statements like 'thou art that', 'I am Brahma') are prototypical 'secrets' in Indian traditions? Did you know, too, that, during the upanayanam (the 'sacred thread ceremony'), the father whispers a secret into the ears of his son, and that that 'secret' is the Gayatri Mantra? Do you have any idea why either of these two is a secret? If you do not, there is no way on earth you can decipher the 'secret' of the tantrik world. You do not even make a distinction between what Indians consider secret (and why they do so) and your own Freudian construction of *events as secrets*. Caught up in your own fantasies about secrets and their nature, and by kicking up so much dust while 'digging' into the 'secrets' of Ramakrishna, you have ended up throwing dust into your own eyes.

Now consider a very different strategy. This is how you describe your attempts: 'I have located a pattern, but only a pattern. There is no linear argument here, no clear-cut revelation. There are only symbolic acts that connect up to symbolic visions, which in turn can be associated with symbolic acts, and so on' (p. 296). And then you go on to announce that you will momentarily step out of the 'symbolic web of texts' to advance a clear thesis, a 'linear argument' (ibid.). All scientific theories are a 'symbolic web of texts'. One does not step out of this web to advance 'a clear thesis'; these theories constitute a web precisely because they are spun by clear theses. The only *contrast* to a 'linear argument' that I can think of is a 'circular argument'. A circular argument might also spin a 'web', but it is an intellectually pernicious trap. Why do you suggest that a linear argument (why do you use scare quotes?) is 'somehow' incompatible with the fact that human knowledge is like a web, where things not only appear interconnected but are also mutually dependent? Linear arguments (as against circular arguments) advance human knowledge. A 'clear thesis' is indispensable to the web that human knowledge is. Why do you counterpose one with the other? In what way or fashion is one aspect of human knowledge opposed to the nature of the totality of human knowledge? Of course, you do not even pause to reflect on the claims you advance. You can no more step out of the web that human knowledge is than you can afford to be circular, if you intend to advance human knowledge. Yet, you appear far too caught up by the image of your own stepping out of a 'web' to become 'linear'. In other words, your image of what you think you are doing (which assumes epic proportions at times) seems to blind you to what you actually do.

At this stage, the following charge can be reasonably levelled against you. *You have not really explained anything.* In that case, why have you used Freud? If you have used him merely to show that it is also possible to describe Ramakrishna as a pathological person, you are indulging in mischief. You add to malicious gossip and such an addition *is not* trivial.

6.3. If this is what you do, you trivialize the experiences of another culture without doing anything to understand them and, what is even worse, *in the guise of providing an explanation.* Isn't this what you, in fact, do? Such an action is hardly without moral consequences. You inflict violence on those fellow human beings whose experiences you talk about.

You trivialize the traditions you speak about, you trivialize enlightenment, you trivialize the phenomenon you want to explain, and your explanation is trivial. In short, your purported explanation *trivializes experiences.*

By virtue of this, experiences are *transformed.* What does the transformation consist of? Such purported explanations *re-describe experiences by twisting or distorting them.* Without explaining anything, you have re-described Ramakrishna's religious life as a cluster of pathological symptoms.

Of course, it is true that scientific theories 'correct' experiences too: we see a stick appearing bent when immersed in water, and we see the movement of the sun across the horizon. Our scientific theories tell us that neither is true. In such cases, it is important to note that these theories preserve our experiences the way they are. In fact, scientific theories explain to us the *necessity* of such appearances. They do not *distort* them, much less *deny* them, whereas your 'explanation' denies *access to experience*.

Here lies the root of the sense of wrongness that many feel. Who or what is denying the access to one's experience? It is not a theory, but a *theorizing of someone else's experience*. Because this point can be easily misunderstood, let me unravel it just a bit.

Long before Freud wrote whatever he did, we had people of other religions coming to India to say the same thing: first from Islam and then from Christianity. They told us that we were worshipping the cow, the monkey, the penis, the stone idol and the naked fakir (not only they, but many Indians in their wake told us the same as well). That is how these people *experienced us and our activities*. Their theologies had prepared them for such an experience long before they came to our part of the world. Of course, they saw only what they expected to see.

The descriptions that missionaries provided, the reports of Christian merchants, the developments within Christian theology ... were the 'facts' that Freud sought to understand. (To the extent that he believed he was laying the foundation of a 'scientific' theory, to that extent these were the 'facts' for which he was accounting.) What did Freud theorize then? He theorized the *European experience* of other cultures and a theological elaboration of these experiences.

Consequently, who or what denies us access to our experience? It is the *experience of another culture* (or, the 'theorizing of such an experience'). Though important in its own right, we can safely drop this distinction. It lies at the root of the feeling of wrongness: *our experiences are being trivialized, denied, distorted, and made inaccessible by someone else's experience of the world*. You have a feeling of moral or ethical wrongness, because such a situation is neither justified nor justifiable. One is made to think that, apparently, there is only one way of experiencing the world: the 'Western way'.

In order to go with the Ramakrishna you sketch, one is obliged to deny one's experiences to oneself. Not only do you try to foist your way of going about the world on others in the name of gaining an 'understanding', but the others, too, have also to voluntarily accept it and actively cooperate in the process. They are *compelled to become volunteers* in the process of denying their experiences of the world to themselves.

If this is not violence, Jeffrey Kripal, what is?

7. Do not tempt yourself into misunderstanding the above points. None of these charges could have been made, if you had indeed provided us with a scientific explanation (Freud did think he was scientific) of the 'life and *teachings* of Ramakrishna'. The point is that you provide no explanation of any sort except a trivial one. And you do that by merely re-describing the saint as a pathological person. You trivialize whatever you touch, including the experience of another culture. In the process, you inflict violence on your fellow human beings.

Thus, some among us protest: this situation is morally wrong. Yet others argue this point of view eloquently and with repeated insistence. But such men and women are easily branded as members of the RSS (Rashtriya Swayamsevak Sangh), or the Sangh Parivar and, of course, are faced with the ever-present threat of being damned as a 'Hindu fundamentalist'. Others, much like the fourteen-year-old boy that I once was, remain silent because another kind of wrongness is involved as well: *a cognitive wrongness*.

Scientific theories, in so far as they explain our experiences, do so without denying or trivializing the latter. But, the explanations of the sort you give, and those I heard, do not explain; they merely trivialize, distort and deny what we experience. They do not shed any light on our experiences, but render them opaque and inaccessible. Galileo did not deny that we see the movement of the sun on the horizon or that we see it rise and set. No one would have taken him seriously, then or later, if he had done either. Instead, he explained the necessity of this perception, while explaining that the world is not structured this way. Sure, he laid down a challenge; but to whom or to what did he address it? It was to a set of *beliefs* about the world and to the authority that defended those beliefs. He did not tell us that we hallucinate every time we see the movement of the sun; he claimed that the geocentric theory *was false*. That is not what you do, Jeffrey Kripal. You tell us we have *false* experiences, *not* that we have a false theory about mysticism. How is this accomplished? You trivialize and deny our experience. And this makes most of us remain silent, striking us dumb the way a boy of fourteen could not think of anything to say when he heard what the Shiva linga 'meant'. Not because it struck a chord with him but because he did not know how to counter it. He remained silent because he did not know how to express the sense of cognitive wrongness he felt, a situation that many among of us find ourselves in.

Today, nearly five decades later, that boy has grown up. He has studied books, thought over questions and analysed relevant experiences. Today, he is able to say what is cognitively wrong: such explanations do the opposite of what scientific theories do. He now knows that these explanations do nothing of the sort they claim; they are merely a way of structuring the experience of a people from another culture. He knows that these *pseudo*-explanations— that is what they are—*sound* fancy; he also knows that many from his culture parrot this exotic product. But since when, he asks himself, are scientific truths decided by means of majority votes? Thus, he claims that your story is wrong not only morally, but also cognitively. That is, you have not produced knowledge. You *could not have* produced it because you have not explained the experience but, instead, provided a trivialized and distorted description of such an experience. You are not even close to capturing (let alone explaining) Indian 'mysticism' or its cultural forms. In fact, you are even blind to seeing it.

8. What an extraordinary thing to say! You have written a book about the mysticism of Ramakrishna and yet, here I am, suggesting that you are not even able to see it. Some explanation is in order. It is tricky, so let us take it by stages.

8.1. Let us step back from the psychoanalytical explanations and ask ourselves the following question: *which problem was Freud trying to solve?* Of course, there were many: he wanted to investigate the nature of hysteria; he wanted to figure out the story behind incest fantasies; he wanted to understand slips of the tongue. I do not mean any of these; what is the problem underlying these issues? Philosophers of science identify this as the 'problem-situation'. What then was Freud's problem-situation? Both the nature of the psychoanalytic practice and the structure (and content) of the psychoanalytical explanations give us ample clues to the direction of an answer. In its blandest form, it is this: 'Is one's experience in the world (especially about oneself and the others) veridical (that is, true)?' If we keep in mind what I have said hitherto and what you implicitly assume, it can be put even more provocatively: *Is the experience of an individual directly accessible to the individual whose experience it is?*

8.2. Freud's answer is known: no, he said, one can access one's own experience *only* through the mediation of another, *in casu*, the psychoanalyst. This is not the only reason why Freud's story appears unbelievable. There is something else of importance as well.

I am sure you will admit that not only the notion of experience, but also its existence is of crucial importance to us human beings. We think that experience is valuable and important; it is both the source of and the precondition for most learning. Given its centrality to human existence, one would naturally expect the Western tradition to be bothered about figuring out what this 'experience' is. Yet, amazingly enough as it turns out, such is not the case. Despite books and articles in many, many disciplines bearing the title, the nature of 'experience' has hardly been studied. More often than not, it is reduced to thoughts, feelings, perceptions, or even physical sensations and actions. None of these, either collectively or jointly, exhausts experience because one *could experience any or all of them as well.* (One can experience thoughts, feelings, and so on.) Then, what is 'experience'? An important question, but very ill-understood.

This being the case, Freud's observation and his sense of the 'problem-situation' are very valuable indeed. Of course, he hypothesized that individual experience is not directly accessible to the concerned individual, and postulated many mechanisms to account for this non-accessibility. We need not take sides on the 'validity' or otherwise of his individual hypotheses here, even though that is important.

8.3. There is, however, another culture in the world which has absolutely made this 'problem-situation' the central focus of its inquiry. All Indian traditions, without any major exception as far as I know, have made experience and its interrogation central to their inquiry. Naturally, they, too, discovered that experience is not 'veridical'; there are 'things' that prevent us from accessing these experiences. Different traditions named them differently: maya, *avidya* and *agyanaare* are the best-known categories in this context. They thought each of these categories was an instance of *paap* or ignorance; in fact, removing this has been their central goal: *gyaanoodaya* or the 'arising of knowledge' (again, this is called differently by different traditions). The hindrances to knowledge were either 'illusions' (of sorts) or ignorance (of sorts). One could eliminate them, they said, and they developed a number of practical ways of doing so. (The plurality of Indian traditions partially expresses the plurality of the ways of removing the veil of ignorance.)

Though ill-understood by most Indologists and philosophers, these notions are crucial. Ignorance is not mere absence of information; it is accorded a role and is seen as a force that actively *hinders* the emergence of knowledge. Maya is not mere illusion; the world exists and impinges upon us too much to make such a facile claim. In any case, these traditions also believed that some kind of mediation would be helpful in accessing one's own experience. They called such a mediator guru and suggested that, in most cases, one needed a guru to achieve enlightenment.

In other words, Jeffrey Kripal, there exist two rival or competing *practical* traditions that address themselves to the same (or very similar) 'problem-situation'. By virtue of this, they become rival or competing research traditions that provide different answers to the same 'problem-situation'.

Why did you not look at Indian traditions this way to understand Kali's child? Why do you speak as though the tantrik 'emphasis on sex' antedates Freud's claims? You say that Tantrism spoke about 'sex' even before Freud, as if you want to compliment Indian culture for its acuity. Actually, it does not sound complimentary but patronizing. Indian traditions *challenge* Freud's theories. Why did you not look at the issue in this manner?

It is not as though you are ignorant of Indian traditions. Even if you are, your mentor Wendy Doniger is supposed to be *the* expert on Hinduism. Why did it not occur either to her or to you that the theories you used were already facing challenges from within Indian traditions? Here is my simple answer: *you have been blinded to the existence of Indian traditions as alternatives to Freud.*

8.4. That is not all. You do something more in your blindness. You use Freudian explanations to characterize a rival research tradition. Such a move can only yield a caricatured, distorted version of the competitor. When I was young, I remember one of my uncles making fun of my exposition of the Darwinian evolutionary theory with the following riposte: 'You might be proud to accept that your ancestors are monkeys. I, however, am not'. I felt like a fool again, because I did not know how to respond to my uncle. When I later read the research and the controversies, I discovered that this is one of the standard ways of ridiculing the evolutionary theory. Who does the ridiculing? Those who belong to rival research traditions, of course! By caricaturing Galileo's theory, Aristotelians ridiculed it; that is how modern medicine looks at Paracelsus or the medical practices of Europe in the Middle Ages. That is what you do as well. To use the stories of the Viennese master to understand Kali's child is like using creationism to portray Darwin's theory. You are blind to this distortion as well. So, how could you describe Ramakrishna, when you cannot see him? You cannot.

This blindness, inherent in your venture, must also render us blind. It does, *but in a different way and for a different reason*. I suppose you have no problem in accepting the suggestion that theories about cultural worlds have their *roots* in the experiences of such worlds. These theories describe experiences; they reflect on experiences; they problematize such experiences and think through them. In other words, if I want to theorize about Indian culture, I need to have *access* to an experience of Indian culture (directly or indirectly). These explanations deny such access by acting as a filter between our own experiences and us.

In one sense, all theories act as some kind of a filter: they select some salient aspect of the experience and focus upon it. In the case we are talking about, the situation is not the same. These purported explanations act as a distorting glass. I knew I had such experiences; I saw that others apparently continued to have the experiences I had earlier (I continued to see adult male friends holding hands; I continued to see people doing puja to the Shiva linga); I knew, too, that I had these but was unable to access them *because of these explanations*. That is, these explanations came actively between my own experiences and me, and *actively prevented* me from describing or reflecting on my own experiences. Did I really 'see' the homosexuality of my friend when he held my hands? No. Did I really 'see' a phallus when I looked at the linga? No, I did not. Our experiences of the world and the explanations that are used are at loggerheads with each other: without speaking about experience, one cannot say what the 'Indian experience' consists of; the (Freudian) stories we reproduce tell us that there is no 'Indian experience' to talk of.

This is the lot and the daily life of cultures and peoples colonized by Western culture. Colonization—as many have pointed out—was not merely a process of occupying lands and extracting revenues. It was not a question of us aping Western people and trying to be like them. It was not even about colonizing the imagination of a people by making them 'dream' that they, too, would become 'modern', developed, and sophisticated. It goes deeper than any of these. It is about denying peoples and cultures their own experiences; of rendering them aliens to themselves; of actively preventing any description of their own experiences except in terms defined by the colonizers.

9. Thus, your stance prevents you from knowing you are blind. But why are you blind? To put it another way, what makes you blind? The answer to this, too, has layers, and let me peel just a few of them. To do that, I shall have to engage you in your own territory, on your own turf. That is, I want to talk to you about your understanding of your own culture and religion. (Isn't this what 'cultural hermeneutics' is all about?) Let me, therefore, play the ventriloquist and displace your voice to ask myself a few questions: is the alienation from our own experience (that I have spoken of) different from what any believer undergoes in the West, when he 'discovers' that God is dead? Is my experience different from that of a Westerner losing his belief in God and the mystic? Are our travails anything other than the story of 'modernity' as it is played out in India?

9.1. *Yes, to all the three questions.* Let me get into an autobiographical mode once again to talk about some of them. I did not quite tell you what happened to me during those decades when we fast-forwarded. Let us rewind a bit and see what happened to the lad between his eighteenth and thirtieth year. You see, he wanted to change the world and became a radical. He left home before he was even twenty, lived in the slums, worked in a quarry, went to the villages and even became a Marxist for a period of time. From an 'orthodox' Brahmin, he metamorphosed into a fire-breathing 'radical': India was backward; the caste system was a curse; Indian traditions were outdated; the 'gods' (though he still wrote it with a 'small g') did not exist (except that they had once walked the lands of Europe!). In other words, a run-of-the-mill progressive. In short, the revolution could not come soon enough for him. However, what brought him to Marxism also brought him out of it: the inability of these stories to make sense of his experience. So, he came to Europe, not in search of the Holy Grail (how could he? He was born a Brahmin after all!), but to study the root cause of the problems of Marxist theory. You see, in those days it was difficult to find the books of Hegel, Fichte, Schelling, and other German philosophers in public libraries. Even as I began to solve my problems with Marx, a new issue was beginning to force itself on me: I had begun to realize dimly that I was an Indian, and that I lived as such in a culture I hardly understood.

This realization turned my world upside down; in doing so, however, it helped me regain access to my own experiences. The world that got turned upside down was the one *I thought* I had lived in all the time. I had thought until then that I knew Western culture like the back of my hand: it was a shock to discover just how far I was from knowing either. I could hold forth on the notions of 'civil society', 'ought' in ethics, the histories of the Renaissance and the Enlightenment and, why, I could even eat meat and drink wine. None of these, I discovered, meant anything: I had remained an Indian, even if I had once thought I was 'modern'. Thus, I reflected on my experiences (fed by reading and yet more reading) until I could begin to grasp the outlines of the question: *What is it to be an Indian?* Seventeen years ago, I formulated these reflections as a research project, titling it after a poem by T.S. Eliot that goes like this: '... *We shall not cease from exploration*, and the end of all our exploring will be to arrive where we started and know the place for the first time'. I had indeed arrived where I had started from: India, Bangalore, a Brahmin family. I, too, began to know the place for the first time because, at last, I could begin to access my own cultural experiences in the way they needed to be accessed. However, the job is not complete and the process not yet over. During all these years, I have been constructing the tools required to gain access to our experiences because I also realized that my individual biography was but the Indian history writ small.

9.2. That is why I can now say that discovering the lingam was called 'penis' did not rob me of my world the same way atheism robs a believer of his world in Western culture. *It could not*. There are so many reasons why these two processes are not even remotely similar that I cannot hope to mention any of them in the course of this letter. Instead, let me recount a story taken from the *Chandogya Upanishad*.

It appears Prajapathi said that he who has found the 'Self' (Atman) and understands it obtains all worlds and all desires. The devas and the asuras both heard these words, and said: 'Well, let us search for that Self by which, if one has searched it out, all worlds and all desires are obtained.' Thus said Indra from the devas, and Virochana from the asuras, and both, without having communicated with each other, approached Prajapathi ... They dwelt there as pupils for thirty-two years. Then Prajapathi asked them: 'For what purpose have you both dwelt here?' They both replied: 'A saying of yours is being repeated ... Now we have both dwelt here because we wish for that Self.' He made them both look in a pan of water and asked them what they saw. They had seen their own bodies reflected. He made them dress up and look again into the water in the pan, and asked them what they saw. They said: 'Just as we are, well adorned, with our best clothes and clean, thus we are both there, Sir, well adorned, with our best clothes and clean'. Prajapathi said: 'That is the Self, this is the immortal, the fearless, this is Brahman.' They both went away satisfied in their hearts. Prajapathi reflected on their absence of critical thought and thought that whoever of the two followed this line of thought would 'perish'.

The story continues: now Virochana, satisfied in his heart, went to the asuras and preached that doctrine to them, that the Self (the body) alone was to be worshipped, that the Self (the body) alone was to be served, and that he who worshipped the Self and served the Self, would gain both worlds, this and the next (Müller 1962: 134–7). The story further continues about what Indra did, but that is not relevant now. What is important are the three *obvious* points in the story.

Both the asuras and the devas seek enlightenment. Quite obviously—as this story makes clear—this state does not consist of 'believing in' some deva or another for the simple reason that they, the devas, too, thirst for enlightenment! Further, to reach this state—as becomes evident when we follow the story further—no 'grace' of any kind of 'God' is required: *one needs to think through*. (Indian traditions speak of any number of other ways, too, but that need not detain us here.) From this, it follows that one's enlightenment is the result of one's own effort. It is a *deserved* 'reward' that is in proportion to the effort one puts in. Between oneself and enlightenment—which is the ultimate goal in life—no one and nothing can counteract one's efforts.

Virochana's *insight* that the body requires worshipping because it is the 'Self' is a wrong answer *because* it is superficial. The answer, however, is *not false*. As the story evolves further, the reader appreciates that the asura's answer is superficial because Indra is provided with a 'deeper' answer. An answer is superficial *only in relation* to a deeper one but that does not make the former a false answer. Virochana's insight *appears* as materialistic and 'atheistic' as they come: yet, the story seems to condone it as a *possible* answer (though superficial) to *seeking enlightenment*. The discovery that all there is to life is the life one has—or the body one has—does not rob an Indian of anything. Very sharply put: in Indian traditions, 'atheism' (of a particular sort, see below) *can also be a way of reaching enlightenment*. This claim is not even remotely similar to the shock of 'discovering' (in Western culture) that 'God is dead'.

What kind of 'atheism' am I talking about? Not the Western atheism: that makes *no sense* to the many Indian traditions because of two things: (a) as the above story suggests, the road to 'enlightenment' does not go through Jerusalem. That is, Prajapathi does not tell Indra that he should 'believe in God' in order to be enlightened; (b) consequently, most of these Indian traditions are not 'theistic' (poly-, heno- or mono-, or whatever) the way Judaism, Christianity and Islam are. Consequently, Western forms of 'atheism' do not have the Western kind of theistic doctrine to oppose, when they come to India.

9.3. The contrast between our asuras and the devil in the Bible cannot be greater. In the classical but simple interpretation, even though the devil is a fallen angel, he does not believe *in God*, but merely *acknowledges* His existence. As the Gospel puts it, 'Thou believest that there is one God; thou doest well: the devils also believe, *and tremble*' (James 2: 19; emphasis mine). The devil makes us *deny* the 'true' God, says the religion that Christianity is. God reveals Himself to save us from the 'clutches' of the devil, it assures us further. To become an atheist in the West is to lose 'faith' in this revelation. Where is this 'atheism' and where are our traditions? Where is the devil and where are our asuras?

Thus, our asuras are not like the devil or his minions in the Bible. Not only do they seek 'enlightenment'—as the above story makes it clear—but some of them are also the biggest *bhaktas* of our *devatas*. The reason why Rama was born, they say, was to kill Ravana—a supreme bhakta. He deserved to die in no other way than being slain by Vishnu himself. To this day, we celebrate the greatest king (an asura) we ever had, and greatest bhakta who ever lived: Lord Bali (an immortal) on whose head Trivikrama (Vaamana, as he is also called) placed his third step. Each year, it seems, he ascends from the bottom of the earth to find out how his subjects are faring: the streets are lit, as are our homes with their doors open, so that he may come in and feel welcome. We call this the festival of lights, Deepavali. You know all this. Why do I tell it to you then? It is to say that our 'atheisms', our 'asuras', the 'immorality' of our devas do not rob us of our traditions the way atheism robs a believer in the West. Devatas may die, be born again, punished, or even be immortal: our traditions do not suffer from any of this but live on precisely because of it. Consequently, today, *without rejecting any piece of knowledge I have ever learnt*, I can access my traditions and my experience in a very profound way. That is why, Jeffrey Kripal, you would be wrong to say that what I felt when I was fourteen is what the believer feels when he loses his faith in the God of Abraham, Isaac and Jacob. *This is another process altogether.*

When people protest against your portrayal of Ramakrishna, the majority of Indians is not saying what you think they are. The language they use may sound familiar to your ears; what they say might remind you of your own experience. To see and understand us this way, however, is to understand very little about what makes us different cultures or even what is interesting about this.

10. During the last two decades, I have not merely built tools to recover my own experiences. I discovered that I could not do this without understanding Western culture either. My attempts at understanding one could not have begun without trying to understand the other. To know my mother better, it appears, I need to know my mother-in-law as well. So, let us look at how *you* have been treating the latter because we know what you have done with the former. How have psychoanalysis, sociology, psychology, anthropology, or whatever else, described what religion is? That is to say, what do they *assume* when they try to explain religion, if they explain it at all? They assume that

religion is a human product, if not a human invention. But, Jeffrey Kripal, this assumption denies them *their study object*: a Christian believer sees the Bible as *the word of God* and not just as a book. You cannot explain this belief by appealing to any sets of natural causes unless you begin with the *assumption* that the believer is wrong about his own experience. Of course, you cannot countenance God in your research; however, if you do not, you are not studying religion as the believer experiences it, but its caricatured representation. In other words, your Freud *cannot explain religion*. He explains it as merely a human product, an assumption for which he has *no grounds*. To formulate simply: atheism is a philosophical option, but this option will *keep* you from doing science. Doing theism, however, will give you theology but not science. To a Christian, the existence or non-existence of Jesus is of great importance, but the answer to the question about the historical Jesus will not tell you anything about his Christ-nature. If he is not the Christ, Jesus of Nazareth is merely a man, not even 'the Son of Man'. But then, of course, you cannot assume that Jesus is the Christ and write a *scientific* tract about it either. Underlying this dilemma is a whole host of other problems. (To write further on this would require a book. I have written one such, *'The Heathen in His Blindness'* (2005), which you might care to read.) Therefore, it appears, *by assuming the stance that you do* towards the study of religion, you do 'unto your brethren what you do unto us as well'. You caricature the experience of the believer in your culture; you caricature the experiences of our entire culture. *It is this that blinds you to what you are doing.*

That means your descriptions of our experiences are doubly caricatured. *First,* you tell us that what we 'see' *is not* what we see: the linga is not the linga but symbolizes something else. As I said earlier, this is what religions like Christianity and Islam have told us. You tell me they are right. This way, you impose your cultural experience upon us and deny our experiences. *Second,* you tell us that, even here, what we do is something else: it transpires that we are not 'worshipping' the linga or falling in love with Shiva. We do not 'worship' at all (one can only 'worship' either God or the devil) and Shiva is but an 'erotic ascetic'. The aspect has two *tails that sting*: why does the imagination of Indian culture express itself in such grotesque forms as the phallus, the monkey, the stone idol with four arms, and an elephant-headed human figure? Why is Western imagination confined to more 'decent' things like visualizing God as the 'Father'? Enter Wendy Doniger and her 'children', who answer these questions in ways known to us all. Is it any wonder people are furious? Are you really that amazed?

Let me bring the case to a conclusion: what are you trying to 'understand' when you use your 'hermeneutic' to understand Ramakrishna? How do *you* see him? How does your culture sees him? Or how do *we* see him? What are you theorizing about? *Your experience*, your culture's experience, or ours? You insist that how your culture experiences the world is also the only possible experience of the world. You want to tell us what Ramakrishna's 'mysticism' is *all about* because that is the only way your *theories* allow you to see it. Your theories, your explanations, your assumptions *deny us* what you would not, as a person, dream of denying to us: that we, too, have an experience—a different one perhaps, but one that is as 'valid and legitimate' as any human experience can be.

How should one look at such an effort and accomplishment? From one side of the Atlantic—where I am now—I look at it with 'shame, disgust', and horror. I am ashamed and upset by the trivialization; I feel disgust and loathing at the gossip; I react with horror to the violence you inflict. From the other side of the Atlantic, the contrast could not be sharper, or so it seems. Here is how your doctoral supervisor, Wendy Doniger, describes her responses in her foreword to your book: 'I found myself smiling often and laughing almost as often as I read it. ... When I took chapters of it with me to the beach ... people offered me to trade their novels ... for a chance to read it, so evident was my pleasure in it. ... I am very proud to have played a small part in this wonderful book.'

While leaving you to munch on this image, let me end my letter with the words you use. You say: 'I at least am ready to laugh again, to exchange gifts, to argue, to apologize, to weep. I always have been.' I believe you. But do you know that people from other cultures also do so? We too laugh, exchange gifts, argue, apologize and weep. You know *that* we do it; you *assume* you know what they are because that is what *you* too do. But do you know *how* we do any or all of these things? Does it occur to you that we might do them *differently*? Do you, Jeffrey Kripal, know *how we cry* or even why? I wonder.

Friendly greetings,
Balu

CHAPTER 6

*Are Dialogues an Antidote to Violence?**

One standard remedy, often proposed for reducing the violence between opposing parties or communities, is to recommend a 'dialogue' between them. This is especially the case when the dispute appears to involve one or another religious doctrine or practice. In the previous chapter—so one could argue—the violence of the kind I have talked about can be ameliorated if a dialogue takes place between the concerned parties. However, this call for 'dialogue' overlooks the *prima facie* evidence from the domain of religious studies which suggests the contrary; intense religious dialogue has often gone hand in hand with much violence. The evidence for violence simultaneously occurring alongside dialogue lies in the history of ancient Christianity and its struggle with the Roman *religio*; the religious wars; the periods of Reformation and Counter-Reformation in Europe and so on. Is this mere contingent correlation? Or is it because these dialogues were either inter- or intra-religious in nature? Or is it because a dialogue with religions is simply impossible? Consequently, do we need 'more dialogue' with and between religions, or 'less' of it, 'none' of it, or a 'different kind' of dialogue altogether? In this chapter, I shall

* An earlier version of this chapter (with Sarah Claerhout) was previously published in 2008 as 'Are Dialogues Antidotes to Violence? Two Recent Examples from Hinduism Studies', *Journal for the Study of Religions and Ideologies* 7(19), pp. 118–143.

interrogate the belief about the alleged role that dialogues play in reducing violence between people.

In the past five years or so, a heated dispute has erupted in the American society. The dispute flared up when two books, both authored by professors at American universities, became issues of contention among Hindu groups in the United States. The first book is by Paul Courtright (1985) and it concerns Ganesha, the elephant-headed Hindu god; the second is by Jeffrey Kripal (1998) on the Bengali saint, Ramakrishna Paramahamsa. In response to these books, several Hindu groups called for public apologies from the authors, withdrawal of their books and their dismissal. Some individuals even threatened them with physical violence. These events have become catalysts for a wider critique of the Western portrayal of Indian culture.

This social context raises explanatory questions about these reactions. The standard answer is about the propagandist role played by Right-wing Hindu organizations—collectively called the Hindutva movement—in the United States and elsewhere. This answer points to the fact that the responses of Hindus in the United States were neither monolithic nor uniform and that not all of them were incensed by these scholars and their explanations. Consequently, they see the hand of the Right-wing Sangh Parivar behind many such angry responses. While such allegations may be true, one major issue has gone largely unnoticed. It concerns the ability of the Hindutva movement to find echoes in the largely politically unaffiliated Hindus in American society and elsewhere. *Into what kind of experience is* Hindutva *tapping?* In the course of this chapter, I will formulate one aspect of what is perhaps a multi-dimensional answer, as it relates to the nature of the dialogical encounter.

There is something more. *Assuming* the need for people of different religious persuasions to live together peacefully, what should they do when they disagree and want to solve their disagreement? The famous philosopher of science, Sir Karl Popper, once formulated the aporia confronting 'humankind' and his solution to it in the following terms: 'If the method of rational critical discussion should establish itself, then this should make the use of violence obsolete: *critical reason is the only alternative to violence so far discovered*' (Popper 1976: 292; emphasis in the original). If people want to solve their disagreements, it seems as though there are only two choices: either people kill each other, or they sit down, discuss with each other, and let ideas die in their stead. 'In the face of argument of such quality,' writes Gellner (1985: 43)—himself a Popperian—'one can only feel embarrassment'. In the course of this chapter, we will also discover what the embarrassment is about.

According to Popper's own meta-theory of science (see Popper 1968, 1972), his bold claim can be temporarily accepted only if it cannot be refuted. I will refute the claim by arguing that, in some kinds of encounters, the kind of rational discussion that Popper has in mind generates violence. If the arguments hold muster, they establish two things: one is that the disjunction 'reason or violence' will not work; the second is that it refutes the assumption that a dialogue, in all cases and in all circumstances, reduces the probability of violence between disagreeing human communities. This assumption is often implicit in the calls for a dialogue between different religions, different cultures, and different nations today.

The Structure

Even though I believe that the substantial thesis of this chapter is not dependent on any idiosyncratic use of language, I will take care to define the notions in the first section, 'Argumentation and Dialogue'. From there on, I will use the word 'argumentation' instead of the word 'dialogue', and maintain this usage consistently throughout. In this task, I draw upon what we consider to be the best theory of argumentation today. This substitution of words is also intended to suggest a very minimal claim: argumentation is at least a subset of dialogue.

In the section 'Studies on Hinduism', I look at two examples from studies in Hinduism studies. Here, the focus is on some passages from the works of Courtright and Kripal merely to show that some of their arguments *could* provide a ground for serious disagreement. At that point, we will notice two facts: one is that some Hindus threaten the two scholars with physical violence; the second is the quasi-total absence of attempts by the incensed Hindu groups to engage critically with Courtright and Kripal.

At first sight, these two facts appear to lend credence to the 'reason or violence' hypothesis. First, there are no attempts by these groups to argue with the two authors and, second, there is the threat of physical violence. In the presence of disagreements and the felt need to solve them, the 'reason or violence' hypothesis suggests a cause–effect relationship between these two. Of course, we also need other accounts that explain the existence of these two facts. For our purposes, it does not matter what form such explanations take; but it does matter that one introduces them *ad hoc*. Instead of going down this route, I formulate a simpler hypothesis that not only explains the relationship between the above two events but also accounts for their existence. The hypothesis merely construes the books of Courtright and Kripal as argumentative moves. This is done in the third section 'A Hypothesis'.

In 'Argumentation and Violence', I analyse the nature of the violence involved in the argumentative situation. Here, I speak of the Hindu experience that the Hindutva movement is tapping into. In this way, my hypothesis also goes some way (though not all the way) in explaining the success of Hindutva.

The fifth section, 'An Asymmetrical Burden' demonstrates *a skew* in the argumentative situation and exhibit some of the logical compulsions responsible for that. This skew consists of putting an *asymmetrical burden of proof* on the participants in an argumentative discourse. I argue that any workable theory of argumentation has to make both substantive and formal assumptions to get off the ground, and that it is epistemically impossible to localize the cause(s) of this skew in all cases. In other words, it is not possible to defend the claim that, in the argumentation between Hindus and Western scholars, one could trace the skew to 'defective' theories or to the 'unreasonableness' of either of the two parties.

'A Methodological Problem', the final section, takes up an allegedly 'methodological' question about studying the 'Other' and show why it is not methodological at all. In the process, we notice the presence of several other asymmetries in what should ideally be a symmetric dialogical situation. Here, I tie up some loose ends and conclude on some general reflections that might help in understanding the spirit and intent of this chapter better.

Argumentation and Dialogue

The field of logic (both formal and informal) has generated the most interesting theories of argumentation in the course of the last three decades. The *Erlangenschule* (Lorenzen and Lorenz 1978) has successfully conceptualized the truth-functional propositional calculus as dialogical logic (see also Barth and Krabbe 1982). The pragma-dialectical approach of Frans van Eemeren and Rob Grootendorst is the most comprehensive in the field of argumentation from which I borrow this definition: 'An argumentation is a phenomenon of verbal communication which should be studied as a specific mode of discourse, characterized by the use of language for resolving a difference of opinion' (van Eemeren *et al.* 1996: 275). If 'verbal' is seen as a synonym of 'oral', then the definition is too narrow because it speaks only of oral communication. All argumentations need not be face to face; e-mails, internet chats and discussions on electronic forums are equally 'face to face' in today's world. Therefore, I shall drop this restriction. Instead, I adopt the above definition with the proviso that 'verbal' includes both 'oral' and 'written' modes of discourse.

When does an argumentation between two or more people come into being? Whenever there is a conflict of 'avowed opinions'. Of course, this situation alone does not suffice for an argumentation to take place: both parties should want to resolve the difference of opinion and do so through a process of critical discussion. Under these conditions, the parties engage in argumentative discourse and arrive at a consensus based on certain *rules* binding upon them. The pragma-dialectical school speaks of these rules as the 'Ten Commandments' of reasonable discussions. The ten rules that van Eemeren and his co-authors (van Eemeren *et al.* 1996: 283-4) suggest are the following:

Rule (1) Parties must not prevent each other from advancing standpoints or from casting doubts on standpoints.

Rule (2) A party that advances a standpoint is obliged to defend it if asked by the other party to do so.

Rule (3) A party's attack on a standpoint must relate to the standpoint that has indeed been advanced by the other party.

Rule (4) A party may defend a standpoint only by advancing argumentation relating to that standpoint.

Rule (5) A party may not disown a premise that has been left implicit by that party or falsely present something as a premise that has been left unexpressed by the other party.

Rule (6) A party may not falsely present a premise as an accepted starting point nor deny a premise representing an accepted starting point.

Rule (7) A party may not regard a standpoint as conclusively defended if the defense does not take place by means of an appropriate argumentation scheme that is correctly applied.

Rule (8) A party may only use arguments in its argumentation that are logically valid or capable of being validated by making explicit one or more unexpressed premises.

Rule (9) A failed defense of a standpoint must result in the party that put forward the standpoint retracting it and a conclusive defense of the standpoint must result in the other party retracting its doubt about the standpoint.

Rule (10) A party may not use formulations that are insufficiently clear or confusingly ambiguous and a party must interpret the other party's formulations as carefully and accurately as possible.

Such rules emphasize the necessity of drawing inferences and incorporate some minimal pragmatic considerations, and some minimal conditions for verbal communication. Consequently, any rational dialogue will have to accept some or another set of rules.

Because a dialogue consists of verbal expressions or linguistic statements, its structure is about the relations between them. If the dialogue is not face-to-face, the pragmatics of the argumentative discourse will at best refer to the context, which is incorporated in the form of statements as well. Henceforth, I use the word 'belief' to speak of the statements involved in an argumentative discourse without, however, making any assumptions about the status and nature of beliefs. Since criticism or justification is at issue, the relations that can hold between these statements are either logical or semantic in nature. That is, some kind of *deductive relation* should hold between such beliefs. In the theory of van Eemeren and his co-authors, this is the eighth of the 'Ten Commandments':

An argument can lead to a resolution of a difference of opinion only if the reasoning underlying the protagonist's argumentation is valid. When the reasoning is valid, the defended standpoint *follows logically* from the premises which are used, explicitly or implicitly, in the protagonist's argumentation. (van Eemeren *et al.* 1996: 285; italics mine)

The 'deductive relation' spoken of here is neutral in nature: no suggestion is made about the kind of logic employed in any given discussion. The logic guiding a discussion could belong to any of the varieties that populate the market place: the classical predicate calculus, intuitionist logic, para-consistent logics, non-monotonic logics, deviant logics, non-standard logics, dialectical logics, adaptive logics, and so on. Each of these logics has its own meta-logical notions of deduction and validity, soundness and proof, and so on. The notion of dialogue is neutral with respect to the choice of logics; it merely proposes that once a suitable logic is chosen, the participants follow its rules of inference.

Unless qualified otherwise, I use the word 'violence' in a generic sense: 'injury by or as if by distortion, infringement, or profanation' (Merriam-Webster online:http://www.merriam-webster.com/dictionary/violence, accessed on 12 April 2012).'Injury' should be seen as 'an act that damages or hurts'. Both words could refer to physical or mental events; this is how I use the word 'violence'. The context of the use of these words clarifies any additional meanings as and when they accrue.

Studies on Hinduism

During the past years, two books, both authored by American professors, have generated strong feelings among the Hindu diaspora living in the United States. One is by Paul Courtright, Professor of Indian religions at the Emory University. It is about Ganesha, the Hindu deity. He is the son of Shiva, who is the lord of destruction among other things. Following an Indian reprint of this book in 2001, a huge controversy erupted. An internet petition signed by hundreds of Indians circulated on the web before it was withdrawn; some of the signatories had called for the death of the author. The famous Indological publisher, Motilal Banarsidass, withdrew the Indian reprint of this book because of the furore the book and the cover photo caused. Many academics issued a call to withdraw their books from the publisher because they felt that academic freedom was threatened by mob violence. Concerned Hindu communities in North America formed groups, circulated petitions, met with the Emory University authorities demanding that Paul Courtright be dismissed from service, his book withdrawn from the shelves of the library, and that his classes discontinued. The story even made it to *The Washington Post* (Vedantam 2004).

The second book is by Jeffrey Kripal, currently professor at Rice University. The subject of his investigation was Sri Ramakrishna Paramahamsa, the teacher of the more famous Swami Vivekananda (who established the Ramakrishna Mission in India and abroad). The mentor of Kripal is the well-known Indologist of the University of Chicago, Wendy Doniger. Having received an award from the American Academy of Religion for the best first book of the year, it has been dogged by controversy ever since its initial publication in 1995.

In both cases, the authors in question and their supporters argue that they treat their subject matter with sympathy and respect. They also insist that the way to knowledge is fraught with disenchantments, and that one should be prepared to embrace unpleasant truths, if one seeks knowledge. Consequently, it is only reasonable that they treat Hindus with a degree of suspicion: either they do not respect academic freedom, or they are Hindu fundamentalists, or both.

These claims do not convince the Hindus; nor are they all Hindu fundamentalists. Some of them are respected academics in their own right. There is a sense of fury amongst them and they feel *violated*. In fact, in any discussion about these books, the undercurrent of violence is barely suppressed and never far away. Why? Before answering this question, we need to take notice of what Courtright and Kripal do.

Courtright's Ganesha

Even though a few passages (Courtright 1985: 110–11, 120) from the book generated outrage among the 'Hindu diaspora', I would like to focus on his enterprise as a whole which involves the use of Freudian psychoanalysis to understand Ganesha. The cognitive status, neither of psychoanalysis nor of this particular reading of Freud (or psychoanalysis) is at issue. Let us assume that one could use Freudian theories to understand cultures, and that Courtright provides us with a justifiable interpretation of Freud and/or psychoanalysis. Such interpretations transform Ganesha and Shiva into symbols. To whom are these figures symbols? Whose psyche expresses the elephant trunk psychoanalytically, or represents Shiva symbolically? There are three logical possibilities here: either these express the psyche of those individual scholars who indulge in such interpretations (we can write this possibility off); or they tell us why some unknown author conceived of Shiva and Ganesha this way (this too can be written off). Alternatively, and this is the third possibility, they are claims about the psyche of the Indians who perform puja rituals to Ganesha and Shiva in these forms.

Let us look at the last and only realistic possibility. A particular *interpretation* of psychoanalysis functions as *an explanation* of the Indian psyche: Indians offer puja to Shiva linga because ...; Indians cook sweets while performing puja to Ganesha because the desire for sweets is an expression of ...; and so on. (The ellipsis can be filled in by a suitable interpretation of psychoanalysis.) In other words, a particular reading of Freudian psychoanalysis functions as an explanation of the psyche of a people. This move from interpretation to explanation is *logically necessary* because psychoanalysis is an explanation of the psychology of individuals. One does not have the freedom to choose a psychoanalytical explanation of the psyche and deny that one is providing an explanation of a psyche. About which Indians is this claim made? All Hindus who were, are, and will be: that is, all those who did, do and will do puja to the linga and to Ganesha. Such an explanation of the Indian psyche, in that case, requires compelling *evidence* before it can be considered true. The author, of course, does not provide this because he thinks he is advancing a psychoanalytical 'interpretation' of Ganesha.

I have already considered Jeffrey Kripal's attempts to understand Sri Ramakrishna Paramahamsa, the teacher of the more famous Swami Vivekananda. As I have argued in the previous chapter, unless one specifies the mechanisms involved in the 'transformation', the explanation is both trivial and ad hoc.

We can now appreciate the prima facie reasons for disagreeing with Kripal and Courtright. Even while we grant that many of the Hindu practitioners have not read either Courtright or Kripal with the care they deserve, we can understand why these authors generate controversy. They do put across controversial claims. However, nothing in their claims tells us why research should generate either suggestions of violence or expressions of hostility. Why does violence raise its ugly head during a discussion about the intellectual merits of certain ideas? Why do attempts at scholarship bring forth invectives, death threats, and engender violence?

A Hypothesis

There are two ways of looking at this situation. The first is to look at it the way I have sketched it so far: two respected scholars have used some or another version of Freudian psychoanalysis in order to understand Hinduism. Surely, it is in the very nature of an intellectual enterprise to try to understand phenomena by using whichever theories one thinks are adequate for the job. Therefore, to deny intellectuals this freedom is to threaten the very process of knowledge acquisition.

When we describe the situation in these terms, the response of the scholars, whether Western or Indian, and the reactions of some Hindus become predictable. The second group challenges the status of psychoanalysis or its ability to understand Hinduism; the first argues in its defence that scholars have used psychoanalysis in understanding other religions too, including Christianity. Some people challenge the mastery of these scholars in the relevant languages and/or of the primary sources; the others reply that these writings have passed academic muster on that score. And so on. In between, most scholars indulge in very loud table thumping, equally vigorous political hand waving and massively sign petitions to protect the virtues of 'academic freedom' from 'mob violence'. And when asked to explain the violent reactions of some Hindus, every scholar worth his or her name will appeal to the favourite bogey-man: 'Hindu fundamentalism'. So, one is supposed to believe that all the incensed 'Hindus' are brainwashed by the Hindutva movement, too stupid to understand the virtues of academic freedom, and, of course, delivered to the mercy of base emotions.

Even if the Hindutva movement has played a role in mobilizing the rage of the Hindus, none of the scholars I have either personally met or read seems to realize that they have a huge explanatory problem on their hands which they are waving away by appealing to ad hoc hypotheses. *Why are the 'Hindus' incensed?* Even though each scholar has his or her own story to tell, all of them take to the moral high ground: the blemish has to be sought on the side of the Hindus. This sense of self-righteousness would be almost sanctimonious, if it were not for the fact that the scholars who take such an attitude do indeed genuinely believe that they are right.

There is, however, a second description of the situation possible. What Kripal and Courtright have done is to *initiate a dialogue* with the Hindus about their religion. That is, I suggest that Kripal and

Courtright make *the first dialogical move by writing their books*. They have not merely studied Hinduism the way a physicist studies the refraction of light through a prism, but are also communicating the results of their research to an audience that comprises Hindus. They are explaining to Hindu practitioners the nature and structure of their practices, whether these involve doing puja rituals to Ganesha or listening to the teachings of Ramakrishna. While continuing to assume that these scholars appeal to theories they find useful, and that they are justified in their choice, let me create a dialogical situation. I will now show that this 'small' transformation suffices to explain the violence in the situation without appealing to any other hypotheses, ad hoc or otherwise.

This transformation requires making a deliberate abstraction from the concrete social and political processes in which both the antagonist and the protagonist are rooted. This is deliberate because only in this manner would one be able to show the structural results of a rational dialogue. In some senses, it is like creating the 'laboratory conditions' for an experiment. I look at the dialogue as though both the parties were sitting in a virtual seminar-class together, doing nothing other than engaging in the process of dialogue. We need to follow the steps in the dialogue without any 'disturbing conditions' and observe their impact. To facilitate this, consider the following fragment of a verbal exchange between a hypothetical 'scholar', and an equally hypothetical 'Hindu'. Both the dialogue and its individual participants are my constructions, meant merely to illustrate the problem. Even though one could distil such imaginary argumentations from the books written on Hinduism, my aim is more modest: outline the possible flow of one kind of argumentative discourse.

> Scholar: What are you doing?
> Hindu: Doing 'puja' (translated as 'worship') to Ganesha (*namaskara* to Ramakrishna).
> Scholar: Why are you doing it?
> Hindu: Ganesha is a 'deva' (translated as 'god') (Ramakrishna is an enlightened guru).
> Scholar: What explains his status?
> Hindu: Ganesha is the son of Shiva (Kali revealed herself to him).
> Scholar: Why does Ganesha have an elephant head? (How did Ramakrishna become enlightened?)

Hindu: It is Shiva's doing. (Here, the story of Ganesha is recounted.)
Hindu: It is due to Ramakrishna's 'tapas' (translated as 'penance').
(Here, the story of Ramakrishna is recounted.)
Scholar: Yes, I know the story too. But you misunderstood my question.
Hindu: What is your question then?
Scholar: Explain Ganesha's head (Explain Ramakrishna's enlightenment).
Hindu: I told you that already (refers to the story).
Scholar: Your story merely narrates and claims to tell us what occurred. My question is about the why.
Hindu: I do not understand you.
Scholar: Why was it an elephant head and not a human one? (Why did Ramakrishna do 'penance'?)
Hindu: I do not know.
Scholar: Here is the explanation why Ganesha has an elephant head and Ramakrishna did 'tapas'. (Now the Freudian explanations are presented.)
Hindu: *Silence*.

Argumentation and Violence

In the previous chapter, I showed how explanations of the sort that Kripal provides engender violence. That argument is fully applicable here. Thus, we can say that the method of rational, critical discussion, *contra* Sir Popper, is not 'the only alternative to violence so far discovered'. In fact, it *engenders violence in dialogical situations involving intercultural encounters*. Reasonableness, it appears, is not an antidote to violence; in certain kinds of encounters, this reasonableness *breeds violence*.

I would now like to suggest that the Hindutva movement is tapping into this experience. The recruiting base of Hindutva movement in the United States and elsewhere is broad; it consists of people who are hardly 'Right wing' in their political leanings. Nor are such people prone to fall prey to the propaganda of some fundamentalist religious movement. But, the issue of 'representation of Hinduism' is a lightning rod that draws well-educated Hindus into the folds of Hindutva because it is able to attach itself to this sense of violation.

If this is the case, the situation raises the even more troubling but fascinating issue of the growth of Hindutva in India itself. It would suggest that one of the sources for the growth of Hindutva has to be sought in the unlikeliest of places: Indian 'secularism'. If this is true, more of 'secularism' in India is not the antidote to the Hindutva and religious violence; such thoughtless remedies merely strengthen the growth of both. (See the Chapter 7 for an elaboration of this argument.)

One aspect of the situation involving violence is now obvious: attempts like those of Courtright and Kripal inflict violence by denying the experience of people whose religions they talk about. Even though we have focused only on these two authors, this observation is true for many, many more works in the West that study Hinduism, and Hinduism is studied mainly in the West. This is also the reason why, increasingly among the Hindu 'diaspora', Western intellectuals studying Hinduism are looked upon with suspicion.

However, this situation raises two questions. One is about the individual motivations of writers like these: are we to say they are inauthentic and are out to inflict pain on their fellow human beings? Even if we accept the logical possibility that some among them do have such psychologies, it is ridiculous to use it as an 'explanation' for this state of affairs. The second question is about the validity of the increasingly vociferous stance that only 'insiders' should study Hinduism precisely in order to prevent such violence. If a practising 'Hindu' studied Hinduism, would such problems never come to the fore?

An Asymmetrical Burden

Now, I want to build a generalized argument that goes beyond the case of Hinduism studies examined so far. To do so, however, I make use of the same strategy; in order to facilitate the process of comprehension and also signal the generality of the argument, I will continue to call the two hypothetical, individual participants in the dialogue as the 'scholar' and the 'Hindu' respectively. This baptism is one of convenience: we could identify them equally well with variables (as 'A' and 'B'), or as the protagonist and the antagonist (using their technical meanings from argumentation theory). However, purely for the sake of readability, I have chosen recognizable names.

I will now argue that in all such encounters, any further
argumentation becomes *tilted or loaded in favour of the scholar* because
the structure of argumentation compels him to indulge in a series
of inter-related cognitive moves. They are: (1) the scholar attributes
some implicit premises to the Hindu; (2) these premises appear to
explain Hindu practices; (3) these explanations presuppose the truth
of a specific psychological theory; (4) this theory structures the nature
of the phenomena requiring explanation; (5) the Hindu is logically
compelled to defend the moves of the scholar. Even though each of
these moves appears intuitively obvious, their combined effect skews
the argumentation as a whole. And this skew stakes the deck against
the Hindu.

The Cognitive Moves

To begin with, there is the *first* move of *attribution of implicit premises*
to the Hindu. If the wish is to have a dialogue, one can have it *only*
by attributing some specific premises to the Hindus. In the case of
Courtright, one can have a further dialogue about performing puja
rituals to the Shiva linga or to Ganesha only by making assumptions
about the 'subconscious' in the Indian psyche. To deny these premises
is to deny the justificatory/explanatory challenge that Courtright
issues. To do so is to refuse further argumentation. In the case of
Ramakrishna, it is obvious that to deny the occurrence of sexual
trauma of the saint is to deny participation in the argumentation. That
is why, in the sequence sketched earlier, I made the Hindu fall silent.
To appreciate this point better, consider two further developments in
the argumentation.
The first one:

> Scholar: Here is the explanation why Ganesha has an elephant
> head and Ramakrishna did 'tapas'. (Now the Freudian explanations
> are presented.)
> Hindu: I do not buy it.
> Scholar: OK. Do you have any explanation at all for the story?
> Hindu: (After some silence.) No.
> Scholar: Your story does not explain Ganesha's head and
> hence justify your 'puja'. Nor does it explain the 'penance' of
> Ramakrishna. My theory explains both. Even if this explanation is

incomplete or defective, you have no other explanation. So, if you want to be rational then you will either accept this explanation or come up with a better one.

Hindu: (Silence.)

Let us now look in the second possible direction:

Scholar: Here is the explanation why Ganesha has an elephant head and Ramakrishna did 'tapas'. (Now the Freudian explanations are presented.)

Hindu: I do not buy the Freudian explanations.

Scholar: Fair enough. There are many who also have problems with Freud and psychoanalytical explanations. However, I consider them illuminating. Therefore, I will continue to use this framework to make sense of Ganesha and Ramakrishna. Either you agree with me or let us agree to disagree. If you disagree, remember that we can only have a meaningful discussion when you come up with a different, alternative explanation.

How can the Hindu keep the argumentation alive now? See how Courtright (2006: 73; italics mine) formulates the two kinds of responses open to the Hindus:

… how do we do our work when some of the Others say, 'you got it right, that's what I mean', or, '*I hadn't thought of it that way before*, but, yes, *that makes sense*', whereas other Others say, 'your interpretation is offensive to me, and to all Hindus. Your book should be banned?'

The Hindu either agrees with Courtright that the latter's explanation makes sense or wants the books banned. These are not just factual alternatives; these are the only possible responses that the Hindus have in such situations. Could there be an argumentation without the scholar attributing such premises? No. *The disagreements arise due to the attribution of such premises*. In its absence, there is nothing to disagree about and hence there is no argumentation.

The *second* move transforms these attributed premises into *explanatory schemes*. That is to say, these explain the actions (or behaviour) of the Hindu:

(a) Because religion and religious worship express repressed libido, the figurative representation of the deities provides clues about repressed urges.

(b) 'In effect, Ramakrishna *took* the "anxious energies" of his early sexual crisis for which he almost killed himself, and *"turned them* around the corner" where they revealed their essentially mystical natures ... he *took* what were regressive symptoms and, through Kali and her Tantric world, *converted* them into genuine experiences of a sacred, mystical realm' (Kripal 1998: 324; italics mine).

In the *third move*, because the scholar assumes the truth of the explanatory schemes, he/she is also obliged to accept the truth of their source. That is to say, the scholar assumes the truth of *one specific psychology*. In the cases presented above, it is important to note that the real object of discussion is some or another human practice. However, the dialogue itself is not about these practices, but regarding the beliefs that the Hindus are alleged to hold about these practices. This shift at the object level is defensible only if we assume that discussing human practices is identical to discussing the beliefs the actors hold about such practices. Better put: if human practices express the beliefs of the actors about these practices, then a discussion of practices is the same as discussing the beliefs the actors hold about such practices. When formulated so explicitly, we recognize the above claim as a part of one specific psychological theory—commonly called the *intentional psychology*. The scholar assumes that such an intentional psychology is true and, therefore, valid for all human beings. Consequently, what are evidenced in the practices of the Hindus are their beliefs about the practices.

To understand the *fourth* move, let us begin by noticing that these explanations identify phenomena by giving them a structure: Ganesha is one of the many Indian *gods*; performing puja rituals is to *worship* Ganesha; stories about Ganesha incorporate *religious beliefs*; the depiction of Shiva and Ganesha are *religious symbols*; and so on. Thus, these explanations specify not only what requires explaining but also *how* such an explanation should look like.

The *fifth* move involves a logical compulsion, *an obligation on the Hindu to defend the moves of the scholar*. The Hindu is *compelled* to defend the moves of the scholar because they are *logical and not psychological* in nature. What is the origin of this compulsion? Because the moves of the scholar claim to identify the implicit logical premises in the claims of the Hindu, the latter has no choice but to defend them. That the scholar imputes these premises thus *making* them implicit, and that they are true only on condition that the implicit psychological theory assumed by the scholar is also that of the Hindu, are issues that never become a part of the dialogue: *they become the presuppositions of the dialogue.*

What kind of presuppositions are they? Some are explicit; some are identifiable implicit premises; and some others function the way the *ceteris paribus* clause (the clause that says 'everything else remaining the same') functions in the formulation of a scientific law. No amount of digging will ever allow us to explicate the *ceteris paribus* clause. In fact, its presence signals that one *cannot* enumerate what 'all the things' are that must 'remain the same' (see Earman and Roberts 1999; Fodor 1991; Pietroski and Rey 1991; Rosenberg 1995; Schiffer 1991). Differently put, a rational dialogue becomes skewed because the party which makes the maximum number of unproven assumptions does not have to demonstrate the truth of these assumptions. The protagonist cannot even ask the antagonist to prove this truth because he is unaware of all the assumptions the latter is making: most are hidden in the ceteris paribus clause. Consequently, all one can say about a 'rational dialogue', even when it is conducted by formulating explicit and prima facie non-partisan, is that it gets skewed even where one does not *want* or *intend* it to happen.

Because of the above considerations, one might want to argue that the problem is with the nature of the additional premises and thus their semantic content. However, this impression is misleading: we cannot make such a claim *on reasonable grounds*.

Given the formal nature of the rules of the dialogue, nothing of substantial interest follows from them unless one adds empirical and theoretical statements with a rich semantic content. All real-world discussions are about such statements, and if a dialogue has to help us anywhere then it is in the actual world that its efficacy is tested. Consequently, to blame the semantic content for the skew is equivalent to saying that a reasonable discussion is not possible in the real and actual world about substantial issues, where differences of opinion exist. Furthermore, it is not possible to localize the specific premise that brings about the skew because of the *ceteris paribus* clause. All we can say is that the dialogue becomes skewed. We cannot proceed any further. Therefore, we cannot show that the skew arises from the semantic content of the subject under discussion; nor can we show that the rules of the dialogue are not the source of the skew. This confirms the result that philosophers of science have called the 'Duhem-Quine thesis', which tells us that no theory is tested in isolation from the background theories or web of beliefs it is embedded in. Consequently, when some experiment or event appears to falsify a theory, it is impossible to say which specific part of this web of beliefs has been falsified.

What would happen if the Hindu refused to accept that he assumes the truth of any of the premises the scholar attributes? He will have to do more than merely say that he does not entertain the premises imputed to him; he will have to provide an alternative assumption that justifies the standpoint he has advanced. For instance, if the Hindus are not willing to accept the assumptions imputed to them, they have to come up with alternate assumptions that justify their beliefs. Such an alternative explanation will have to be about what 'religion' is, what the relation is between beliefs and human practices, what it means to do puja to the Hindu deities, how this is a justifiable explanation and so on and so forth. In other words, they have to be intellectual experts, who have explanations about many, many facets of their culture. The Hindu must not only have explanations for cultural phenomena, but he must also accept that such explanations constitute the implicit premises of his argumentation.

It is here that we see the skew in the dialogue in its sharpest form: *the onus of proof is distributed unevenly between the participants in the dialogue.* The scholar makes a series of cognitive moves and his defence is that they are logically necessary, if one wants a rational, critical discussion. The Hindu, for his part, has to have *explicit alternatives*, if he disagrees with the implied (or implicit) moves. *The only way the non-Western peoples can show they are not 'stupid' is by explicitly providing alternate explanations that make them appear intelligent.*

Let us also see where this has brought us. First, it is obvious that one cannot accuse scholars like Kripal and Courtright of bad faith; nor could one hold their 'psychologies' accountable for their portrayal of Hinduism. Their use of psychoanalysis cannot be localized in their desire to 'demean' Hinduism; nor can one 'explain' their writings as a part of some nefarious anti-Hindu plot and propaganda. Second, by the same token, if 'insiders' do research and teach Hinduism, these problems do not get solved. *They too would face the same set of issues.*

Given this, it is obvious that the so-called 'insider/outsider' problem is barren as far as this situation is concerned.

Violence is involved *in* the argumentative situation not because Kripal and Courtright are 'outsiders'. We should appreciate the logical compulsion in the argumentation that forces them into making some cognitive moves. These moves, in turn, inflict violence on the experiential world of the Hindus. The latter, for their part, react violently because they are violated. Of course, this situation does not justify violence, but it teaches us not to go around apportioning moral blame on the participants with nonchalance.

A Methodological Problem

In my analysis thus far, I have deliberately ignored the many discussions on this topic. Many before me have said much about the effacing of the 'Other', the scholarly responsibility of allowing the 'Other' to speak, the 'right' to speak about a religion, the nature of scholarly representation, and so on. It is often suggested that these are 'methodological' questions or issues of 'normative' epistemology. I will now argue that they are neither.

In a recent article, Russell McCutcheon (2006) notices three facts about the scholar of religion in the study of the 'Other', especially from within the 'liberal humanistic tradition':

1. The scholar indulges in a remarkable role switching: while, as liberal humanist, he wants to give a voice to the Other, simultaneously, he also speaks in place of the 'Other' (McCuctheon 2006: 741).
2. In the case of someone like Courtright, he notices a change from the early Courtright who wanted to efface himself as a scholar to the new Courtright who chooses to affirm himself at the risk of effacing the 'Other' (ibid.: 728).
3. The inability of the scholar to digest dissent when the 'Other' speaks back (ibid.: 746).

While one can resonate with the issues that McCutcheon raises, one cannot accept either his diagnosis of the situation or the remedy he proposes. To my mind, his diagnosis makes these scholars inauthentic: they employ a different set of tools when they focus on 'Others' for whom 'they feel little affinity' as against what McCutcheon calls the 'no cost Others'. If 'feeling affinity' is why someone chooses one set of intellectual tools and not another, then Kripal and Courtright are not scholars but charlatans. If true, they *do not desire* to generate knowledge at all. However, such condemnations require more proof and evidence than produced by anyone so far.

Reconsider what Courtright and Kripal claim they do: they indulge in 'interpretations'. Let us leave aside what they are 'interpreting', but merely focus upon how they can be challenged. Regarding the acceptability of their interpretation, any challenge that the Hindu can issue to either of these two scholars can only take the form of questioning *the explanatory adequacy* of their psychoanalytical theories. Does Courtright's use of psychoanalysis explain why Indians do puja rituals to Ganesha adequately or not? Does Kripal explain Ramakrishna's religious life or not? We need to note that explanatory adequacy is a peculiarly *comparative notion* in this dialogical context: the Hindu cites a story about Ganesha's elephant head; Courtright, as the scholar, explains the *'meaning* in the selection of the elephant head'. Clearly, Courtright wins because a puranic *story* is not an alternative to a Freudian *explanation* of that story.

Even though the scholar claims to assume an 'interpretative' stance, his use of theories put an *explanatory burden* on the Hindu. To challenge either Courtright or Kripal is to challenge either their use (or the theory) of psychoanalysis. That is, one can only challenge the explanatory power of these theories and, as we have seen, the Hindu cannot do that unless armed with an alternate explanatory theory. The scholar, by contrast, can challenge the 'interpretation' of the Hindu by dismissing it as mere minority opinion, or as the ravings of a 'Hindu fundamentalist', or by assuming an *explanatory stance*. The scholar can switch between interpretative and explanatory stances, whereas the Hindu can only assume an explanatory stance. This asymmetric relationship is cognitive in nature: even though Courtright or Kripal use explanatory theories, only their 'interpretation' is the subject matter of the argumentation. Moreover, their interpretations acquire the status of unchallengeable opinions. To challenge their interpretation, one has to challenge the status of psychoanalytical explanation; doing the latter, however, enables these scholars to defend it *as their opinion*: 'I find that psychoanalysis illumines dreams, stories, and cultures. You do not. So let us agree to disagree.' The reason for this is not difficult to seek: the explanatory theories they base their interpretative stance upon is a presupposition of the dialogue and not its subject matter.

Finally, something even more remarkable happens. Because the Hindu can only challenge the explanatory adequacy of the theory provided he has an alternative, he is excluded from the dialogue itself. The scholar ends up having a dialogue with a 'surreal' Hindu. Such are the logical and cognitive compulsions that the Hindu is banished from the dialogical situation, and plays merely a pre-dialogical role. The scholar becomes a ventriloquist.

In other words, additional asymmetries in a 'symmetric dialogue' come into focus: the Hindu is saddled with an explicit explanatory burden and is forced to assume a pre-dialogical role, whereas the scholar has the 'choice' of (or the 'freedom to choose' between) being interpretative or explanatory. Concomitant to this asymmetric cognitive burden, there is a corresponding asymmetry in their dialogical roles.

We can now see why the role switching comes about: the scholar has both an 'interpretation' and an explanatory theory at hand. The alleged 'inconsistency' of Courtright has to do with the nature of the dialogue and is not due to his lack of authenticity or 'lack of affinity'. The scholars do not employ different sets of tools depending on their affinities; the explanatory theories they use end up becoming the presuppositions of the dialogue. Our problem, in short, has to do with *what happens to a rational dialogue in certain kinds of encounters*.

Having taken a neutral conception of dialogue, I have construed two writings on Hinduism as a *dialogue about a religion*. Without adding any ad hoc and arbitrary hypotheses, such a construal has enabled me to not only exhibit the violence involved in the situation but also identify its two different sources: one is the requirement of reason; the other is a reaction to the inflicted violence. Even limited analysis of the situation raises important and disturbing questions—about the relation between 'reason' and violence, the need for dialogue, the morality of 'reason' as it is embodied in a dialogue, and so on. If we think deeper and dig further, we encounter different kinds of dialogue in the history of religions: dialogue between religions, dialogue within a religion, dialogue between atheists and believers, and so on and so forth. What other lessons do the conclusions here hold in store for us? Whatever they might be, we should not simply go around issuing clarion calls for 'more dialogue' with and between religions—which is what the common-sense, the media, and the politicians advocate—as though that suffices to reduce the violence we hear and read about every day. *At the minimum, some of these 'dialogues' exacerbate violence; they do not reduce it.* I am not suggesting the absence of dialogue as 'the' remedy for violence. Nevertheless, I submit that we would do well to study the history of religions in a different way than hitherto.

In the last following chapters, I have circled around the notion of colonial consciousness in different ways. These considerations open up a different kind of reflection in the next chapter. In so far as colonialism is a political event, its product (in our case, the colonial consciousness) has a very serious consequence in the realm of normative political theorizing as well. That is what I shall look at now.

CHAPTER 7

Intercultural Encounters, Reasonable Dialogues, and Normative Political Theory

In the previous chapter, I took two examples from Hinduism studies to raise issues about dialogues and their relation to violence. In this chapter, I shall broaden the nature of the examples and focus on their implications for political philosophy. More concretely, I want to examine the consequences of the previous two chapters for some theories of political liberalism. In the process, it must become clear why we cannot rely upon received wisdom, if we intend to rethink India studies today.

With the publication of *A Theory of Justice*, John Rawls (1971) gave a new lease of life to normative political theory. Today, it is a flourishing academic discipline. While one notices this with some satisfaction, it is a puzzle why students of culture have largely kept away from this important debate.[1] After all, because it is normative, such a political theory is universalizable and the norms proposed by it (about fairness, justice, and such like) *ought to* hold universally. Given the presence of different cultures in the world, it is of importance to find out whether such differences are of any consequence to normative political theorizing. Even if the 'universe of discourse' of normative political theory is restricted to American society by means of a philosophical fiat, the presence of cultural minorities in that society is an indisputable fact. Nevertheless, cultural difference has not been taken seriously as a basic conceptual issue of normative political theory. This lacuna becomes even more glaring when we turn to Rawls's later work *Political Liberalism* (1996).

The aim of both the later Rawls and thinkers like Charles Larmore is to build a political conception of justice that will find backing among all reasonable people in spite of their adherence to incompatible comprehensive doctrines or conflicting views of the good life.[2] The basic structure of society should be organized and justified according to the tenets of a minimal moral conception which stands free from the different comprehensive doctrines, but is legitimized by an overlapping consensus among them. In contrast to the 'non-public' reasons of the various comprehensive doctrines, this political conception of justice expresses the common 'public reason' of the citizens; it is shared as 'a basis of a reasoned, informed, and willing political agreement' (Rawls 1996: 9). It guides the citizen's *reasoning and debating in the public forum* about constitutional essentials and basic questions of justice.

However, this political conception of justice is one of the two pillars that guide such reasoning and debates. The other pillar involves considerations about the very nature of such debates. That is to say, inquiries into how public dialogues are to be conducted also become essential to political liberalism. To Rawls, agreement about the nature of a reasonable discussion is a 'companion agreement' to the one regarding the political conception of justice as fairness:

... [A]n agreement on a political conception of justice requires is to no affect without *a companion agreement on guidelines of public enquiry and rules for assessing evidence*. The values of public reason not only include the appropriate use of fundamental concepts of judgment, inference, and evidence, but also the virtues of reasonableness and fairmindedness as shown in abiding by the criteria and procedures of common sense knowledge and accepting the methods and conclusions of science when not controversial. (Rawls 1996: 139; italics added)

Elsewhere, he states that these values of public reason are necessary to distinguish reasoning from rhetoric or means of persuasion. All ways of reasoning 'must incorporate the fundamental concepts and principles of reason, and include standards of correctness and criteria of justification' (ibid. 220). Rawls argues that in providing justifications 'we are to appeal only to presently accepted general beliefs and forms of reasoning found in common sense, and the methods and conclusions of science when these are not controversial' (ibid. 224). Yet, except for the minor hand waving in the direction of the precepts of reasonable discussion, he does not seem to consider it his task to fill in this important idea.

To Larmore, the norm of rational dialogue is one of the two pillars of his theory of liberal neutrality—the other being the norm of equal respect for persons:

In discussing how to solve some problem (for example, what principles of political association they should adopt), people should respond to points of disagreement by retreating to neutral ground, to the beliefs they still share, in order either to (a) resolve the disagreement and vindicate one of the disputed positions by means of arguments which proceed from this common ground or (b) bypass the disagreement and seek a solution of the problem on the basis simply of this common ground. (Larmore 1990: 347)

The role of dialogue, then, is to try and convince others of the validity of our own views of the good life by means of arguments or enable a retreat to a neutral ground, where it fails. Other champions of political liberalism confirm that the commitment to reasonable public dialogue lies at the heart of this normative framework (Ackerman 1994: 367). Dialogue is especially central to the political domain, Ackerman suggests, because politics concerns the vital issue of 'how people who disagree about the moral truth might nonetheless solve their ongoing problem of living together' (Ackerman 1989: 8).

The liberalisms of Rawls, Larmore, and Ackerman are not identical; one presumes that the same consideration holds as far as their implicit understandings of a dialogue and its scope are concerned. Rawls, for instance, is interested in the role of such a dialogue only in the public forum about constitutional essentials and basic questions of justice. Nevertheless, such is his confidence about the nature of reasonable dialogue that he allows 'the criteria and procedures of common-sense knowledge' to decide about its structure. Rawlsian theory cannot be parasitic on any one particular notion of dialogue any more than one can claim that 'common-sense knowledge' contains only one specific notion of dialogue. The only demand is that all participants abide by the same criteria and procedures, and this exhibits their reasonableness and fair-mindedness. The belief that a rational dialogue could work in debates on constitutional essentials and basic questions of justice and *yet not pervert the cause of justice* can only be justified, if there is some kind of a 'guarantee' (nothing less than a logical certainty would do in this case) about *the nature, structure and the results of a rational dialogue*. Something about such a dialogue necessarily prevents perversions. To put it even more simply, the rational dialogue that Rawls wants must itself be 'just', an exemplar of the kind that Rawls defends. That is why it can work in public debates. *Otherwise, it cannot.*

Analogous points hold good for Larmore and Ackerman. Even where we take into consideration the debate between Habermas and Rawls about the nature of dialogue, there too the same considerations are valid. Rational dialogues will incorporate some or other criteria or principles that are logical and semantic in nature. Such criteria or principles will guide a sound discussion and arbitrate about unsound steps. Consequently, even though I focus mostly on Rawls and Larmore in this chapter, the lesson is broader in scope: it equally affects all political theories that emphasize the role of rational dialogue, whether of a Habermas or of an Ackerman.

Given the importance of the above considerations, why have political liberals nonetheless neglected the notion of rational dialogue?[3] One reason could be its familiarity: Larmore remarks this norm has been a central element of western thought for centuries (Larmore 1990: 354–6). However, familiarity is a very dubious justification unless one can show that what is familiar is also well-understood. Another reason might have to do with the intellectual domain under consideration. One could say that it is not the task of normative political theory to say what a 'rational dialogue' is; disciplines like argumentation theory are more suited to develop this notion into a workable theory. *Working under this assumption*, I will continue to use the best available theory from the field of rhetoric or argumentation theories. This theory satisfies the structural demands that we might want to put on the notion of 'rational dialogue': it is reasonable, the rules of discussion are transparent and they are neutral with respect to the participants in a discussion. However, when we apply this apparently reasonable set of rules to *actual discussions* between members of different cultures, peculiar results emerge that undermine the claims of political liberalism.[4]

Since I have already discussed the nature, structure, and the rules of such a dialogue in the previous chapter, I shall not repeat myself here. Instead, let me ask: is such a notion of dialogue also a 'reasonable' one? A Rawlsian creature is 'reasonable' if it possesses two properties: (a) it accepts fair terms of social cooperation; (b) it accepts the 'burdens of judgment', that is, accepts that reasonable pluralism is the inevitable result of the exercise of reason by reasonable creatures: 'Persons are reasonable in one basic aspect when, among equals say, they are ready *to propose principles and standards as fair terms of cooperation and to abide by them willingly, given the assurance that others will likewise do* so' (Rawls 1996: 49; italics added). Or, in other words,

... the first basic aspect of the reasonable ... is the willingness to propose fair terms of cooperation and to abide by them provided the others do. The second basic aspect ... is the willingness to recognize the burdens of judgment and to accept their consequences for the use of public reason. (Rawls 1996: 54)

A reasonable discussion as outlined above is not only a form of social cooperation, but its structure also satisfies the first condition of reasonableness. The reasonable is also public:

... [I]t is by the reasonable that we enter as equals in the public world of others and stand ready to propose, or to accept, as the case may be, fair terms of cooperation with them. These terms, *set out as principles*, specify the reasons we are to share and publicly recognize before one another as grounding our social relations. (Rawls 1996: 53; italics added)

In a way, one could say that the paradigmatic case of the application of such dialogical rules is a well-conducted scientific discussion. Such a setup does not privilege either the protagonist or the antagonist in the discussion. Consequently, it generates a reasonable discussion that does not violate fairness *in the minimal sense* that the discussion does not favour any one particular party. Does this continue to remain the case, if we apply it to what one might call 'intercultural encounters'?

Some Inter-cultural Dialogues

The theory of John Rawls is pitched at a high level of abstraction, something, Rawls says, he does not 'apologize for' (ibid. lxii). There is nothing wrong with abstraction, of course; most of our theories in the natural sciences describe objects at a high level of abstraction, as well.

However, such abstract descriptions must 'approximate' the concrete, embedded objects with respect to what they describe. That is, the concrete objects must approximately behave the way the abstract descriptions indicate. The same holds good for Rawls's theory too.

We will now take up some real examples of intercultural discussions. The protagonists in all these cases are people from cultures other than the modern Western culture; the antagonist represents the modern western culture. Let us also circumscribe the goal of these discussions: the scholar from the West is merely trying to understand people from other cultures. We will not allow either of the parties to go beyond this explicit goal.

Cicero's *On the Nature of the Gods* is one of the earliest and finest treatises on the nature of religion, gods, belief in them, and so on. From that dialogue, consider the following fragment, where Gaius Cotta, the academic sceptic, is speaking:

> I am considerably influenced ... by the plea that you put forward at the conclusion of your discourse, when you exhorted me to remember that I am both a Cotta and a pontiff. This is no doubt meant that I ought to *uphold beliefs* about the immortal gods *which have come down to us from our ancestors*, and the rites and ceremonies and duties of religion. For my part, I shall always uphold them and have always done so, and no eloquence of anybody, learned or unlearned shall ever dislodge me from the belief which I have inherited from our forefathers ... You are a philosopher, and I ought to receive from you a proof of your religion, *whereas I must believe the word of our ancestors even without proof.* (III, ii: 290–91; emphasis mine)

The same point is made even more strongly later: 'Although I for my part cannot be persuaded to surrender my belief that the gods exist, nevertheless you teach me no reason why this belief, *of which I am convinced on the authority of our forefathers*, should be true' (ibid. 293; emphasis mine). Addressing the need to prove the existence of gods felt by Quintus Lucillus Balbus, his stoic opponent, Cotta says the following:

> You did not really feel confident that the doctrine of the divine existence was as self-evident as you could wish, and for that reason you attempted to prove it with a number of arguments. *For my part a simple argument would have sufficed, namely that it has been handed down to us by our forefathers.* (III, iv: 295; emphasis mine)

How would a twenty-first-century intellectual continue the dialogue with Cotta? He or she could challenge the belief that belonging to a tradition or the authority of one's forefathers is an adequate justification for continuing a practice. After all, many practices (like owning slaves for example) in the same tradition are abhorrent. Consequently, to say that one believes in gods because one's ancestors also believed in them is an inadequate justification.

Consider now the relation between the intellectuals of this culture and the religious practices of their day. There was no dearth of books and philosophical schools decrying, denigrating, and dismissing the importance of gods, or even denying their existence. Though dangerous, even individuals dared it: Lucian, the famous satirist from the second century, openly challenged the cult of Glycon—visiting its chief priest, poking around its shrine, asking questions with a grin on his face. The danger—Lucian's life was endangered—lay in mockery and not in the challenge. Even mockery, in so far as it was directed against the credulous, like Plutarch's *On Superstition* for instance, was welcome (MacMullen 1984: 15).

We do not need to go further than Cicero to be convinced of this fact. The social, psychological, and epistemic speculations put across in *De Natura Deorum* to account for the origin of religion have not been bettered to this day. Even those inclined to treat this evaluation as an exaggeration will have to admit that the arsenal of arguments, which supported the attack of eighteenth century European intellectuals against religion, came primarily from this one single work. Yet, Cicero himself was a priest. Though a sceptic and a critic of augury, he retained his membership in the board of Augurs of the Republic. Epicurus urged his followers to take part in sacrifices, himself participating in the religious festivals of Athens, and was initiated into the Eleusinian mysteries. His follower, Lucretius, followed the master's example in venerating ancestral gods. Plutarch, author of the famous essay against superstition, spent his later life as a priest in Delphi composing tracts on divine punishment and evident terrors of the next world. From today's optic, the same Gaius Cotta, who is himself a priest, beautifully exemplifies this curious division between what they said and what they did:

I, who am a high priest, and who hold it to be a duty most solemnly to maintain the rights and doctrines of the established religion, should be glad to be convinced of this fundamental tenet of divine existence, not as an article of faith merely but as an ascertained fact. *For many disturbing reflections occur to my mind, which sometimes make me think that there are no gods at all.* (Cicero, I, xxii: 61; emphasis mine)

How to have a dialogue with people, who participate in religious activities and sacrifices (oftentimes even lead them), and yet claim not to believe in the gods and the deities to whom such sacrifices are offered? How could one deny the existence of gods and yet officiate in religious ceremonials? The enlightenment thinkers took up this issue nearly 1800 years later.

To Montesquieu, it simply reflected the genius of Roman politics: Rome used rational means to govern irrational masses. Neither fear nor piety was at its foundation, but simply the recognition that all societies need religion—a mechanism required to govern the masses by taking advantage of their credulity. Diderot varied on this theme a bit: he suggested that Cicero was irreligious, but then 'in his time, the people hardly read at all; they listened to the speeches of their orators, and the speeches were always filled with piety toward the gods; but they did not know what the orator thought and wrote about it in his study' (cited in Gay 1973: 156). Hume was even more explicit, suggesting a fear of persecution if not downright dishonesty:

If there was ever a nation or a time, in which the public religion lost all authority over mankind, we might expect, that infidelity in ROME, during the CICERONEAN age, would openly have erected its throne, and that CICERO himself, in every speech and action, would have been its most declared abettor. But it appears that, whatever sceptical liberties that great man might take, in his writings or in philosophical conversation; he yet avoided, in the common conduct of life, the imputation of deism and profaneness. Even in his own family, and to his wife TERENTIA, whom he highly trusted, he was *willing to appear a devout religionist;* and there remains a letter, addressed to her, in which he seriously desires her to offer sacrifice to APOLLO and AESCULAPIUS, in gratitude for the recovery of his health. (Hume 1964: 347; emphasis mine)

Gibbon, in his magisterial *Decline*, accepts the theme wholeheartedly. With an ease that can only surprise the modern mind, he transforms pagan thinkers into actors in a charade:

How, indeed, was it possible, that a philosopher should accept, as divine truths, the idle tales of poets, and the *incoherent traditions of antiquity;* or, that he should adore, as gods, those imperfect beings whom he must have despised, as men! ... In their writings and conversation, the philosophers of antiquity asserted the independent dignity of reason; but they *resigned their actions to the commands of law and of custom.* Viewing, with a smile of pity and indulgence, the various errors of the vulgar, they diligently practised the ceremonies of their fathers, devoutly frequented the temples of the gods; and sometimes condescending to act a part on the theatre of superstition, they *concealed the sentiments of an Atheist* under the sacerdotal robes ... It was indifferent to them what shape the folly of the multitude might choose to assume; and they approached, *with the same inward contempt, and the same external reverence,* the altars of the Libyan, the Olympian, or the Capitoline Jupiter. (Gibbon 1952: 13; emphasis mine)

This is not merely the opinion of the old masters. Peter Gay, our contemporary, endorses these opinions. To him, the attitude of Cicero was a conscious compromise: 'Cicero was urging the Romans to stand fast against new cults and oriental superstitions, but Cicero did not see, or did not say, that his policy sanctified practices which he scorned privately as vulgar and absurd' (Gay 1973: 155). Even when they did not believe in the divinity of their deities or in their existence, Epicurus, Cicero, and Plutarch not only participated but also led religious practices. In having a dialogue with them, either one transforms them into inauthentic intellectuals ('they do not believe in what they themselves say') or attributes some or another reason for their outward behaviour ('fear of persecution' or 'prudence' or 'expediency').

We can already observe the skew in the dialogue: it favours the scholar from the West. The process of trying to understand the ancient Roman culture by the modern Western mind is generating prejudice and bias against the representatives of the Roman culture: their intellectuals appear inauthentic and inconsistent, irrespective of what generates these two attitudes in them.

Now consider a modern-day intellectual coming across a group of people performing a rain dance. To the query about the reasons for the dance, he gets to hear a story. Invariably, this story will refer to a situation where the rains did not come, where the people performed the rain dance, and where rain followed this event. Thus, this intellectual believes that this particular group attributes *causal efficacy* to the performance. Any further dialogue will involve discussions about the efficacy of the rain dance in producing rain. As an example of such a dialogue, here is Livingstone (the medical doctor) talking to a Kwena practitioner (the rain doctor).

Medical Doctor: So you really believe that you can command the clouds? I think that can be done by God alone.

Rain Doctor: We both believe the very same thing. It is God that makes the rain, but I pray to him by means of these medicines, and, the rain coming, of course it is then mine ...

Medical Doctor: But we are distinctly told in the parting words of our Saviour that we can pray to God acceptably in his name alone, and not by means of medicine.

Rain Doctor: True! But God told us differently ... God has given us one little thing which you know nothing of. He has given us the knowledge of certain medicines by which we can make rain ... We don't understand your book, yet we don't despise it. *You* ought not to despise our little knowledge, though you're ignorant of it.

Medical Doctor: I don't despise what I am ignorant of; I only think you are mistaken in saying that you have medicines which can influence the rain at all.

Rain Doctor: That's just the way people speak when they talk on a subject which they have no knowledge. When we first opened our eyes, *we found our forefathers making rain and we follow in their footsteps* ...

Medical Doctor: I quite agree with you as to the value of the rain; but you cannot charm the clouds by medicines. You wait till you see the clouds come, then you use your medicine, and take the credit which belongs to God only.

Rain Doctor: I use my medicine, and you employ yours; we are both doctors, and doctors are not deceivers. You give a patient medicine. Sometimes God is pleased to heal him by means of your medicine; sometimes not—he dies. When he is cured, you take the credit for what God does. I do the same. Sometimes God grants us rain, sometimes not. When he does, we take the credit for the charm. When a patient dies, you don't give up trust in your medicine, neither do I when rain fails. If you wish me to leave off my medicines, why continue your own? (John and Jean Comaroff 2002: 499–500; emphasis mine)

At first sight, it looks as though two religious conceptions (in Rawls's term, two 'comprehensive doctrines') have met each other in a dialogue about an issue of no great significance or political importance. Nothing is further from the truth. Even though Dr Livingstone was a missionary, we could easily make appropriate substitutions in his contribution to the dialogue and have a natural scientist or an intelligent layperson carry on a similar conversation with the Kwena practitioner. Should we do so, the skew becomes more apparent: the only way to understand the Kwena practitioner is to deny him any conception of natural causality. Having a reasonable dialogue with this African requires us to transform him into an irrational and superstitious creature.

Nietzsche does precisely that to the Indian culture of his time. In India, there is a festival, which involves people performing puja to all kinds of implements they have at home: from bicycles to cars; from bookcases to utensils; from ploughs to pens. Nietzsche read about this festival called the *Ayudhapuja* in the writings of Sir John Lubbock, an English historian:

In India ... a carpenter is accustomed to make sacrifices to his hammer, his axe and his other tools; a Brahman treats the crayon with which he writes, a soldier the weapon he employs in the field, a mason his trowel, a labourer his plough in the same way. (Nietzsche 1986, §111: 63)

He notices this fact in the following context:

In those ages one as yet knows nothing of natural laws; neither earth nor sky are constrained by any compulsion; a season, sunshine, rain can come or they can fail to come. Any conception of *natural causality* is altogether lacking. When one rows it is not the rowing that moves the ship: rowing is only a magical ceremony by means of which one compels a demon to move the ship. All illness, death itself is the result of magical influences. Becoming ill and dying never occur naturally; the whole conception of 'natural occurrence' is lacking ... When someone shoots with the bow, there is ... an irrational hand and force at work in it; if the wells suddenly dry up, one thinks first of all of subterranean demons and their knavery; it must be the arrow of a god through whose invisible action a man suddenly sinks down. (Ibid.; emphasis in the original)

The only way to understand this wide-spread festival in India is by transforming the Indians living either today or in Nietzsche's period into exemplars from 'primitive times'. The skew is even more apparent. The process of understanding and exploring how 'reasonable people' could come to different 'reasonable' conceptions (the 'burden of judgement' in Rawls) is compelling the modern Western mind to deny (to an entire culture and its people) even elementary understanding of social and natural events. Adults from this culture are not even in a position to understand that the pen does not write without an author, something that even a child in the Western culture knows. Surely, if this is the case, there is something fundamentally wrong with the Indian psychology. In the earlier chapters, we have already seen what is 'wrong' with the Indian psychology, if we follow the psychoanalytical stories of Courtright and Kripal.

What do these examples have in common, and why are they relevant to a consideration of a theory of political liberalism? What they have in common is this: when the modern Western mind tries to 'understand' members from other cultures, the dialogue becomes skewed in favour of the former. Invariably, people from other cultures emerge as inferior specimens. Even though we have set up a 'reasonable' dialogue, the results of this process are anything but fair.

They are relevant because this situation raises challenges to the theories of political liberalism. If a reasonable dialogue generates skewed results in such diverse matters as the above, why should we believe that the same would not happen when political issues are at stake? Setting up 'fair terms' of social cooperation (the way we did it with the dialogical rules) does not provide any *cognitive guarantee* that it also works fairly. If the reasonable rules of dialogue lead the Western mind (which is also a reasonable creature) to understand others the way it does, how can we assume that the exemplar of 'public reason', the Supreme Court, will be fair in understanding and judging? *It might be in the nature of a reasonable discussion itself to skew the process.*

If cognitive mechanisms, which exhibit a cultural bias tilted towards the western culture, embed a 'freestanding' notion of rational dialogue, it makes sense to suspect such a dialogue of making implicit assumptions that are not obvious at the outset. In the same way, justice as fairness might be implicated as well. It is possible that when Rawls speaks about its appeal to those who share a common 'political culture' of democratic institutions, the suggestion is something much narrower: the appeal of justice as fairness has less to do with 'reasonableness' than with sharing the western culture. A 'political conception of justice is formulated *so far as possible* solely in terms of certain fundamental intuitive ideas viewed as implicit in the *public political culture* of a democratic society' (Rawls 1999: 480; emphasis added). This notion could be less freestanding and embedded more in the western culture than it is in a 'democratic society'.

The Skew in the Dialogues

Why are these dialogues skewed? As I have noted in the previous chapter, it has to do with the cognitive mechanisms involved in the process. To understand the others, the Western mind has to make a series of dialogical moves. In so doing, a systematic distortion occurs as an inevitable result. In each of the dialogical cases sketched above, we face similar problems. If the wish is to have a dialogue, one can have it *only* if one attributes some specific beliefs to the protagonists. (Even though more than one belief is required in some cases, let us continue as though one belief is sufficient to continue the dialogue.) Let us identify these in the above examples as well.

In the first case, one has to assume that Cotta is defending his belief in the gods because it is a part of his tradition to believe in them. In the case of Cicero, one has to come up with some assumption about the relation between his belief and practice that either renders him consistent or makes him inauthentic. In the third case, one has to attribute a belief about the causal efficacy of rain dance to its practitioners. In the fourth case, one has to say that the Brahmin believes that his pen writes and that it is the author of his tracts.

Is one justified in attributing these beliefs to one's opponents? If yes, one renders the opponents into idiots: Cotta really thought all beliefs sanctioned by his forefathers are justified because they are so sanctioned; there are cultures, where people really do believe that their jumping up and down in some form causes the rains to come; the Brahmins really do not know that without a human hand and brain directing it, the pen cannot write coherent tracts. Of course, it is possible that such people (mostly from non-Western cultures) are stupid, but it is not plausible. The reason why it fails to have plausibility is that the very same people exhibit behaviours in other domains, which contradict the beliefs one is imputing to them in this particular case. As Wittgenstein puts it in a similar context, in his *Remarks on Frazer's Golden Bough*: 'The same savage who, apparently, in order to kill his enemy sticks his knife through a picture of him, really does build his hut of wood and cuts his arrow with skill and not in effigy' (Wittgenstein 2002: 87).

However, could one have a dialogue without attributing such beliefs? A moment's reflection will make it clear that one cannot. What is one *disagreeing* with, if not with the belief that traditionally sanctioned beliefs are justified by virtue of that fact alone? Or with the belief that rain dance does cause the rains to come? Could Nietzsche have disagreements with a Brahmin without attributing to the latter the belief that holding a pen is 'a magical ceremony that compels a demon to write'? *The disagreements arise precisely due to the attribution of such beliefs.* Otherwise, there is nothing to disagree about. In a dialogue, one draws the attention of the protagonists to the fact that such beliefs constitute the *hidden* premises of their argumentation. In the interests of a rational argumentation, one is logically compelled to impute such beliefs.

Here is the *first issue,* then: on the one hand, by attributing premises to people from other cultures, one renders them unfit for being dialogue partners; on the other hand, the only way to have a dialogue is by attributing such premises and by transforming them into idiots.

What would happen if the protagonist suggests that he is not willing to accept the beliefs imputed to him? For instance, if a Cicero or an Indian is not willing to accept the imputed assumptions, they have to come up with alternate assumptions that justify their beliefs: in one case, Cicero has to show how he could deny the existence of gods and still remain a priest; in the other case, the Indian needs to explicate the assumptions that justify worshipping the 'crayon'. This compulsion arises because of the fact that any dialogue is a rule-governed activity, even if it is us who formulate the rules. These rules belong to the 'ten commandments' of an argumentative discourse. Consequently, one has to say, amplifying the fifth rule for the rational argumentation, that 'a difference of opinion cannot be resolved if a protagonist tries to withdraw from the obligation to defend an unexpressed premise ... To resolve the difference of opinion, the protagonist must accept the responsibility for implicit elements in his or her argumentation' (van Eemeren *et al.* 1996: 285).

Let us now examine the nature of the beliefs imputed to the protagonists. They are, above all, explanatory in nature.

(a) 'Because Cotta believes that the ancestral practice lends validity to beliefs, he is arguing that he believes in the existence of gods on the basis of ancestral authority.'

(b) 'Because Cicero was afraid of being accused of "deism", he knowingly and falsely officiated in religious ceremonies.'

(c) 'Because people believe that their rituals have a (magical) causal efficacy, the group performs rain dance in order to cause the rains.'

(d) 'Because Indians think that all the implements possess some kind of divine power, they also believe that it is the divine

nature of the pen to write. Therefore, Indians do believe that
the author is merely the means through which the pen writes.'

Each of these (or similar) explanatory hypotheses becomes the
assumption (or implicit premise) in the argumentation. Consequently,
the protagonist has to come up with an alternate *explanatory hypothesis*.
Consider what this demand really implies. If a Cicero has to provide
an *alternative* explanation, it will have to be about what 'religion' was
to the Roman culture, what the relation is between beliefs and human
practices, what being a priest entails, what it means to believe in gods,
how this is a justifiable explanation, and so on and so forth. In other
words, he needs to be an intellectual expert, who has explanations about
many, many facets of his own culture. The same demand holds good
with respect to Nietzsche quizzing the Brahmin about Ayudhapuja.
Clearly, it can be no demand of a rational, critical discussion that the
protagonist has explanations for cultural phenomena and that such
explanations constitute the premises of his argumentation.

On the one hand, it must be obvious that by formulating one's
hypotheses as beliefs of the actors, one is imputing assumptions
that are not there. By doing so, one violates the fifth rule of the
argumentative discourse: 'A party may not falsely present a premise as
an accepted starting point ... ' (van Eemeren *et al.* 1996: 284). On the
other hand, without violating these rules, one cannot have a rational,
critical discussion at all. It is thus that we come to the *second issue*.
A rational, critical discussion is not possible if the rules of dialogue
are violated; but without a violation of such rules, no intercultural
dialogue appears possible.

One might be inclined to suggest that one needs to 'understand' what
the protagonist is saying before disagreeing with him. What has gone
wrong in these dialogues is that people have jumped to conclusions
without really ascertaining what the other was saying. This *ad hoc* claim
is not an objection to what I am saying: of course, a rational, critical
discussion is impossible without understanding the protagonist; at
times, such a discussion itself is a means to 'understand' the standpoint
of the protagonist. The issues are independent of the phase in which a
specific dialogue finds itself in. Even though I will address this question
at the end, let me illustrate it by taking up the third issue.

In the cases presented above, it is important to note that the real
object of discussion is some or another human practice. Whether it is

about worshipping the pen, or whether performing the rain dance, or officiating as a priest, the discussion is about the nature of a practice. However, the dialogue itself is not about these practices, but regarding *the beliefs that the protagonists are alleged to hold about these practices*. The only way one can have a rational, critical discussion about a practice is by reformulating it in terms of the beliefs the practitioners 'ought to' hold about these practices. This is inevitable: the dialogue can only be about a conflict of 'avowed opinions'. The opinions express the beliefs held by the parties in a dialogue about these practices.

This is the *third issue*. At a meta-level, it is obvious that such a dialogical stance presupposes the following: *human practices are embodiments of beliefs*. Only because such a relation is postulated between practice and belief could we think in terms of an intercultural dialogue. As Wittgenstein puts it in his remarks on Frazer's work:

Even the idea of *trying to explain the practice*—say the killing of the priest-king—seems to me wrong-headed. All that Frazer does is to make this practice plausible *to people who think as he does*. It is very queer that all these practices are finally presented, so to speak, as stupid actions.

But it never does become plausible that people do all of this out of sheer stupidity.

When he explains to us, for example, that the king must be killed in his prime because, according to the notion of the savages, his soul would not be kept fresh otherwise, we can only say: where that practice and these views go together, *the practice does not spring from the view*, but both of them are there. (Wittgenstein 2002: 86; emphasis mine)

Or again:

... [O]ne might begin a book on anthropology in this way: When we watch the life and behaviour of men all over the earth we see that apart from what we might call animal activities, taking food, &c., &c., men also carry out actions that bear a peculiar character and might be called ritualistic.

But then it is nonsense if we go on to say that the characteristic feature of *these* [emphasis in the original] actions is that *they spring from wrong ideas* about the physics of things. (This is what Frazer does when he says magic is really false physics, or as the case may be, false medicine, technology, &c.) (Ibid. 89, emphasis added)

One does not have to agree with everything Wittgenstein says in order to appreciate that there is a genuine insight here: when describing human cultures, if we formulate cultural practices as embodiments of beliefs, we will only make it plausible to those who do think this way.

Not only does one make a meta-level assumption about the relation between belief and practice, but such a dialogical stance also *compels* the protagonist to accept the same. The dialogical partners *ought to* accept that practices are embodiments of beliefs; if they do not, one cannot have a dialogue. The factual assumption of a specific culture is transformed into a (cognitive) *moral rule* that all cultures *ought to accept*. Notice that the factual assumption could be true or false. However, notice the status it has taken as well: it is obligatory for the rest of humankind to accept it as true. The prejudices of a culture are transformed into an obligatory rule for all to follow. This is the *fourth issue*. Critical discussion enjoins the involved parties to thoroughly argue and defend the positions they put across; yet, to enable a dialogue, one party is *compelled* to accept uncritically the positions of the other party *as its own*.

We can now raise the *fifth issue* in intercultural dialogues. These explanations *structure the description* of practices in other cultures. They identify the nature of the phenomena and give them a structure. Thus, in these dialogues, one is not just attributing some explanations as the implicit premises of a discussion, but doing something more. *One is identifying the phenomenon under some particular description*, which happens to be one's own. To have a dialogue, the others have to accept these terms of description.

What appears a logically consistent set of rules generates some kinds of inconsistencies, when used in situations involving intercultural encounters. Instead of clearing up misunderstandings, intercultural dialogue *generates* them. The process and the result of these dialogues achieve the opposite of their intended *goal*: instead of clearing up misunderstandings between members of different cultures, intercultural dialogue breeds misunderstanding. The interaction between the structure of rational dialogue and the cognitive mechanisms that embed them is clearly the locus of these misunderstandings. In other words, the structure of rational dialogue compels the modern western mind to take recourse to his common-sense conception of what people are. These are very much part of the Western culture. They guide not only our theorizing, but also the way we relate to people from other cultures. They are an implicit part of our common sense and not, in any sense, the result of what scientific psychology has to tell us about people.

In addressing the issue of the stability of political structures, Rawls suggests (see also his 1996: 142) that those who live within justice as fairness will want to continue to live within it: 'The idea is that, given certain assumptions specifying a reasonable human psychology and the normal conditions of human life, those that grow up under basic institutions that are just ... acquire a reasoned and informed allegiance to those institutions sufficient to render the institutions stable' (Rawls 1999: 487). While such a claim requires making empirical assumptions about human psychology, it also requires the presence of a logical assumption: ceteris paribus, a fair structure (that is, a structure set up by reasonable persons) will work fairly. On the basis of what we have seen so far, we can suggest that this assumption is *not a logical truth* and that no such cognitive guarantees can be given. A structure, which appears reasonable and fair in the Rawlsian sense, namely rational dialogue, generates results skewed in favour of one particular party and, therefore, cannot hope to retain allegiance of those who participate in it. These results show that the problems of stability and legitimacy are not solved within Rawlsian theory of justice as fairness. The favoured solutions are merely presupposed.

Moreover, a Rawlsian reasonable person is capable of tolerating only some minimal variants of his own experience. In the process, all claims to the contrary notwithstanding, equal respect is not accorded to others who are different. What constitutes the 'tolerable' differences is not specified explicitly either. Larmore argues that in 'discussing how to solve some problem ... people should respond to points of disagreement by retreating to neutral ground, to the beliefs they still share, in order either to (a) resolve the disagreement ... or (b) bypass the disagreement ... on the basis simply of this common ground' (Larmore 1996: 134–5). What would constitute neutral ground in these dialogues? What kind of a common ground could one propose in such contexts, where one of the norms (the norm of rational dialogue) leads to the violation of the other norm (the norm of equal respect)? One might want to say that the antagonist is trying to treat the protagonists with 'equal respect', because he is appealing to the protagonist's 'capacity of thinking and acting on the basis of reasons' (Larmore 1996: 139). As we have seen, indeed, he tries to find the 'reasons' for the actions of his protagonist. However, in the *way* he does so, he violates the norm of equal respect. Even in Larmore's theory, the norm breaks down when people are different from some unspecified notion of what 'difference' implies.

The Implications of the Skew

Based on the foregoing, I would like to formulate a minimal set of observations. In situations of intercultural dialogue, certain kinds of 'reasonable discussion' not only generate misunderstandings, but also breed violence. The nature of these dialogues entails a violation of the rules of dialogue; but without such violations, dialogue cannot proceed. In the process of such dialogues, one imputes explanations as the implicit presuppositions, which are actually non-existent. These explanations, in their turn, make assumptions about the nature of human practice and its relation to belief, the structure of human psychology, and the nature of human beings. A scientific understanding of human cultures and individuals does not sanction these assumptions; they belong to the common-sense of a culture. In the deepest sense of the term, they are a part of the metaphysical and religious conceptions of a culture.

How many of these implications are due to the nature of rational dialogue? How much is owed to the nature of the themes involved in these discussions? How much is to due the structure of intercultural dialogue? Even though, today, we have no means of answering any of these questions adequately, one could still make an attempt.

A reasonable discussion requires some kind of a logical and semantic coherence, even if one is willing to embrace a loose notion of 'coherence'. Because every discussion makes presuppositions, one will be working with implicit premises. As Rawls makes it explicit, normative political theory is about *justifying* practical arrangements. The importance of public reason to political liberalism is that its exercise allows citizens to explain to each other *the reasons* for the policies and practices they advocate (Bohman 1995: 260). From this, it follows that the disputes about practices have to be necessarily formulated as disputes regarding beliefs about practices. Furthermore, these disputes will appeal to specific notions about the relation between theory and practice, the nature of beings who entertain such beliefs, and so on. In other words, the notion of a rational dialogue *compels* one to accept a specific conception of human psychology *as true*. This psychology postulates a particular kind of relation between reasons and actions, beliefs and behaviour. As a folk psychology, however, it belongs to the set of 'folk psychologies'; it is the folk psychology of one particular culture. That is to say, the implicit premises that the antagonist attributes to the protagonist are true, if and only if the common-sense conceptions of the antagonist (regarding human psychology) are also true.

Where do these notions come from? Quite obviously, they have but one lineage: the history of the culture in question. The history of western culture is also the history of Christianity and its secularization (Balagangadhara 1994). To the extent the principles of rational dialogue draw upon these notions, to that extent they are drawing upon the frameworks of Christianity and its secularization. That is to say, in the absence of scientific theories about people, drawing upon commonsense notions forces one to draw upon the ideas present in some or another 'comprehensive doctrine'. An intercultural dialogue brings to the fore an assumption of political liberalism: it assumes the truth of the western cultural folk psychology. This folk psychology has crystallized in the course of the history of one specific comprehensive doctrine, namely, Christianity. Consequently, political liberalism is forced to derivatively assume the truth of one particular 'comprehensive doctrine'.

Even if one disagrees here, one cannot justify the claim that one's notion of 'political liberalism', which includes a much vaguer notion of 'reasonable discussion', is independent of comprehensive doctrines. If it transpires that the *very idea* of a reasonable discussion appeals to culture-specific assumptions about human beings, as we believe it to be the case, then Rawls's belief about his theory's neutrality will have been ill founded. The onus is on the advocates of political liberalism to show how the *structure* of 'reasonable discussion' in the public political sphere is independent of conceptions arising from specific 'comprehensive doctrines'.

Let us recollect that the structure of dialogue with its ten rules does not violate any notion of fairness or justice. In fact, it satisfies their requirements admirably. However, we have also seen that using these rules in real situations violates requirements of both reasonableness and fairness because the dialogue gets skewed. Let us also recollect what the skew consists of: it distributes the burden of proof unevenly between the participants in the dialogue. This is a consequence of using a set of rules in a dialogue which does not, prima facie, seem to imply such an uneven distribution. On the contrary, these rules are devised precisely in order to prevent such a consequence. Where then does this additional and unexpected consequence come from? Here is one possibility: certain other premises which have been added in the course of the dialogue make this dialogue a skewed one. In short, reverting to the language of normative political philosophy, while we might observe the emergence of injustice from an apparently just structure, we are unable to localize the cause of injustice.

This has a very serious and troubling consequence to Rawlsians and other advocates of political liberalism. I shall explore its nature shortly. For now, let us notice that the above conclusion brings us to the 'Duhem-Quine thesis': theories are never tested in isolation from the background theories they are embedded in. The relevance of the Duhem-Quine thesis to our present endeavour is this: in the process of proposing and justifying a political structure, we need to appeal to our current 'common-sense' beliefs about a host of other issues, which cannot be explicated. That is to say, such a justification is founded on assumptions borrowed from other domains of human endeavour. Not only are these assumptions the co-foundations of a just structure but, together, they could also eventuate in unjust consequences. In this sense, how can one build a just structure given the nature of human knowledge? Justice as fairness cannot constitute the foundation of a society; such a structure itself will require foundations from elsewhere. Taken together, they might well make for a travesty of justice.

Political Liberalism and Violence

The 'burdens of judgment', Rawls claims, compel any reasonable being to accept the reasonable pluralism of comprehensive doctrines (Rawls 1996: 54–61). He does not 'deny that prejudice and bias, self- and group interest, blindness and wilfulness, play their all too familiar part in political life', but, he adds, 'these sources of unreasonable disagreement stand in marked contrast to those compatible with everyone's being fully reasonable' (Rawls 1996: 58). Similarly, Larmore states that 'at the heart of what should be the self-understanding of liberal thought' lies 'the recognition that reasonable people tend naturally to disagree about the comprehensive nature of the good life' (Larmore 1994: 62).

If the burdens of judgment indeed entail accommodating the inevitable plurality in the world, how does the denial of (and the attendant violence upon) the experiences of other people square with this? It does not. Consequently, a reasonable discussion can take place only between people who share the implicit common-sense conceptions or the same folk psychology comprising of unspecified assumptions.[5] Therefore, people from other cultures or those who share such a history only partially (like the new immigrant groups in the US) have to be *a priori* excluded from building the 'overlapping consensus'. To put it very explicitly: only those members sharing a *common Western history* are competent to enter into a reasonable discussion. Furthermore, because it is impossible to say what should be in 'common' between such people on any reasonable grounds, both the inclusion and the exclusion from becoming a part of the 'overlapping consensus' become *entirely arbitrary*. It appears as though the theory of political liberalism is *intolerant to the point of being arbitrarily tyrannical*.

Contrary to what people insist, I believe that the current notions of pluralism are far too weak to address the nature of pluralism in the world adequately. The issue is not one of recognizing that many different cultures populate the planet today. This is a banal fact that nobody disputes. However, the possibility that the difference between cultures might be plotted differently is not taken into account. *Cultures not only differ from each other; they differ from each other differently.* To describe such differences in terms of differing beliefs or differing practices is merely one way of describing the differences. The notions of cultural differences that exist today are those that come from the western culture. Surely, one cannot argue that the way some culture experiences its difference from other cultures is the universal framework for describing differences between cultures.

There is also a different kind of incompatibility in the theory of Rawls. It has to do with his notion of 'reasonableness' itself. As said, a Rawlsian creature is reasonable if it possesses two properties: (a) it accepts fair terms of social cooperation; (b) it accepts the 'burdens of judgment', that is, accepts that reasonable pluralism is the inevitable result of the exercise of human reason. These Rawlsian criteria also enter into conflict with one another. The rules of dialogue, as the pragma-dialectical school formulates them, are eminently fair terms of cooperation as they apply to both parties. However, as we have seen, these fair terms of dialogue entail that the antagonist makes assumptions about the *truth* of his cultural common-sense and hence about the *falsity* of alternate folk psychologies. (One cannot accept the truth of intentional psychology without making its opposite false.) That is to say, accepting condition (a) leads one to the denial of condition (b). One could be reasonable in one aspect, that is, accept fair terms of social cooperation and yet in the name of that very reason end up denying the second condition. To the framework of political liberalism, these intercultural examples are not mere examples. In their generalized form, they entail some damaging and debilitating consequences.[6]

Justice and Dialogues

These issues have a greater reach than might appear at first sight. Let me make use of the known disagreements between Gandhi and Ambedkar on the nature of the Indian caste system in order to formulate another question. To come to it quickly, let me set the context first. It is this: Gandhi argued that the current Indian caste system was a distortion of the *varna* system; Ambedkar felt that Gandhi did not recognize the intrinsic injustices in the Indian caste system. Gandhi claimed that Ambedkar's position was divisive in that it would pit one community against another; in this diagnosis, Gandhi has been proved right because such is the case in India today. According to Ambedkar, however, Gandhi failed to see the extent to which social humiliation is an institution in Indian society and an integral part of Hinduism. One wanted changes in the caste system; the other strove for its total abolition. Whatever their differences—and, indeed there were many—both agreed that the Indian society of their time was unjust (because of the presence of social, political, economic, and sexual discriminations) and wanted to create a just society, where such discriminations would no longer exist.

We know for a fact that neither Gandhi nor Ambedkar clearly articulated and theorized their conceptions of justice. Through what can be gleaned from their highly unsystematic writings, it is a safe bet to say that they had different ideas of what constitutes 'justice' in society. But, these differences have to do with their substantive notions of justice. However, neither denied that each sought justice in society and recognized similar strivings in each other, notwithstanding the problems that Ambedkar had with Gandhi. However, what enabled them to recognize this in each other? More generally put: how could we possibly talk of the presence of multiple theories of social justice, when they are all so different from each other? I suggest that the answer should be sought in the formal notion of justice. That is, we have some intuitions about certain properties that justice has by virtue of its form. No matter how we define the English word 'justice', we identify that we are talking about the same phenomenon in so far as we agree that what we seek exhibits certain properties that we think belongs to justice. Only because we share some common beliefs about the formal properties of justice that we can disagree with each other about the way we define substantive notions of justice. Let me now enter the issue I want to address by formulating a question about one such formal property of justice.

Just Structures, Unjust Consequences

What guarantees that a just society, once built, will continue to remain just? Because this question might sound absurd, or can be easily dismissed with a rhetorical flourish ('there are no guarantees in life'), a brief explication is required.

Consider the question 'Why build a just society?' with the understanding that (a) one is not asking for a justification why justice is preferable to injustice; (b) one is not asking for the reasons why one has to be just. If we agree that we are all against flagrant injustices that occur in a society, from this consideration alone, it does not follow logically that we should build a just society. This can be illustrated with the help of an analogy. Because one does not have any reason to live, it does not follow, therefore, that one has reasons to commit suicide. In this sense, the claim that those who oppose injustice in society should strive to build a just society is a *non sequitur*. One needs a separate motivation in order to build a just society.

So, why should building a just society be a goal? The best answer is also the simplest one: 'Because a just society will *always* eventuate in just consequences'. This answer belongs to the formal notion of justice: we recognize some structure as 'just' if and only if all its consequences are also just. In this sense, the formal notion of justice is a meta-level predicate (much like the notion of 'truth') that enables us to judge whether or not some structure embodies some or another substantive notion of justice. Perhaps, an example can make this point perspicuous: if we treat human beings as our equals (and continue to do so repeatedly) then, through this action, no consequence comes into existence that makes us treat human beings unequally. That is, if it is suggested that just structures could have unjust consequences, our basic intuitions about and our best theories of justice would become flatly contradictory or nonsensical. *Justice entails consequences that are also just.* Of course, it is obvious that circumstances external to a just structure (natural disasters, war, conquests, revolutions) can always *deform* such a structure. In this sense, actions and events other than us treating our fellow human beings equally might eventuate in a situation where we are forced to treat the others unequally. But, the ground intuition is that a just structure, functioning ideally, cannot possibly eventuate in unjust consequences. In simpler terms: a repetitive just action cannot, on its own, have unjust consequences. Even though this looks like a logical claim, there is an empirical question here: *is this also the case?*

As we have seen so far, if we allow a 'reasonable' dialogue to unfold by following the transparent and fair rules of the dialogical structure, such a rational dialogue not only inflicts violence but also becomes unfair. Its unfairness consists of the fact that such a dialogue distributes the onus of proof unequally between the dialogue partners and brings about a skewed (thus, prima facie unjust) consequence. Furthermore, it also results in an asymmetric division of dialogical roles. A reasonable and just structure built on fair and transparent rules of dialogue eventuates in a skewed, unfair and unreasonable structure. That means to say, *we have no logical grounds to suggest that, when left to itself, a just structure cannot have unjust consequences.* A just structure might have just consequences; it might have unjust consequences. *This is an empirical issue.* Even if someone provides normative (and factual) arguments to suggest that one ought not to be unjust, this does not allow us to extend the argument further. One might be against injustice all the time, and yet consistently oppose the creation of a 'just' society in some particular case.

Thus, while one could oppose the 'caste system' in India (because of the unjust consequences associated with that system), one could also consistently oppose the creation of a 'caste-less' society. The argument for one is not an argument for the other. One has to empirically demonstrate that building a caste-less society in India will not have unjust consequences. No thinker, whether Indian or western, who opposes the 'caste system' has ever addressed himself to this task. All of them commit the same fallacy: they simply demonstrate the unjust consequences of the caste system and send out clarion calls (or implement irrational policies) to 'abolish' such a system and bring about a 'just' society. Such a stance is the rule because they assume that a just structure could never have unjust consequences, unless external circumstances disturb the structure. This is a false premise. I have shown that *there exists at least one structure, which is reasonable and fair, that generates unjust consequences*. This proves that whether or not a just society 'ought' to get built (whatever be the substantive notion of 'justice') is an empirical issue: one has to show that a particular kind of 'just' society will not generate unjust consequences. one has to provide independent arguments as to why such a society ought to be built. Otherwise, one presupposes what requires a proof of its truth: that building a just society is normatively praiseworthy and should factually be pursued. In this context, consider, for example, the challenges that Ambedkar formulates:

Under Gandhism, the untouchables may study law, they may study medicine, they may study engineering or anything else they may fancy. So far so good. But will the untouchables be free to make use of their knowledge and learning? Will they have the right to choose their profession? Can they accept the career of lawyer, doctor or engineer? To these questions the answer that Gandhism gives is an emphatic 'no'. (In Ambedkar 2002: 169)

Today, through the reservation policies pursued by the Central and the state governments in India, Ambedkar's preoccupations have been answered in the affirmative. If we accept a consequentialist notion of justice, then it is easy to show that the requirement of justice conflicts with the requirement of rationality. Under the assumption that the reservation policy is a just measure to set earlier wrongs right, we can easily show that a society that follows this principle is bound to collapse. Because neither the 'high' nor the 'low' caste has any reason to expend more energy or effort than is required for a particular outcome (this is the rationality assumption), none will put in the effort to become competent and capable: the reward and the punishment is utterly indifferent to the capacities of the individuals, but is sensitive only to the caste they are born in. The inefficiency and the irrationality in all those Indian institutions that follow the reservation policy is an ample demonstration of this fact. Whatever Ambedkar's assessment of 'Gandhism' might be, Gandhi too shared the former's desire to uplift the downtrodden through corrective moral and political measures. In this sense, the current reservation policy in India is an empirical example of how an argument against injustice can never serve as an argument for a 'just' society.

I think both Gandhi and Ambedkar shared a flawed notion of justice as something that applies to social structures and institutions. In this, they are not alone. In some senses, this is a history shared by most of us. We, too, think in terms of social justice and argue with each other as though such discussions make perfect sense. However, there might be something wrong with this way of looking at social arrangements.

Let me sum up. Theorists of political liberalism assume that their theories are independent of specific philosophical and metaphysical doctrines. I have argued that 'reasonable discussion' or 'rational dialogue' is not a neutral mechanism to settle disputes but, instead, is dependent on specific philosophical and metaphysical conceptions about a host of other issues. In this sense, even if it transpires that the minimal theories of political liberalism do not directly incorporate parts of 'comprehensive doctrines', the notion of 'reasonable discussion' or 'rational dialogue' does. Unlike other liberalisms, which are explicit about their assumptions, the notion of political liberalism merely occludes its compromised nature. Our discussion of intercultural dialogues is meant to bring the suppressed assumptions into the foreground. It might be the case that the theory of political liberalism is itself 'just another doctrine'.[7]

Political theories, whether normative or empirical, have to make factual assumptions about many facets of human psychology, if they are to get off the ground. Surely, one of the flaws of political liberalism is precisely the assumptions it makes about human psychology. By implicitly calling a particular cultural folk psychology, *as it is rooted in one 'comprehensive doctrine'*, reasonable and thus in assuming its truth, one merely transforms different cultural folk psychologies into false and hence 'unreasonable' exemplars. Reasonable pluralism, which assumes the inevitability of reasonable people coming to different reasonable judgments, is forced to bow to the logic of its cognitive mechanisms and deny pluralism. It too affirms the familiar theme of western superiority. So, what makes this liberalism any different from the nineteenth-century liberalism, which explicitly stated that all other cultures in the world are inferior to Western culture (Mehta 1999)? One of its advocates states that 'political liberalism remains humanity's best hope in a world where cultural diversity is not only a fact of life, but a joy of living' (Ackerman 1994: 386). If this is true, humanity should perhaps realize that this situation reflects despair rather than hope.

Notes

1. An exception is the work of Seyla Benhabib (especially her 2002), which concerns the neglect of culture in normative political theory. Another effort to inscribe cultural diversity into political theory is Parekh (2000). For an attempt to trace the implications of deep cultural conflicts for Rawls's account of public reason and toleration, see Bohman (1995, 2003).

2. For helpful summaries of Rawls's argument, see his own introduction to the paperback edition of *Political Liberalism* (Rawls 1996: xxxvii–lxii) and Davion and Wolf (2000: 4–8). Buchanan offers an analysis of Rawls's notion of reasonableness in his 2000: 73–8. An overview of Larmore's argument for political liberalism is found in his 1990 work.

3. This neglect stands in stark contrast with the attention received by the notion of 'public reason' in the debates about political liberalism: See Bohman (1995), D'Agostino and Gaus (eds. 1998), Frohock (1997), Habermas (1995), Quong (2004).

4. Throughout the chapter, when the context permits, 'rational' and 'reasonable' are used interchangeably. Rawls distinguishes between these two, but I have taken care to see that his distinction does not affect the points made (Rawls 1996: 48–54). I also use 'dialogue', 'discussion' and 'argumentation' as synonyms. As far as I can tell, the subtle differences in meaning have no consequences for our argument.

5. Different critiques of Rawls's notions of the reasonable and public reason, which reach similar conclusions, can be found in Bohman (1995) and Friedman (2000).

6. The consequences go far beyond the theories of political liberalism alone. In his critique of Rawls, Jürgen Habermas summarizes his framework

of 'discourse ethics' as follows: 'Under the pragmatic presuppositions of an inclusive and noncoercive rational discourse among free and equal participants, everyone is required to take the perspective of everyone else, and thus project herself into the understandings of self and world of all others; from this interlocking of perspectives there emerges an ideally extended we-perspective from which all can test in common whether they wish to make a controversial norm the basis of their shared practice; and this should include mutual criticism of the appropriateness of the languages in terms of which situations and needs are interpreted' (Habermas 1995: 117). From my argument it follows that the structure of rational discourse prevents a Western participant from taking the perspective of non-Western participants. In cases of intercultural encounter, then, Habermas's requirement neither follows from—nor can it be presupposed by—the norms of rational discourse. Consequently, the further steps he describes can never be taken.

7. For an analogous conclusion see also Marilyn Friedman (2000: 16–33).

CHAPTER 8

The Secular State and Religious Conflict*

In the previous chapters, I have outlined the nature of colonial consciousness, the Western descriptions of aspects of the Indian culture, and the violence surrounding both. What happens when these phenomena are institutionalized? That is, what happens when cognitive and psychological phenomena take on institutional forms? The Indian 'secular' state, which is a continuation of the British rule after Indian independence, provides us with answers to this question. In this chapter, I look at the nature of the Indian 'secular' state and relate its workings to the growth and sustenance of violence in India. The violence I want to talk about is the so-called 'communal' violence, one of the forms that religious violence takes in India. I shall argue that the so-called neutral liberal state, which the 'secular state' in India is, actually *feeds* the violence it is supposed to contain or neutralize.

There are few places in the contemporary world where the problems of cultural pluralism are as acute as they are in India. The

* An earlier version of this chapter (with Jakob De Roover) was published in 2007 as 'The Secular State and Religious Conflict: Liberal Neutrality and the Indian Case of Pluralism', *The Journal of Political Philosophy* 15(1), pp. 67–92.

Indian case poses fundamental challenges to the political theory of toleration. By tackling the problem of religious conversion, my analysis shows that the dominant way of conceiving state neutrality becomes untenable in the Indian context. The Indian state, modelled after the liberal democracies in the West, is the harbinger of religious conflict in India because of its conception of toleration and state neutrality. More of 'secularism' in India will end up feeding what it fights: the so-called 'Hindu fundamentalism'.

The Participants and the Issues

In the Indian debate on the Hindu–Muslim conflict, three parties claim to offer a solution. The secularists argue the need for a secular state in India; the Hindu nationalists or advocates of Hindutva plead the case for a Hindu state; and the anti-secular Gandhians claim that the Indian culture has the resources to handle the question of religious pluralism. For the sake of argument and convenience, I will divide these parties into two groups, namely, secularists and anti-secularists.

On the one hand, there are the proponents of secularism: they propose that Hindus and Muslims (and other communities) should accept a common framework of secular law. This framework claims neutrality with respect to all religions. The position of secularism in India is generally associated with the ideas of her first Prime Minister, Jawaharlal Nehru, who once said 'no state can be civilised except a secular state' (Chandra 1994: 75). The Indian secularists defend a position well-known to political theory: the obligation of religious neutrality of a liberal state.

On the other hand, there are the opponents of secularism: they refuse to accept the Western theories about the religiously neutral state and offer an alternative system of traditional values. The different communities, they feel, should accept this system as a common framework. Its fundamental principle is the equality of religions: since all religions are incomplete manifestations of a supreme truth, all of them are equal. This group consists of advocates of Hindutva on the one side and Gandhian anti-secularists on the other. Although significant differences exist between these two parties, they agree on one issue: in India, politics should not be separated from religion because the Indian traditions yield a more tolerant politics than Western secularism. One of the Hindutva spokesmen voices a widespread opinion when he says that 'Hindu secularism' is superior to Western secularism:

... [A]ll through the history, the Hindu state has been secular. All Hindu rulers were expected to live up to the ideal of 'Sarva Panth Sama Bhava' in their dealings with the people. This concept of 'equal respect for all panths or ways of worship' is a positive concept with a much wider and broader meaning than what is conveyed by the concept of secularism as accepted in the West. (Madhok 1995: 116)

Or, to let the most distinguished among the anti-secularists, Ashis Nandy, explain the moral of his story:

... [I]t is time to recognize that, instead of trying to build religious tolerance on the good faith or the conscience of a small group of de-ethnicized, middle-class politicians, bureaucrats, and intellectuals, a far more serious venture would be to explore the philosophy, the symbolism, and the theology of tolerance in the faiths of the citizens and hope that the state systems in South Asia may learn something about religious tolerance from everyday Hinduism, Islam, Buddhism, or Sikhism rather than wish that ordinary Hindus, Muslims, Buddhists, and Sikhs will learn tolerance from the various fashionable secular theories of statecraft. (Nandy 1998: 338)

The anti-secularists challenge the belief that different religious communities can live together in a society only within the framework of a religiously neutral state. Thus, the debate revolves around one of the basic tenets of contemporary theories of toleration, namely the belief that state neutrality is necessary for a peaceful and viable plural society.

One should not reduce the clash between secularism and anti-secularism to a clash between a tolerant, progressive left and an intolerant, conservative right. Instead, it is a clash between two frameworks, both claiming to provide a solution to the problem of conflicts between the different communities in Indian society. Both parties agree on the objective of a peacefully diverse society. Both allow people to worship in whichever way they prefer and to whatever god(s) they prefer. Both allow the followers of the various religions to visit their mosques, churches, gurudwaras, temples, or stay home. Both allow people to believe in one God, or in three or five thousand gods, or claim that there is no God. If there is agreement on these issues, what then is the clash about?

I would like to address this question by taking up the issue of religious conversion. Hindutva wants a ban on conversion in India. It feels that the state should enact a law constraining the proselytising drive of Christianity and Islam. This proposal is anathema to the secularists, who insist that the state should protect the religious liberty of the individual. Why does Hindutva feel such strong aversion towards religious conversion? One suggestion is that the movement consists of religious fanatics. However, this fails to take into account that many Hindus, hardly illiberal fanatics, hold similar views. Mahatma Gandhi, for instance, said at one point that if he had the power to legislate, he would ban all proselytizing: 'If I had the power and could legislate, I would stop all proselytizing ... In Hindu households the advent of a missionary has meant the disruption of the family coming in the wake of change of dress, manners, language, food and drink ... ' (*Harijan*, 5 November 1935). This view is still prevalent among contemporary Gandhians. In the words of Manikan Ramaswami:

In a pluralistic society if people have to live in harmony, one group that believes its assumed form of God is superior and tries to convert the thinking of others will not certainly help. One group trying to impose its views on others based on its unconfirmable assumptions will certainly cause social tension and should not be permitted in a secular society. The pseudo seculars who call it religious freedom to convert, if they apply their mind will understand banning conversion, forced or otherwise, is not a Hindutva agenda; on the other hand not banning conversion is the agenda of the aggressive religions. (Ramaswami 2002)

While secularists agree with the Muslim and Christian minorities that the latter must be free to proselytise, most of the anti-secularists intend to defend the interests of the Hindus. Hindutva backs a Hindu state; the secularists strive for a secular state, which is neutral towards all religions. As noted, the secularists defend a *normative* principle of state neutrality. They say that one ought to separate politics from religion because without such a separation, the state cannot treat all religions in a neutral or symmetric manner. The secularists offer several rationales and, together, these bring them to the belief 'that secularism in India, as elsewhere, is indispensable' (Bhargava 1998: 2). My questions are these: could the Indian state remain neutral on the issue of religious conversion? If yes, what would neutrality mean in the Indian context?

Secularism and Religion

Religious conversion is a problem in India when Islam or Christianity tries to convert people from Hinduism. That is, it is not an issue of converting Muslims into Christianity or the other way round, but one of converting Hindus into either of the two. If the secular state has to be religiously neutral, it must have a symmetrical attitude toward all religious conversions and not favour one type of conversion over another. That is, it must treat conversions between the Semitic religions and from Hinduism to the Semitic religions in the same way, namely, as conversions between different religions. In that case, it confronts the following problem. Are the Semitic religions and the Hindu traditions *phenomena of the same kind?* A religiously neutral state has to *assume* a positive answer to this question, if it has to treat Hinduism and the Semitic religions symmetrically. However, this assumption *has no warrant*. If anything, the prima facie evidence points to the *falsity* of this assumption. A random selection of claims put across by the students of the Hindu traditions ought to suffice in this context.

In the second of the multi-volume *Historia Religionum*, an Indian (Dandekar 1971: 237), talking about Hinduism, says that:

Hinduism can hardly be called a religion in the popularly understood sense of the term. Unlike most religions, Hinduism does not regard the concept of god as being central to it ... Hinduism does not venerate any particular person as its sole prophet or as its founder. It does not ... recognize any particular book as its absolutely authoritative scripture.

Similar thoughts occur in a handbook, written by experts in the area, aimed at a more general public:

Hinduism displays few of the characteristics that are generally expected of a religion. It has no founder, nor is it prophetic. It is not credal, nor is any particular doctrine, dogma or practice held to be essential to it. It is not a system of theology, nor a single moral code, and the concept of god is not central to it. There is no specific scripture or work regarded as being uniquely authoritative and, finally, it is not sustained by an ecclesiastical organization. Thus it is difficult to categorize Hinduism as 'religion' using normally accepted criteria. It is then possible to find groups of Hindus whose respective faiths have almost nothing in common with one another, and it is also impossible to identify any universal belief or practice that is common to all Hindus. Confronted with such diversity, what is it that makes Hinduism a single religious tradition and not a loose confederation of many different traditions? (Weightman 1984: 191–2)

Indeed. The problem is not confined to Hinduism. Collins, a Buddhologist, is not sanguine about Buddhism either. Speaking of the mistake of using emic categories of Christian thought, as though they were etic categories of description and analysis in the academic study of religions, Collins (1988: 103) adds in parentheses, 'perhaps the most pervasive example of this is the concept of "religion" itself'.[1]

Citations like the above could be multiplied indefinitely, but I trust the point is made. There are prima facie grounds to suspect that the Hindu traditions and the Semitic religions are phenomena of different kinds. Nevertheless, without providing arguments to the contrary, the secular state assumes that the Semitic religions and the Hindu traditions are instances of the same kind. Students of religion almost routinely make such remarks as the above and go on to study the Hindu and Buddhist traditions as 'religions' *of a different kind*. We need not discuss here whether their attempts are satisfactory or not. The point is that no student of religion is willing or able to argue that Hinduism and the Semitic religions are phenomena of the same kind. Consequently, the onus is on those who want to argue that these two phenomena are instances of the same kind. In other words, the secular state cannot assume the opposite of scientific wisdom without compelling arguments.

However, there *is* one story or one compelling argument that opposes the scientific wisdom. It comes from the theologies of the Semitic religions. Let me recount the simplest version of that story. There was once a religion, the true and universal one, which was the divine gift to humankind. The biblical God installs a sense or spark of divinity in all races (and individuals). During the course of human history, this sense is corrupted. Idolatry, worship of the devil (namely, the false god and his minions) was to be the lot of humankind until the biblical God spoke to Abraham, Isaac, and Jacob, and led their tribe back on to the true path. Of course, it is possible that this story is true; after all, those who follow these religions do believe in its truth. Is this *enough* for a secular state to accept the truth of this claim? In answering this question, the secular state cannot be neutral. The choices are but two: (a) the state accepts some variant of the above *theological story* and treats Hinduism and the Semitic religions as phenomena of the same kind; or (b) it gives in to the prima facie difference, and (in the absence of better arguments) treats the Semitic religions and the Hindu traditions as phenomena of a different kind.

Religions as Rivals

Abstractly speaking, the freedom to convert people into some religion or the other might indicate the presence of a desirable value in a society, namely, the value of the freedom of religious expression. What such a value logically presupposes, in any case, is the truth of the assumption that *these religions are rival movements*. This is a factual assumption, whose factual nature can be brought to light by noticing that no logical difficulties are created if we assume the existence of multiple religions without postulating that they compete with each other. However, this factual assumption requires justification because history tells us the opposite.

It is a matter of historical fact that Christianity and Islam have been rivals, wherever and whenever they met each other. Could we say the same about the contact between the Hindu traditions and these religions? A Protestant writer from the late eighteenth century, drawing upon the work of François Bernier, the seventeenth-century French merchant and explorer, reports the following:

When the Brahmins have been pressed by the arguments of the Christians, that their law could only be observed in their own country, on account of its peculiar ordinances, their answer has been uniform, 'that God had only made it for them, and therefore they did not admit into it strangers; that they pretended not that Christianity was false; and since God could make many roads to heaven, it was not thence to be presumed that their religion was mere fable and invention'. (Chatfield 1984: 324)

As a Hindu Brahmin of coastal Tamil Nadu assured Bartholomaeus Ziegenbalg, a Lutheran missionary, during the early eighteenth century:

I believe all you say of God's Dealings with you White *Europeans*, to be true; but his Appearances and Revelations among us Black *Malabarians*, have been quite otherwise: And the Revelations he made of himself in this Land are as firmly believ'd here to be true, as you believe those made in your Country: For as Christ in Europe was made Man; so here our God *Wischtnu* was born among us *Malabarians*; And as you hope for Salvation through Christ; so we hope for Salvation through *Wischtnu*; and to save you one way, and us another, is one of the Pastimes and Diversions of Almighty God. (Ziegenbalg 1719: 14)

The famous Muslim traveller to India, Alberuni, also noted the absence of religious rivalry among the Hindus in the eleventh century: 'On the whole, there is very little disputing about theological topics among themselves; at the utmost, they fight with words, but they will never stake their soul or body or their property on religious controversy' (Sachau [ed.] 2002: 3). Although Alberuni continued to say that the Hindus directed their fanaticism against foreigners, it was clear that the Hindus did not do so because they considered the latter to be propagators of false religion. In fact, an analysis of Hindu Sanskrit sources on the Muslims from the eighth to the fourteenth century reveals that 'the construction of the other is made neither in religious nor in territorial terms; in other words, although the term dharma is used in the sense of religion, the Muslims are not projected as a community practising a religion which is the antithesis of recognized religious practices' (D.P. Chattopadhyaya 1998: 90). Thus, traditionally, Hindus did not even identify Muslims along religious lines, let alone consider them as religious rivals.

In other words, the Hindu traditions refused to accept that theirs was a false religion and that Christianity or Islam was the true one. Nor were they willing to say that Christianity or Islam was false. They merely maintained that these traditions could co-exist *without competing* with each other as rivals. This is the Hindu view of the matter. The Semitic religions, on the other hand, advance the claim that they and the Hindu traditions are competing or rival movements. Between these two positions, again, *there is no neutral ground*: (a) the Semitic religions and the Hindu traditions are competitors with respect to each other; or (b) they are not. The secular state has to choose *between these two logically exclusive premises* as well.

Religion and the Question of Truth

Consider the following two propositions about religious truth: (a) religion revolves around the truth of its doctrines; (b) the predicates 'truth' and 'falsity' do not apply to human traditions. These views have been held by two different kinds of groups: the Semitic religions that Christianity and Islam are; and the 'pagan' traditions of classical antiquity and the Hindu Indians.

On the one hand, Christianity and Islam claim that because they are *the unique revelations of the biblical God* to humankind, they are true. They believe that there is one true God, who is the creator and sovereign of the universe. Everything that happens in the universe expresses His will or purpose. In other words, this biblical God has a plan and the universe is the embodiment of this plan. According to each of these religions, their respective doctrine is the true self-disclosure in which the biblical God reveals His will or plan to humankind. Only through a genuine belief in this doctrine and in a total surrender to this Divine Will can human beings hope for salvation.

A random citation, from an epistle said to have been composed around 124 CE, the period of the Apostolic Fathers, illustrates how Christians described their religion from the very beginning. In *The Epistle to Diognetus*, purporting to be a 'reply to an inquiring heathen's desire for information about the beliefs and customs of Christians', an anonymous writer explains:

The doctrines they (the Christians) profess is *not the invention of busy human minds* and brains, nor are they, like some, adherents of this or that school of *human thought*. As I said before, it is *not an earthly discovery* that has been entrusted to them. The thing they guard so jealously is no product of *mortal thinking*, and what has been committed to them is the stewardship of no *human mysteries*. The Almighty Himself, the Creator of the universe, the God whom no eye can discern, has sent down His very own Truth from heaven, His own holy and incomprehensible Word, to plant it among men and ground it in their hearts. (Staniforth 1968: 176–8; italics added)

Naturally, this *self-description* also carries with it a description of the other. Other religions are heresies, false religions, or idolatry and worship of the devil. After living thirty years among the Hindus in the 'headquarters' of Hinduism, Benares, this is how Reverend M.A. Sherring formulated the issue in the nineteenth century:

[Here] idolatry is a charm, a fascination, to the Hindu. It is, so to speak, the air he breathes. It is the food of his soul. He is subdued, enslaved, befooled by it. The nature of the Hindu partakes of the supposed nature of the gods whom he worships. And what is that nature? According to the traditions handed about amongst the natives, and constantly dwelt upon in their conversation, and referred to in their popular songs—which perhaps would be sufficient proof—yet more especially according to the numberless statements and narratives found in their sacred writings, on which these traditions are based, it is, in many instances, vile and abominable to the last degree. Idolatry is a word denoting all that is wicked in imagination and impure in practice. Idolatry is a demon—an incarnation of all evil—but nevertheless bewitching and seductive as a siren. It ensnares the depraved heart, coils around it like a serpent, transfixes it with its deadly fangs, and finally stings it to death. (Urwick 1985: 133)

All these traditions are nothing but attempts of the false god to deceive the gullible and to corrupt the true religion.[2] Thus, the Semitic view has it that religion revolves around the crucial question of the truth and falsity of a set of doctrines.

On the other hand, there is the pagan self-description, as evidenced both in the Hindu traditions and in the *religio* of the ancient Romans. These self-descriptions see the various traditions as a *human search* for 'truth', and they see the different religions as paths in this ongoing quest. As Gandhi (1942: 2) writes: 'Religions are different roads converging to the same point. What does it matter that we take different roads so long as we reach the same goal?' Or in the famous words of Quintus Aurelius Symmachus, the last pagan prefect of Rome: 'Everyone has his own customs, his own religious practices ... What does it matter what practical system we adopt in our search for truth? Not by one avenue only can we arrive at so tremendous a secret' (Barrow 1973: 37–41). Though there are many differences between the ancient Roman pagans and today's Hindus, they share a common attitude which distinguishes them from Christians and Muslims alike. They do not approach the diversity of human traditions in terms of doctrinal truth.

In the pagan view, there is no one true God opposing whom stand many *false gods*. There are different 'deities'; there are different stories about them; different traditions differentiate communities from one another. Although this view might countenance the belief of the followers of the Semitic religions, it cannot but see this as the story of some particular traditions. That is, it inevitably transforms the revelation of the biblical God into another *human* avenue. Let us assume that both the pagans and the Christians are in agreement with the premise that 'all things in human affairs are doubtful, uncertain, and unsettled'. By virtue of this, religions also share this attribute, say the pagans. Their religion does not, say the Christians, because it is the truth itself, as revealed by the Divine mind. Better put: the religions of antiquity were false religions because they were inventions of 'busy human minds', whereas Christianity was the Truth because none other than the biblical God had entrusted stewardship of His truth to the Christians. In other words, Christians opposed their true religion to the false *religiones* of the Roman period and later to the 'pagan idolatry' of the Hindus.

To most Hindus, on the contrary, the question of 'truth' in tradition does not even make sense. The Hindu practices generally revolve around a series of puja rituals and traditional stories about Shiva, Krishna, Rama, Kali, Durga, and other *devatas* or 'deities'. In the same way as it does not make sense to inquire whether the Western practice for men to wear trousers is true or false, so is it a category mistake to pose truth questions about human traditions in general, from the Hindu perspective. This incomprehension towards the notion of 'religious truth' has given rise to the claim that Hindus look at the truth of religions in a different way. The Hindu view does involve the ascription of truth-predicates to religions, it is said, but in a 'pluralist' manner: 'all religions are true'. However, it is unclear what it means for truth to be conceived pluralistically.[3] More importantly, this attribution of a pluralistic notion of religious truth to the Hindus threatens to turn them into beings lacking the basic capacity of consistent reasoning. If all religions are true, both Christian and Islamic doctrines have to be true at the same time. This claim then entails that Hindus fail to see that one religious doctrine which claims that God is Father, Son, and Holy Spirit, and that Jesus Christ is the Son of God stands in contradiction to another which asserts that God is one and cannot have a son who is both divine and human.

In contrast, my explanation avoids transforming Hindus into logical cretins. It agrees that, today, English-educated Hindus have learnt to talk in terms of 'religion' and 'truth'. Historically, pagan traditions have generally tried to make sense of the Judeo-Christian claims about 'religious truth' from their traditional perspective. The result is the often-repeated claim that 'all religions are true'. This does not reflect a peculiar notion of religious truth, but an attempt to translate the attitude of one culture into the language of another. Even though Hindus have discussed 'truth' in Indian languages also, this 'truth' appears to be of a completely different kind than the doctrinal truth claimed by the Semitic religions. Until we have a clear insight into its nature, it is best to stress that the Hindu view does not see the different traditions of humanity as either true or false.

Conversion is possible from the false to the true only if one assumes that both the traditions of antiquity and Christianity opposed each other with respect to truth and falsity. This holds not only regarding the traditions from classical antiquity, but also with respect to the Hindu traditions of today. Consequently, the secular state that allows for the possibility of conversion is compelled to *choose* between the following: (a) both the Hindu traditions and the Semitic religions are epistemic candidates with respect to truth and falsity; or (b) they are not.

Proselytization versus Non-interference

The Semitic self-description contains a universal truth claim, which gives rise to a dynamic of proselytization. When the biblical God reveals His plan, it covers the whole of humankind. Those who receive this revelation should try to convert the others into accepting the message in this divine self-disclosure. That is, proselytizing is an intrinsic drive of Islam and Christianity. The pagan view, on the contrary, implies that every 'religion' is a tradition—that is, a specific set of ancestral practices—characterizing a human community. The traditions are upheld not because they contain some exclusive truth binding the believer to God, but because they make some community into a community. Any attempt at interfering with the tradition of a community from the outside will be seen as illegitimate, since all traditions are part of the human quest for truth. We can again turn to the pagan prefect Symmachus's justly famous letter to the Christian Emperor Valentinian II:

Grant, I beg you, that what in our youth we took over from our fathers, we may in our old age hand on to posterity. *The love of established practice is a powerful sentiment* ... Everyone has his own customs, his own religious practices; the divine mind has assigned to different cities different religions to be their guardians ... If long passage of time lends validity to religious observances, we ought to keep faith with so many centuries, *we ought to follow our forefathers who followed their forefathers and were blessed in so doing* ... And so we ask for peace for the gods of our fathers, for the gods of our native land. It is reasonable that whatever each of us worships is really to be considered one and the same. (Barrow 1973: 37–41; italics added)

Given this opposition between proselytization and non-interference, consider the situation in India. Here, citizen *x* is a Hindu who endorses the pagan claim that all traditions are part of a human quest for truth; while citizens *y* and *z* are a Muslim and a Christian respectively, who believe that their religion is the true revelation of the biblical God, while all other 'traditions' are false religions. This situation involves a deep conflict of values. The value of non-interference is central to the tradition of citizen *x* and it is unethical for him to allow Muslims and Christians to interfere in the traditions of human communities. Thus, he opposes conversion. At the same time, the value of proselytization is central to the religions of citizen *y* and *z*. They have to propagate the true message and show to the adherents of other 'traditions' that they are practicing idolatry, the greatest sin according to these religions. Since non-compliance implies that they disobey the biblical God's will, it would be profoundly immoral not to spread this message and try to save heathens or *kafirs* from eternal damnation. Thus, they strongly feel conversion ought to be allowed.

How can the Indian state be neutral with respect to the *attitudes* of the citizens *x*, *y*, and *z*? Either the state agrees with citizen *x* that 'religion' is a human quest, *no 'religion' could be false*, and, therefore, ban conversion; or it will have to agree with citizens *y* and *z* that religions could be the revelation of the biblical God, therefore, *some 'religions' could be false*, and thus allow for conversion. In other words, the secular state has to *choose* between the following two premises: (a) no religion could be false; or (b) some religion(s) could be false. There is no neutral ground *between these two logically exclusive premises*.

These aspects of the Semitic religions and the pagan traditions—namely, proselytization and non-interference—are bound to collide in a society where the Semitic religions encounter pagan traditions *as a living force*. This is exactly what is happening in India today. Though a growing number of Hindus speaks in such terms, the widespread discontent about conversion is not generally caused by the fear that the whole of India will become Christian or Muslim. Some groups may take this scenario seriously, but it does not explain the equally strong aversion towards conversion among those who do not. Many reasonable minds, who do not see an imminent threat of India becoming an Islamic country, still consider religious conversion to be a violation of the social fabric, for it goes straight against the traditional Hindu stance of non-interference.

The anti-secularist movement has adopted the pagan view of the Hindu traditions, and this implies that one community should not interfere in the tradition of another. Naturally, the proselytizing drive and exclusive truth-claims of Islam and Christianity become extremely problematic in a society where non-interference has the force of self-evidence. The pagan view about the traditions of human communities explains why the Hindutva movement and some Gandhians argue for a ban on conversion. The secularists reply that such a measure would simply make a principle of the Hindus into a 'religious rule' to be followed by all others, while a truly neutral framework should allow the Muslim and Christian minorities to propagate and spread their religion. The secularists are not as neutral as they think they are. Their plea for conversion indicates that they have made their choice.

Let me now summarize the four choices the Indian secular state has to make. (a) The 'Hindu traditions' and the 'Semitic religions' are phenomena of the same kind, or they are not. (b) As such, they are religious rivals, or they are not. (c) As rivals, they compete with each other regarding truth or falsity, or they do not. (d) They can do that because some religion is false, or they cannot because no religion is false. In each of the four cases, these claims are those of the Semitic religions and the Hindu traditions respectively. Each of these assumptions carves the universe up into two exhaustive partitions, because, in each case, one statement is the logical negation of the other. So, what should a liberal state do in such a situation? What choices are open to it, if it wants to remain neutral and secular?

The Liberal State and Religious Neutrality

In the context of ethics and normative political theory, one could conceivably[4] endorse Kant's famous dictum 'ought implies can'. That is, if a normative system prescribes some moral rule or another, this implies that human beings or institutions are able to follow that particular rule. If we accept this principle while framing our account of state neutrality, the proposition that the state ought to be neutral implies that the state can be neutral. Thus, on this construal, liberal neutrality is obligatory only if the state *can be neutral* toward the different religious and cultural traditions in a society. However, the choices that the Indian state confronts are logically exclusive. Furthermore, each term in the different choices represents a different point of view: the Semitic or the pagan, which means to say that the state *cannot* choose between these alternatives without sacrificing the very principle of state neutrality. However, the Kantian dictum, that 'ought' *logically implies* 'can', generates the following valid theorem: 'cannot' logically implies 'ought not'. This means that the Indian state *ought not to be neutral* with respect to religious conversion in India because it *cannot be neutral*.

The above statement is odd, to put it mildly. We can bring the 'oddness' to light by formulating it as a logical statement: *with respect to religious conversions*, if a liberal state ought to remain neutral, and if the Indian state ought to be a liberal and neutral state, then the Indian state can be neutral. However, the Indian state cannot be neutral on this issue. Therefore, either (a) a liberal state ought not to remain neutral or (b) the Indian state ought not to be liberal and neutral or (c) both. We can eliminate the choices (a) and (c) rather quickly: the obligation of state neutrality with respect to religious conversion is a cornerstone of liberal political theory. Consequently, there is only one choice left: with respect to religious conversions, theories of state neutrality oblige the Indian state not to be liberal and neutral.

The validity of the above argument requires that at least one of the following is true. (a) The relation between 'ought' and 'can' is one of *logical implication*; (b) some particular interpretation of the notions 'liberal' and 'neutral' leads us to the above conclusion. Some logicians differentiate between 'logical' and 'deontological' implications, and suggest that the Kantian dictum is about deontological implications.[5] Consequently, one reason for the 'oddness' might have to do with the confusion between logical and deontological implications. Nevertheless, it is an empirical truth that theories of state neutrality have hitherto obliged the Indian state *not* to be neutral. The post-independent Indian state implemented a series of reforms to 'the Hindu religion and its law', while it did not interfere with Islam and Christianity.[6] This suggests that some interpretation of 'neutrality' and 'liberalism' is at stake here. Theories of state neutrality that interpret this notion to mean neutrality of justification force us to compromise the notion of a neutral state. Such interpretations either generate odd conclusions or try to defend indefensible positions.

Neutrality of Justification

Andrew Mason formulates an often made distinction between two kinds of state neutrality as follows:

Neutrality of justification requires that the state should not include the idea that one conception of the good is superior to another as part of its justification for pursuing a policy. Neutrality of effect, in contrast, requires that the state should not do anything which promotes one conception of the good more than another, or if it does so, that it must seek to cancel or compensate for these differential effects. (Mason 1990: 434)

Is it possible for the Indian state to have a *neutral justification* of its policy towards conversion, if we assume that it permits religious conversion as a part of the freedom of religious expression? Could it justify this choice in a neutral manner? As we have seen earlier, in order to decide about conversion, the Indian state has to make four choices. If it chooses between them, it chooses for some specific conception of the good, whether pagan or Semitic. Then there is no possibility of neutrality of justification. However, if there is a possibility for the state to suspend its judgement about the truth-value of the statements, then it can play the agnostic with respect to the choices and remain neutral. In other words, could the state plead truth-indeterminacy with respect to these choices?

In a very trivial sense, it is possible to play the agnostic because one could plead ignorance with respect to the truth-value of any knowledge-claim. However, if the state pleads ignorance on some issue, it cannot legislate about the same issue. It cannot play the agnostic and feign ignorance about the question as to whether or not religion revolves around truth, for this would imply it cannot even begin to legislate about the phenomenon of religious conversion. Ignorance about a phenomenon can never be a ground for legislation, since one would not even know what to legislate about. Any legislation regarding religion presupposes some knowledge about this phenomenon. Where it concerns the issue of religious conversion, the knowledge on the basis of which one legislates will inevitably contain either a denial or a confirmation of the claim that religion is a matter of truth.

The Indian state has made provisions in its constitution about the freedom of religion that includes the issue of conversion: Article 25 of the Indian Constitution states that 'all persons are equally entitled to freedom of conscience and the right freely to profess, practise and *propagate* religion'. This has generally been interpreted to mean the following: '[I]n the context of secularism and religious pluralism conversions are legitimate, well within the Constitutional provisions, and entirely a personal affair of the citizens' (Radhakrishnan 2002). From this, it follows that the Indian state has taken a stance on these issues. It endorses the belief that religion revolves around doctrinal truth.

More proof is available. The secular state in India and elsewhere puts certain legal restrictions on religious conversion. Most importantly, it prohibits all forms of coercion in conversion. It says that religious conversion can take place by means of persuasion alone. But, if one takes conversion from one religion to another to be a matter of persuasion, one must presuppose that religion involves the question of doctrinal truth. One can be persuaded to convert only in so far as one accepts the truth of one religion as opposed to the falsity of another. Therefore, the secular state's restriction on religious conversion again reveals it has taken a position on the question whether or not religion is a matter of truth. It may not accept the truth claims of any one particular religion, but it does assume that religion revolves around truth claims. This conclusion shows that the failure to be neutral towards the issue of conversion is not specific to the Indian secularists. It is a general malfunction of the neutrality of the model of liberal secularism. Even when its theorists take a critical attitude towards proselytization, they reproduce the theological assumption that religion revolves around truth and therefore support a principle of religious freedom that entails the freedom to convert.

The Liberal State and Religious Truth

Admittedly, not all forms of liberalism—John Stuart Mill's advocacy of liberty, for instance—emphasize the necessity of state neutrality. Therefore, one cannot conflate liberalism and neutrality. But, all forms of liberalism do agree that a state should not base its policies in any one religion, because this would violate principles such as religious liberty and the equal rights of all citizens. In the case of conversion, it appears the liberal state cannot but implement a policy which either presupposes Semitic theology or the pagan stance towards religion and tradition. Hence, it will fail to grant equal rights to all citizens, since the notion of religious liberty itself is disputed. To one group, it implies the freedom to convert; to the other, freedom from conversion. Could not the Indian state merely subscribe to the right to freedom of thought, conscience, and religion, as proclaimed in the Universal Declaration of Human Rights and follow the example of Western democracies? Surely, one could argue, what works for Western democracies should also work for the Indian polity.

Looking at the theory and practice of state neutrality in the European democracies, we can say the following. In principle, a state can be atheistic, theistic, or agnostic, and yet remain liberal and neutral. As long as people enjoy the freedom of religious expression (used in the broadest sense here), and all religious groups are treated symmetrically, it does not matter much what the sovereign or the constitution declares the state to be. Of course, one might prefer an agnostic state to an openly atheistic or theistic state, but that cannot automatically lead us to question the neutrality of the state. Therefore, one could say that a symmetric treatment of all religions and the freedom of religious expression of the citizens are necessary conditions for the existence and functioning of a liberal state.[7]

More important for my purposes is the prevailing agreement. While a theist admittedly believes in the truth of his religion, the atheist believes that no religious claim is true. The agnostic suspends judgement about the truth-value of specific religious claims because of a confessed epistemic inability to ascertain their truth. Despite their differences, they *share* the premise that religion involves the question of truth. This is a factual premise of the liberal state. That is to say, the *very possibility* of a state being neutral with respect to religions hinges on the issue of whether or not religions involve the question of truth. In other words, although the liberal state ought not to make decisions about the truth of religions, it *must decide whether religion itself is a matter of truth*. I claim that the Western liberal, neutral states have historically so decided.

When Christianity underwent divisions (to speak only of Western Christianity), Catholics and Protestants came up with competing truth claims. They defined the terms of the debate as a discussion about true and false religions. Islam and Judaism do the same as well. Whether they accuse each other of being false religions or merely that the others are deficient in worshipping the biblical God, the point is that each of them advances the claim that their beliefs are true. Further, as histories tell us, this way of framing the issue retained its stability when they met with traditions elsewhere: Judaism and Christianity called the Roman *religiones* false; Islam and Christianity did the same with respect to the Hindu traditions many centuries later. A liberal state can remain *neutral* with respect to the *competing truth claims* of each and every of these religions. That is, the notion of state neutrality can be made sense of by saying that where there are competing 'truth claims', one does not assume a pro-stance with respect to any one of them. However, this does not preclude the liberal state from accepting that religion is a matter of truth. The Western democracies have accepted this position, as history testifies.

The claim that religion is a matter of truth is *not an epistemological thesis* about the beliefs present in different religions. Instead, it is *a theological meta-claim* advanced by each of the Semitic religions about itself. When each is convinced that it is the truth and the rest are false, and each of them explicitly states that the difference between truth and falsity constitutes the difference between salvation and damnation, then each one of them is asserting not only that its beliefs are true, but should also be so believed. And, therefore, that religion is a matter of either truth or falsity. *The liberal state in the West has accepted a Semitic theological meta-claim as its factual assumption.* It is able to play the agnostic with respect to the truth-value of religious claims because it shares the Semitic beliefs about religions.

Could not a liberal state be 'agnostic' with respect to the issue of truth itself? At first blush, it seems as though such a possibility exists. However, what does it mean to say that a liberal state ought to be agnostic with respect to the issue of truth? It could mean that the state is unable to say which of the competing religions is true. Such an attitude presupposes that the state believes that 'truth' and 'falsity' are sensible predicates with respect to religion. As I have said, this is Semitic theology and there is nothing neutral about it. Alternately, it could mean that the state does not take a stance with respect to the issue whether religion itself is a question of truth. In that case, how does the state respond to the issue of conversion, and the 'freedom' to proselytise? The only option, if the state wants to play the agnostic, is to remove the entire issue from the sphere of legislation and let the communities decide about it. But then the state can neither interfere with religious violence nor strive to reduce religious conflict. Such a state will have to remain 'neutral' with respect to *religious violence* and *religious freedom*. Because Western liberal democracies endorse religious toleration and legislate about the issue, quite obviously, they are not playing the agnostic. As I said, they cannot play the agnostic because they have presumed that religious truth is cognitive in nature, and that, for example, coercion is *not* the way for a religion to persuade people of its truth.

Consequently, the Indian state cannot merely follow the example of Western democracies and hope to remain 'neutral'. It cannot play the agnostic and yet legislate about religious freedom. It confronts choices, which Western democracies never had to face.

The Secular State and Religious Violence

The framers of the Indian constitution took over the theory of liberal state as it emerged in the West and tried to transplant it into Indian soil. In the process, they also endorsed the theological claim that religion is an issue of truth. While such a stance makes sense in a culture where the problem of religious tolerance arises because of the competing truth claims of the Semitic religions, it does not do the same in another cultural milieu where the pagan traditions are a living force. Consequently, the Indian state is subject to contradictory demands. It must look at the Hindu traditions the way the Semitic religions do, as I have argued, while simultaneously playing the 'agnostic' with respect to the issue whether religion itself is a matter of truth. The first impels it to legislate on the issue of conversion; the second compels it to remain 'neutral' and let the communities decide. The first stance results in *violence generated and sustained by the state*; the second stance forces the involved communities to solve this problem on their own. The first attitude results in forcing the interaction between the Semitic religions and the pagan traditions to take the form of religious rivalry; the second forces the state to withdraw.

Let me begin with the colonial state, whose foundations are also those of the modern Indian state. An unremitting hostility towards the Hindu traditions sustained the colonial state. Its legislations were meant to curb the superstitions and the cruelty 'inherent' in Indian heathendom. Spinning the state policy around the Protestant-Christian criticisms of the Indian religions, the colonial state created stories about 'priests' of Indian religions, the nature of Hindu temples, the reactionary role the Indian 'religions' played in the evolution of Indian society and such like. The colonial representation of India, which was fundamentally a Protestant description of India, became the guiding mantra of the 'secular' politicians of India. As Nehru said himself, he came to India via the West to some extent, and therefore he approached her 'almost as an alien critic, full of dislike for the present as well as for many of the relics of the past that [he] saw' (Nehru 1988a: 50). The intention and effects of his description could be summarized as systematic attempts to uphold the claim that the Hindu traditions are degenerate, corrupt and in need of transformation. In other words, it upheld the Semitic claim about the inferiority of false religion and therefore wanted 'to scrap much of [India's] past heritage' (ibid.). The secularism of Nehru and his followers was, quite simply, a negative attitude towards Hindu traditions. There is nothing 'neutral', in any sense of the word, about the Nehruvian 'secular' state.

When pursued systematically, such policies are bound to have their impact on society. Eventually, once the seduction of this 'secularism' wore off, representatives of the Hindu traditions began to articulate a defence of their own traditions. However, this defence did not take the form of reflections on Hindu traditions and their ability to address the problems of modern society. Instead, it took the inevitable form of defence against attacks, that is, a *militant defence* of the Hindu traditions against the 'secular' state of the Nehruvian variety.

When looked at from a pagan perspective, there is *no religious rivalry* between the Hindu traditions and the Semitic religions. However, the opposite is the case when viewed from the perspective of the Semitic religions. When the Indian state assumes the truth of a Semitic theological claim, and further accepts this claim as its own epistemological position, then it actively creates and promotes the religious rivalry between the majority (that is, those who belong to the Hindu traditions) and the minority (Muslims, Christians, and so on). That is to say, the state *creates religious rivalry* where there is none (if viewed from the majority perspective). As a matter of state policy, it creates and sustains opposition between religions and traditions. Consequently, it *transforms* the conflict between different groups *into a religious conflict*.

In his introduction to an important collection of articles on secularism in India, Rajeev Bhargava writes that many critics of the secular state have reached the following conclusion:

There is perhaps as much, if not greater religious bigotry today than before. Religious minorities continue to feel disadvantaged and often face discrimination. The scale and intensity of religious conflict does not seem to have declined: if anything it has proliferated, touching people who have never known it before. The verdict against secularism appears unequivocal: *it failed to realize the objectives for which it was devised.* (1998: 2; italics added)

I disagree with this verdict. The secular state provides a readymade dress into which social tensions between groups in a society can legitimately fit. The secular state in modern India assumes the truth of a religious perception (even if the perception is that of the minority) without submitting such a perception to any kind of scrutiny. The exacerbation of religious violence does not tell us that secularism has failed in India. Its intensity tells us that secularism has been *entirely successful in India*. The secular state, which the secularists continue to wish for, does not prevent religious conflicts: *it actively promotes them.*

By forcing the framework of the Semitic religions on the Hindu traditions, the 'liberal' state in India is also coercing the communities to solve their internal conflict in a religious manner. That is to say, it is forcing the pagan traditions in India to mould themselves along the lines of the Semitic religions. The growth of the so-called Hindu fundamentalism is *a direct result* of this coercive straitjacket. Traditions, which never *systematically persecuted* the other on grounds of religious truth, are *forced* into a systematic persecution of religions precisely on this basis. When secularists fight 'Hindu fundamentalism' by appealing to liberal theory, they feed and strengthen what they intend to fight. It is precisely *a liberal 'secular' conception* that *generates* the phenomenon of 'Hindu fundamentalism' in the pagan Indian culture.

Toleration as a Harbinger of Conflict

Naturally, this theoretical claim requires empirical support also. I will develop an empirical argument in the near future; within the confines of this chapter we can only sketch its outlines. The British colonial state in India saw religious toleration as one of its basic duties. In 1858, the Queen of England proclaimed the following:

Firmly relying ourselves on the truth of Christianity, and acknowledging with gratitude the solace of religion, we disclaim alike the right and the desire to impose our convictions on any of our subjects. We declare it to be our royal will and pleasure, that none be in anywise favoured, none molested or disquieted, by reason of their religious faith or observances; but that all shall alike enjoy the equal and impartial protection of the law. (Thomas 1988: 287)

Inspired by the values of toleration and religious liberty, the colonial state argued that Hindus ought to be left free in the spiritual realm of religion, in the same way as the believers in Europe. No human being, said the principle of Christian freedom, could arrogate the authority of God over human souls and consciences.

The resulting policy, however, systematically compelled the Hindus to prove that a particular practice was founded in 'the true religious doctrines of Hinduism'. This was the case, because the liberal colonial state would tolerate a practice only if it had been demonstrated to belong to the realm of religion. Thus, in the nineteenth-century controversy over the practice of sati or widow-burning, the Governor-General in Council decided in 1812 that 'The practice ... being ... recognized and encouraged by the doctrines of the Hindoo religion, it appears evident that the course which the British government should follow, according to the principle of religious toleration ... is to allow the practice in those cases in which it is countenanced by their religion ...'[8] In the same controversy, a British observer commented that 'the true interpretation of the religious law ... will no doubt diminish, if not extinguish the desire for self-immolation. The safest way of coming to a right understanding on a point so interesting to humanity, is a rigid investigation of the rules of conduct laid down in the books which are considered sacred by the Hindoos'.[9] Consequently, the orthodox Hindu community began to aggressively defend the practice of self-immolation by demonstrating its foundation in the 'religious doctrines' and 'sacred texts' of 'Hindu religion'.[10]

Following this route, the policy of religious toleration gradually transformed the self-confidence and vibrancy of the Hindu traditions into a fanatical defence of their alleged 'religious doctrines'. Before the early nineteenth century, Hindu spokesmen had protected their traditions from the missionary onslaught by pointing to the antiquity of their ancestral practices. Or they insisted that 'every one may be saved by his own Religion, if he does what is Good, and shuns Evil', as a Malabar Brahmin told Ziegenbalg in the early eighteenth century.[11] This changed once the liberal colonial state implemented its policy of religious toleration: now these traditions had to prove that they were proper religions with their own sacred doctrines in order to be legitimate. In the same way as its colonial precursor, the secular state of post-Independence India has forced the Hindu traditions to identify and stand up for themselves as religious doctrines—variants of Islam and Christianity. The result is the Hindutva movement: a militant attempt to establish the doctrines of 'Hinduism' as the superior and dominant form of religion in Indian society.

Even though it is incomplete, this argument points to a common mistake in the current analysis of 'the world-wide phenomenon of religious fundamentalism'. As argued in the above, the contemporary liberal framework assumes that the Hindu and other Asian traditions are variants of the same phenomenon as Islam and Christianity, namely religion. In the same way, the current analysis presupposes that all cultural movements in the contemporary world can be classified into two basic categories: the liberal tolerant movements and their counterparts of religious fundamentalism. When one assumes that all the movements in question—Islamic fanaticism in the Arab world; Christian fundamentalism in the United States; the Hindutva movement in India; violent Buddhist groups in Sri Lanka—are variants of one and the same phenomenon, one's analysis and research projects will indeed confirm that we confront a worldwide threat of 'religious fundamentalism' or 'religious violence'.[12] However, this does not give us a fruitful understanding of these various movements. It merely shows how the fallacy of *petitio principii* allows one to uphold a crude conceptual framework, which reduces all cultural movements into variants of either liberal pluralism or religious fundamentalism.

I propose a first step towards an alternative understanding of the so-called 'Hindu fundamentalism' in India. When the Indian liberal state accepts the Semitic notion of human traditions as so many competing religious doctrines (which enables it to grant the freedom to convert), and does nothing more, the pagan traditions are forced to defend their value of non-interference by reacting to those who interfere with them. That is to say, when the state actively promotes only the Semitic conception of the good and the pagan communities want to strengthen their conceptions of the good, a conflict between the two is inevitable. This conflict is not only between the pagan communities and the state but also among the communities in society. To the extent that some one particular type of community— namely, those belonging to the Semitic religions—is perceived to enjoy the protection of the state, the conflict could only take the form of opposing the state violence with civic violence. That is to say, the so-called religious violence between communities and the cry to ban religious conversion arise from the 'neutral' 'secular' policies of the Indian state during the last fifty years or more. The seeds of religious violence *are sown* by the liberal state; however, it is the communities that harvest them.

Beyond the Liberal State

Does all of this mean that state neutrality is impossible in Indian society? This depends on the kind of neutrality one strives for. It has become clear that a neutrality of justification is *logically impossible* for the Indian state. This option is not available because (a) the choices of the state are logically exclusive and (b) the state cannot play the agnostic. However, other conceptions of state neutrality exist: neutrality of effect and neutrality of aim, for example. Drawing on Joseph Raz's formulations of state neutrality, the foremost liberal political theorist of the twentieth century, John Rawls, suggests that neutrality might mean any of the following:

(1) that the state is to ensure for all citizens equal opportunity to advance any conception of the good they freely affirm; (2) that the state is not to do anything intended to favor or promote any particular comprehensive doctrine rather than another, or to give greater assistance to those who pursue it; (3) that the state is not to do anything that makes it more likely that individuals will accept any particular conception rather than another unless steps are taken to cancel, or to compensate for, the effects of policies that do this. (Rawls 1999: 459)

When it legislates in favour of religious conversion, the Indian state cannot live up to the first two principles of neutrality of aim. This policy promotes 'the comprehensive doctrine' or 'conception of the good' of the Semitic religions at the expense of the Hindu traditions by making the four choices that correspond to the Semitic view. This leaves the third option of neutrality of effect. But this, Rawls claims (1999: 460–1), is 'an impracticable aim', because

... it is surely impossible for the basic structure of a just constitutional regime not to have important effects and influences on which comprehensive doctrines endure and gain adherents over time, and it is futile to try to counteract these effects and influences, or even to ascertain for political purposes how deep and pervasive they are. We must accept the facts of common-sense political sociology. (See also his 1996: 193–4)

Thus, the effects of state policy in a liberal regime may well bring about the decline of some religions and their conceptions of the good. We may indeed lament the limited space of social worlds, Rawls continues (1999: 462), but 'no society can include within itself all forms of life'. Rawls has in mind cases of minority religions that go against his conception of political justice: for example, conceptions of the good that require the repression or degradation of certain persons on racial or ethnic grounds or religions that need the control of the state apparatus in order to survive. The predicament becomes somewhat more dramatic in the Indian case. Here, if we accept 'the facts of common-sense political sociology' (whatever these may be) and abandon neutrality of effect as 'impracticable', then it simply becomes impossible for the Indian state to be neutral. Neutrality of effect is the only option left for the liberal state in India in the face of the predicament of religious conversion. If it continues its current policy without trying to neutralize the effects, the cultural traditions that do not conceive of religious diversity as a rivalry over truth will continue to decline.

How could the Indian state neutralize the effects of its policy towards religion and conversion? Such a strategy becomes conceivable when we consider a common description of the co-existence among different religious and cultural traditions in the Indian society. Many authors have claimed that a reasonably stable and plural society existed in India, which far surpassed the cultural diversity of the West at any point during its history. This phenomenon of pluralism, it is said, took a shape different from anything known to modern western culture. There were violent clashes, but these never developed into the systematic persecution of some particular tradition or the other. Alongside these clashes, there was a tendency in each of the religious traditions to absorb or adopt elements from the other traditions. Certain saints, festivals and artistic traditions were shared by Hindus, Muslims, and Christians. In many parts of India, scholars point out, this kind of positive interaction lives on today.[13]

It remains to be seen how far this picture of traditional Indian pluralism will correspond to a social-scientific theorizing of the same phenomena. It could be pure nostalgia, or a naïve conception of societies where Hindus really set the basic rules and compelled others to comply. That is what research will have to show us. Anyway, our contemporary ignorance of the nature of, and the mechanisms behind, this pluralist social structure is tragic, given the fact that it is in fast decline. Social-scientific research should examine the successes and failures of stable diversity in the Indian culture. This research can reveal the mechanisms behind the traditional forms of pluralism and show how they could be stimulated. One thing the Indian state could do in order to neutralize the effects of its policy towards religion is to promote such research projects. It could help create a fertile soil for innovative research into the Indian cultural traditions, including Indian Islam and Indian Christianity, so as to disclose the mechanisms and dynamics that could be stimulated in order to have the Indian pluralism flourish.

In other words, only by actively generating the neutrality of effects could the Indian state hope to become neutral. To give up religious freedom and ban religious conversions is both undesirable and retrograde. It would deny freedom to those groups in India who follow the Semitic religions. Instead of doing this, the Indian state could look elsewhere to become neutral. In response to the economic exigencies of the global market, it has actively stimulated the growth of engineering and allied disciplines. It could do the same with respect to stimulating explorations into the histories and theories of the Indian cultural traditions. The state could make career prospects in such areas exciting, and entice intelligent minds to explore the possibilities of cultural rejuvenation.

At this point, a common misunderstanding may emerge. Let it be clear that I am not in any way suggesting that political structures and processes in India should become 'faith-based', 'theocratic', or 'religious'. This understanding of my argument commits a fallacy: it assumes that because I criticize the notion of a liberal secular state in India, I intend to defend its mirror image of a religious or faith-based state. This is neither a logical implication nor a hidden agenda of my argument. Rather, I wish to challenge the entire framework of liberal political theory on conceptual grounds. This framework first makes all cultural traditions into variants of a common phenomenon of religion. Then it tends to reduce all political models to an opposition between the impartial and secular versus the partial and religious ones. I contest the framework at two levels. Firstly, in spite of its pretention of neutrality, the liberal model of toleration and state neutrality is itself not a secular, impartial model. In reality, it is a Semitic theological entity which has been dressed up in 'secular' philosophical garb.[14] Secondly, the prima facie evidence indicates that the Hindu traditions cannot be variants of the same phenomenon as Islam and Christianity. Hence, the suggestion that an attempt to examine the traditional pluralism of the Indian culture as the source of a potential alternative to the liberal model of toleration is equivalent to the advocacy of faith-based politics misses the point. I do not intend to study the Hindu traditions as a religious doctrine or faith, because this approach captures neither their basic nature nor their distinct structure.

Ultimately, it is not the aim of my argument to prescribe to the Indian state what it should or should not do. I do not even propose that the Indian state is under a moral obligation of neutrality towards the various cultural and religious communities in its society. What I have argued is that the dominant notion of state neutrality of liberal political theory threatens to collapse once it is confronted by a case like the Indian, where pagan traditions and Semitic religions co-exist. The issue of religious conversion shows that neutrality of justification and aim are logically impossible in such a case. Naturally, neutrality could still be possible with regards to different issues. But, the fact that the liberal secular state fails to be neutral in an issue as crucial as that of religious conversion indicates that we should re-examine its success while dealing with other problems of the Indian society also—for instance, its controversy about a uniform civil code.

In so far as the normative theory of the liberal state intends to provide a universal model to solve the problem of diversity in society, it is bound to fail, for it suffers from a profound ignorance of the structure of plural societies other than those of the Christian West. Moreover, my analysis has revealed that the dominant conception of the liberal state—'neutral' and 'secular'—does not allow space to pagan traditions, which do not conceive of religious diversity as a rivalry of truth claims. Perhaps, as Rawls says, no society can include within itself all forms of life. But, when the epistemic premises of the liberal state prevent it from accommodating cultural traditions that form the majority in many Asian countries, it is high time to re-examine the cultural roots and limitations of this particular form of life.

Notes

1. The distinction between 'emic' and 'etic', as it is made in anthropology, refers to how one accounts for beliefs and behaviours. An 'emic' account is meaningful to the actor because it uses categories from within that actor's culture. An 'etic' account, by contrast, is applicable to all cultures, a 'neutral' account as it were.

2. This Christian understanding of the Hindu traditions lives on today. During oral evidence given before the members of the Select Committee of the House of Lords on Religious Offences in November 2002, Ramesh Kallidai, speaking on behalf of the Hindu community, pointed out an article by the Christian Medical Fellowship's Pastor Juge Ram: 'There is another example which I recently came upon which may not be incitement to religious hatred, but in our opinion it is vilification and ridiculing the Hindu belief system. This is an article published in July 2000 by the Christian Medical Fellowship and the article was written by Juge Ram who is a convert from Hinduism to Christianity' and I quote from his article which was published in July 2000 and is at present on their web site. The article says as follows: "Hindus are lost and spiritually blind. They are without hope in this world and in the next. Only Christ can release them. *Hinduism is a false religion.*" So in our humble opinion we think this is definitely vilification and ridiculing one billion Hindus worldwide who are established in a particular religious system' (italics added).

Responding to this statement, the Earl of Mar and Kellie, a member of the Select Committee, said, 'Following on the question about the Christian Medical Fellowship, it struck me from what you read out was that they were just making unpleasant statements, to put it mildly, but they were *not actually telling any lies* about the Hindu religion in the sense that *they were not actually putting out any false remarks* which were possibly going to distort people and miseducate them'. The *Minutes of the Select Committee of The House of Lords on Religious Offences in England and Wales—First Report* (http://www.parliament. the-stationery-office.co.uk/pa/ld200203/ldselect/ldrelof/95/2112706.htm; italics added; accessed 10 April 2011).

3. See Lynch (2001) for a helpful collection of articles.

4. 'Conceivably', because not all deontic theories accept this principle.

5. See, for instance, Jaakko Hintikka's 'Deontic Logic and its Philosophical Morals' in his 1969 work. See also the articles of Hintikka and several others on the nature of deontic logics in Risto Hilpinen (ed.), 1981.

6. See Chatterjee (1998).

7. No attempt will be made to formulate the necessary conditions more precisely because nothing in my argument revolves around them.

8. This statement occurs in a reply from the Governor-General in Council to a letter requesting clarity on the official colonial policy towards the practice of self-immolation by widows, in Majumdar (ed.) (1988: 102).

9. From an 'appreciative notice of Raja Rammohun Roy's first *Tract on Suttee*' in the *Calcutta Gazette* of 24 December 1818.

10. See Lata Mani's interesting work on this issue in her 1986 and 1989 works.

11. Ziegenbalg (1719: 15).

12. See Appleby (2000) and Juergensmeyer (2000) for two recent examples.

13. On this traditional Indian form of pluralism see Apffel-Marglin (1999); Burman (2002); Hasan (1993); Narayanan (2001).

14. See Jeff Spinner-Halev's interesting piece on 'Hinduism, Christianity and Liberal Religious Toleration' (2005) which presents a related argument.

Conclusion

Ah, yes,
We shall not cease from exploration.
And the end of our exploring
Shall be to arrive where we started
And know the place for the first time.
—T.S. Eliot, 'Four Quartets'

In one sense, the title of this book captures the nature of the task facing the contemporary generation, whether in India or in the diaspora. The problems that the Indians of the diaspora (the NRIs) confront are perhaps about a decade ahead of the problems confronted by the same generation living in India. So, I will also focus on the NRIs in concluding this book. Both belong to the same generation. Members of this generation—unlike many from mine—are confident and self-assured; perhaps, they are proud, too, about the strength of their culture and traditions. Rightly so. However, personal convictions about the value of our traditions and culture do not automatically guarantee the truth of such convictions. Not only that. It is also the case that the history of both India and of humankind requires that we should be able to say and show what is valuable and what is not in our traditions. This history, however, is also the history of colonialism, subservience, and is further weighed down by the scientific, technological, economic, and military weight of Western culture. Today, we need more than mere practice and a further continuation of our traditions; we also need to examine them honestly and critically in order that we may transmit what we find valuable in them.

In the past, we chose multiple ways of undertaking such a task: from one extreme—that of wholesale rejection of everything Indian—to the other extreme of total endorsement of everything Indian. There were reasons for both these extremes and for the varieties that lay in between. Though understandable, none of these attempts brought us much by way of understanding Indian traditions. For all their answers, we remain where the earlier generations were: trapped in the framework that refuses to budge or go away. What is the nature of this framework? Why does it entrap? How do we get out of it? Where should we go when we get out of the framework? These are the questions that face us now.

With due respect to us Indians, there is one thing we need to keep constantly in mind. We are the products of colonialism. True, we have been overrun by many conquerors, but they did not all colonize us. As I have argued, colonialism is not merely about conquering territories, ruling over people and extracting revenues. It is a far more inhuman process, involving violence of all sorts: from the purely physical to the purely psychic. Colonialism alters the way we look at the world and, with sheer violence, displaces native ways of experiencing the world. To the colonized, there is no simple or naïve return to the lost world possible. Though tragic and reprehensible, this is what colonialism does, and we need to understand this truth about ourselves in the first place.

British colonialism introduced a new framework for experiencing the world. More than that, it introduced a new way of talking about our experience of the world. This framework told us many new things about ourselves: that we were backward and primitive, steeped in superstition, and dominated by antiquated structures. The British also taught us what these structures were: the caste system was the Indian social structure, and 'Hinduism', 'Buddhism', 'Jainism', 'Sikhism' were our religious structures. We took to this way of talking the way ducks take to water. In the colonized field that the Indian mind had become, many set up tents to sell their merchandise: an attack on the Indian caste system; an instant mixture of reform that could cure the ills of Indian 'religions'; tracts and books that told tales of the tyranny of the Brahmin 'priests'; and, of course, the sale of the seductive siren songs of modernization and progress. On the other side of the Ganges, so to speak, rival merchants set up their tents as well: to sell the waters of the Ganges in cheap plastic bottles so that Indians could wash away all their 'sins'. In the bustle of the marketplace and the excitement of selling exotic goods, the generations before us 'forgot' to ask the one question which they should have: *'Did the tales of the British describe Indian culture and traditions, or did they indicate how the British experienced India?'*

Therein lies the rub. The British descriptions had more to do with their experiences of an alien culture than with the truth about India and her people. Yet, they spoke as though their experience of India was synonymous with facts about India. When we took over the reins of our country from them, we did not inherit only colonial buildings and colonial bureaucracy. We also actively took over their descriptions as though the experiences of the British were incontestable facts about India. So convinced are we about these 'facts' that challenging their status today provokes the ire of the most well-intentioned and educated among us. Yet, perhaps, the strangest of all is this: those who defend the factual status of British descriptions hardly know or understand what they are defending. Let me return to two of these. One: that the caste system dominates Indian society and that it must be abolished; two: 'Hinduism', 'Buddhism', and so on are the religions of India.

Let me begin with the caste system. The British did not merely say that there were *jatis* in India. No Indian could ever deny this. They, and all the subsequent social sciences, said something far more than this: the claim was that all the different jatis in India constituted a coherent totality; that this totality formed the social structure of Indian society; and that some of the Indian religions (sometimes, it was exclusively 'Hinduism') and some of the jatis (it is mostly the Brahmins) provided the ideology supporting such a social structure. This is what is meant by 'there is a caste system in Indian society'. That is, the British—like the current social sciences—did not make an empirical claim about the presence of jatis in India; *they put across meta-theoretical claims about the jatis.*

If we want to assess the truth of these theoretical claims (make no mistake about this: through and through, they are theoretical in nature), then the evidence cannot be what we routinely come up with: the horror stories of 'caste discrimination'; the social humiliation of groups in a society; the phenomenon of 'untouchability'; the presence of poverty, and such like. None of these can serve as evidence for the claim that the nature of the Indian social structure is identical to 'the caste system'. Why not?

As I have said earlier (in Chapter 4), the phenomenon of discrimination (whether individual or social) is neither unitary nor monolithic. It exists in different ways in different parts of the world. If its presence is evidence of the existence of 'the caste system', then the latter is present everywhere in the world. The same applies to poverty and humiliation. These phenomena do not provide evidence for the presence of a specific social structure. Discrimination, poverty, and social humiliation of groups can be found in slavery, in the feudal societies of Europe, in the capitalist societies of today, and so on. In other words, these phenomena are compatible with multiple social structures: *they do not indicate that one kind of a social structure is present in some society or another.* So, on their own, these phenomena are not evidence of one specific social structure, namely, 'the caste system'. We need some facts to be uniquely present in India, absent elsewhere; and these facts must tell us about the fundamental divisions in society. One could say that India is a mishmash of caste, class, social and power groups, and so on (or any such combination). In that case, we are not saying anything more interesting or profound than to notice that jatis exist in India. Who has ever denied this fact?

If there is a problem about the specification of a social division along the lines of caste, it gets compounded by a further theoretical claim: that 'the caste system' is a coherent whole. This is merely an assumption. No one in the world has so far shown how and in what fashion 'the caste system' is a coherent system. The British could not even classify the caste divisions, let alone demonstrate their coherence. They gave up the attempt after trying for nearly thirty years and introducing all kinds of weird categories (like sub-castes, and sub-sub-castes).

If no one has shown that the caste system is a social structure in India or that it is a coherent whole, then what about the claim that it has a specific ideology? Here, sensationalism rules the day: some lines from Manu, some anecdotes of a few people, constitute the evidence. Not one person has laid this alleged ideology bare; not one person knows what the components of this ideology are. How do we even know there is a single ideology? How do we know that there are not exactly 2,371 and a half ideologies present? Again, your guess is as good as anybody else's. Come to think of it, do we even know what an ideology looks like? Is Hitler's *Mein Kampf* an example of an ideology? Is Marx's *Das Kapital* an example of an ideology? Are

Yajurveda or the *Kama Sutra* an example of an ideology? Is Amartya Sen's *The Argumentative Indian* an example of an ideology? Or, is ideology something that people never put down in writing? Scientific research cannot be substituted by coffee-shop talk; it has never been.

Similar considerations apply to the way some of us talk about 'religions'. Everybody seems to know what 'religion' is and knows, too, that 'Hinduism' is an ancient religion. Instead of thoughtfully studying the framework of religious studies, which happens to be Christian theological in nature; instead of trying to understand the theory, the practice, and the history of Christianity, which requires considerable intellectual labour; that is, instead of trying to understand how and why 'Hinduism' is portrayed the way it is in Western culture, many people are beginning to tell the rest of us what 'Hinduism' is. But, what they tell us does not go beyond what eighteenth-century Jesuits told about our 'religions' in terms of its content. The only difference between such people and the Christian missionaries is the valuation: these religious-studies people speak 'positively' of Hinduism and the missionaries spoke 'negatively' of Hinduism.

There is a reason why these people are such experts on 'the caste system' and 'Hinduism'. That is because they have simply taken over the European descriptions of their experience of India as though they were facts about India and her traditions. They do not know this fact, which is excusable. What makes it tragic is that *they do not want to know it*. This combination is the result of colonial consciousness.

Please do not mistake me. I do believe that we need people to realize how the West has been describing us for the last four hundred years or so. We do need diaspora organizations like the HAF (the Hindu-American Foundation), which want to do something about this state of affairs in the United States. My problem is about how they are doing it: by trying to gain recognition for our traditions and customs by transforming 'Hinduism' into a pale variant of Christianity, Judaism, and Islam. These three religions understand neither India nor her traditions. Looking through their theological prisms, they transform our religions into false religions. Paradoxically enough, organizations like the HAF and many 'Hindu' NRIs whom I know accept this judgement. Having accepted this, they want to make us appear 'respectable'. How? Our 'Brahman' begins take the shape of the biblical God, the God of Abraham, Isaac, and Jacob. The Semitic religions (Judaism, Christianity, and Islam) ridicule and heap scorn on our traditions because our 'gods' are not like the biblical God: some accept this stance and transform our 'gods' into 'manifestations' of 'Brahman' who looks like the biblical God. I would like to recount an anecdote that should tell you how deep this attitude has sunk into the minds of Indian intellectuals.

A few years ago, at an international conference in India, we attended plenary sessions in a room, in one corner of which, two reasonably big statues were present: one of a dancing Kali and the other of a dancing Ganesha. During one of the plenary meetings—the last session if I remember correctly—a foreign delegate asked what those statues were and what they were doing. The organizer of the conference, an Indian woman, said they were statues of Kali and Ganesha. 'What are they doing?' After some uncomfortable shuffling of feet, this woman (who had studied in the US and got her PhD from the University of California, Berkeley) said that they were 'aesthetic objects'. Needless to say, I was annoyed and stood up and explained to the other delegates that these statues were not 'art objects' of any kind, but that they were the representations of our *devatas*. Because this woman and many like her are embarrassed by the questions which foreigners ask, they transform us into aesthetic imbeciles who believe that non-human forms exhaust our notions of human beauty. Instead of telling stories about Kali and Ganesha, this woman and others of her kind show us up as people who have no aesthetic sense at all. Or force us into a mould that resembles the Semitic religions. How far should we travel down this road before we realize that we are on the wrong route?

Today, multiple tasks face us. We need to translate our traditions into the language of the twenty-first century. To do so, we need to shake off our sense of complacency in the first place. In the second place, we need to realize that we 'talk the talk and walk the walk' of the colonizers. We need to break out of this. Third, we should recognize that our traditions will not become ours just because we are brought up as Indians: we need to put in the hard intellectual labour of reacquiring these traditions.

The NRIs and their Story

Very often, I hear NRI parents in the USA make the following remark: 'When I came to the US so many decades ago, I knew very little about Hinduism. My ignorance was driven home when I had children and they began to ask what Hinduism was. Because I had to educate them, I ended up learning more about Hinduism in the US (thanks to this or that organization or swami) than during all the years I spent in India.'

Let us reflect on this experience. When Indians come to the US, they feel that they are confronted with their ignorance of 'Hinduism'. To account for this state of affairs, they blame either their earlier lack of interest (in learning about their 'religion' while they were in India), or the absence of education (in India) in this regard. Of course, neither of the two quite explains why they need explicit instruction in 'Hinduism' in order to transmit traditions to their children. After all, the transmission of Indian culture over the millennia depended (and continues to depend) upon ordinary people who have 'learnt' their traditions from their parents and peers, and not from any pandits. One's 'knowledge' and 'ignorance' when one came to the US, in this sense, is comparable to the similar 'knowledge' and 'ignorance' of ordinary Indians. In all probability, had they remained in India, their lack of knowledge would not have worried them as much as it worries them now. They would have transmitted their tradition and culture the way millions do in India: without any explicit instruction in the 'religion' called 'Hinduism'. Peer groups, family circles, friends and relatives, would have also played a role in this process no doubt.

However, what works in India fails when Indians come and settle down in the US. Here, they feel the need for some sort of an explicit education about 'Hinduism'. Clearly, this is due to the environment in which they find themselves: not only does their new environment not help in the transmission of Indian culture and traditions, but it also forces individual Indian parents to school themselves in Indian 'religions' in a particular way. That is to say, unlike the Indian environment where cultural transmission can take place without an explicit education in their 'religions', people are forced to articulate what their religion is when they come to live in Western culture. Therefore, unlike (most of) our parents and peers, Indians living in the West appear to face a different kind of challenge: coming up with an explicit understanding of 'Hinduism', if they intend to transmit their culture and traditions to their children.

Yet, what appears to work for them (namely, codifying 'Hinduism' in terms of either its beliefs or practices, or by spelling out the 'Ten

Commandments') does not seem to work for their children who are born and grow up in the United States: what satisfies their parents does not satisfy the needs of the children. While the parents are quite happy to meet in self-study classes, read Patanjali and feel good that they have arrived somewhere because now they can talk about *pramaana* and *anumaana*, their children do not share the parents' sanguinity. The children feel that they are left to fend for themselves and face questions from their peers and teachers which they do not understand or cannot answer.

In other words, there seem to be three different kinds of problems. First: the Indian ways of transmitting traditions and culture appear to break down when Indians come and settle down in the West. Second: Indians seem to feel a compulsion to codify their traditions in some form or another because of the pressure exerted by the cultural milieu in which they live. Third: such codifications—while they seem to satisfy the needs of the parents—do not seem to help the children in their daily interactions with their peers and society at large. Because of these three problems, a fourth problem also comes to the fore: such codifications have a tendency to downplay both the importance and the necessity of the kind of diversity and pluralism that the Indian traditions have. I want to reflect on this situation.

Setting the Context

When the British East India Company consolidated its hold over many parts of India, and their administrators assumed the position of rulers, a very peculiar kind of hostility towards Indian traditions became the hallmark of the colonial administrative policy. Of course, this hostility was there from the very beginning: in 'Hinduism', the 'religion' of the Hindus, they found everything that was reprehensible and repugnant. This hostility arose not merely because they 'discovered' that some Indian practices, like child marriage, sati, and what-have-you, were intolerable or immoral. Their repulsion had a deeper root: their understanding of religion taught them that such perversions were integral to false religions. Because 'Hinduism' was a false and degenerate religion, its perversions were not mere accidents but a necessary feature.

We need to understand this well because the notion of false religion does not make sense to us. Therefore, let me put it in very simple terms. To the followers of the Semitic religions, only God can be the object of worship. When they speak of 'God', we need to keep two things very firmly in mind.

The first is this: this 'God' is the God of Abraham, Isaac, and Jacob. According to their scriptures, (the biblical) God created the world (as it is described in the book on Genesis in the Old Testament). He is the God of the Israelites (of Abraham, Isaac, and Jacob, and their descendants), who punished the Jews, scattered them across the world for forgetting Him, and also promises to save them. In the hands of the Christians, (the biblical) God's promise to save the Jews got transformed into the salvation of entire humanity; the 'God of Israel' also became the singular, unique, and unqualified 'God', even though He continued to be the God of Abraham, Isaac, and Jacob. His promise—so the Christians claimed—was redeemed by Jesus of Nazareth, who was the promised messenger of this God. ('Christ' means the promised one or the Messiah.) The Jews did not think that Jesus of Nazareth was the Christ, whereas the followers of Jesus claimed that he was precisely that.

The second point is this: Satan, or the devil, is continuously attempting to seduce 'people' to stray from the path of worshipping (the biblical) God. In the hands of the Christians, 'people' refers to entire humankind. Satan, or the devil (he has many names and his followers are 'legion'), undertakes this task of seduction by making the credulous believe that he, the devil, is the 'true' (biblical) God. Of course, he is not the 'true God'; he is the 'false god'. In this task, he is immensely helped by the human followers of the devil: the 'priests'. These 'priests' create all kinds of 'rituals' and mumbo-jumbo, deceive the credulous, hide the 'true message' of (the biblical) God, and so on and so forth. By doing all this, they encourage the ordinary people to worship the devil and his lieutenants: these are the 'false gods'. So, we have one 'true God' (the biblical God, the God of Abraham, Isaac, and Jacob) and multitudes of 'false gods'. Because religion is the worship of God, we get two kinds of religions: the 'true' religion that worships the 'true God', and false religions that worship the 'false gods'.

To the British Christians (and to the Islamic rulers before them), the 'religion' of the Hindus could only be false religion. Our *devas* and *devis* were false gods and merely different representations of the devil and his lieutenants. To the Protestants (and to most of the

Catholic missionaries), such a false religion could only be understood in terms of the seductive power of the devil and the machinations of the devil's 'priests', namely, the Brahmins. Such a false religion not only delivered the credulous into the clutches of the devil and sent them on a one-way ticket to hell, but it also had to be intrinsically immoral. Consequently, any phenomenon that they thought they saw in India—whether it was sati or child marriage—had to do with the immorality of 'Hinduism' and the wickedness of the priests of this false religion. They believed that such a false religion could only exist because a cunning and devious group of people (these are the 'priests' of the false religions) succeeds in deceiving the majority: in the Brahmins, they found such 'priests'. How did these priests gain and maintain their power? In the 'caste system', they found the answer to this riddle. Somehow or the other, the Brahmin priests invented the 'caste system' and somehow or the other, they imposed this immoral system on the larger society. Thus, this 'caste system' became an integral part of the false religion that 'Hinduism' was.

You must remember that the foundation and the framework of these 'discoveries' were not empirical investigations but their theological beliefs. Everything they 'discovered' was fitted into this framework. Discovery of the Upanishads and the Buddhist (and the Jain) traditions merely strengthened the framework. Thus, they came up with the three stages of the decay and degeneration of the 'Indian religion': Vedic religion, Brahminism, and Hinduism. The Vedic religion retained the intimations of (the biblical) God and His original message; Brahminism was the corruption and decay of this religion in the hands of the Brahmin priests; 'Hinduism' is a further degeneration and corruption of the already-corrupt religion of Brahminism. The Buddha fought the 'Brahmin priests' and, because of this, in the eyes of the Protestants, 'Buddhism' was less 'corrupt' than Brahminism. But 'Hinduism' was the most degenerate and corrupt 'false religion', which, unfortunately, was embraced by the majority of the gullible in India.

Therefore, all the ills of Indian society and culture were traced back to 'Hinduism'. They were intrinsic to this religion—the British claimed—and they were integral parts of the same. A lie, if repeated often enough, becomes accepted as the truth; nonsense, when propagated widely, begins to make sense. Such has been the case with respect to Indian 'religions', especially 'Hinduism'.

Drawing a Parallel

The Indian intellectuals of yesteryear swallowed this story hook, line, and sinker. Thus, two extreme reactions came into existence: at one end of the spectrum, some people wanted to 'reform' the religion of the Hindus. They wanted to go back to the 'purer' religion of the Vedas and the Upanishads. At the other end of the spectrum, rabid defenders of 'Hinduism' also came into existence. As is usual in such cases, any number of intermediate positions between these two extremes also crystallized.

The 'reformers' tried to build a purer form of Hinduism: they accepted that pujas in the temples and at home constituted 'idol worship' and, therefore, were intolerable; they discovered that, indeed, the Upanishads did not talk about the 'rituals' that the people were practising and, therefore, the 'Brahmin' priests had corrupted the purer religion of Indians; and so on. Having agreed with the British about almost everything they said, these intellectuals began the process of constructing a pure religion called 'Hinduism' that was modelled upon their understanding of Protestant Christianity. They discovered the 'Nirguna Brahma' that some people had spoken of earlier; they found out that Indians, too, had spoken of 'God' in the singular. In short, their only 'disagreement' with the Protestant Christians was this: Could the 'Indian religion' be reformed to resemble some or the other respectable variant of Christianity or not? The Brahmo Samaj, the Arya Samaj, the Prarthana Samaj, began to create 'respectable' versions of 'Hinduism' that would not overly shock the sensibilities of Protestant Christians. Like all 'respectable religions', these versions of Hinduism identified their 'scriptures' and codified them into clear sets of beliefs; they also had 'God' at the centre of their 'doctrines'; their own versions of 'ethical commandments' and their 'vocation' of service to fellow human beings. And, much like their Protestant brethren, they wanted to 'reform' Hinduism, abolish 'the caste system' (and all such ills). They looked down upon the 'ignorant' mass of Indians who were not knowledgeable about the subtle tenets of the Upanishadic doctrines and were sunk in superstitious practices.

Thus, in many ways, these reformers merely acquiesced in the demands and criticisms of the British, and tried to sculpt a 'Hinduism' that could meet the criticisms. However, in the midst of all these, they *failed* to do that one thing which would have helped them: *understand the culture of the British and the nature of their religiously inspired criticisms.* They merely assumed that the British were justified in the criticisms of the 'Hinduism' of their time, and tried to show that underneath the contemporary corruption, a 'purer' form of religion was waiting to be found. In this, too—although they did not know it well—they followed the British and European portrayal of India and of the degeneration of her 'religions'.

Why is this story important to us today? There are two reasons. The first is this: the portrayal of Indian culture and of the nature of her traditions, which Western culture has provided over the centuries, has become the standard textbook trivia today. Though the picture which the West has painted is incomprehensible without presupposing the truth of Christian doctrines, the claims about the so-called 'religions' of India appear comprehensible even to those who do not know anything about Christianity. Intellectuals in the West and in India believe in the truth of Western descriptions of Indian culture. Most of us believe that 'the caste system' exists in India; that the Brahmins have oppressed the Dalits in India over the millennia; that Buddhism was a rebellion against the 'ritualistic' domination of the Brahmin priests; and so on. Indian intellectuals, too, believe this story: witness our 'reservation policy' and the 'conversion' of Dalits to Buddhism, as mere examples of our commitment to the truth of these Western stories about India. Today, most Indians respond to the questions and challenges they encounter in the same way that Indian reformers responded to the British criticisms and challenges.

Two Different Ways

Consider the following questions which are routinely asked in the West about our culture and which I have mentioned in the third chapter. Why do you wear a bindi? Why do you not eat beef? Is it true that you worship the phallus? What do you think about the caste system? Do they still practise sati in India? Why do your gods have six or eight arms? What is your religious symbol? Do you worship the statue in that temple? Do you believe in God? Are you religious? What does one do when one faces these questions?

Broadly speaking, there are two ways of responding to this situation. The first would be to try and answer these questions by assuming that (a) the questions are intrinsically intelligible and that

(b) one also understands them. That is the route chosen by most of us and by Indian reformers. We now need to notice what happens if we tread this route today because, unlike the reformers of yesteryear, our milieu is not only the Indian, but also the Western, culture.

1. The first requirement, of course, is that we come up with satisfactory answers. However, *satisfactory for whom?* Should it satisfy us—first-generation Indians in the West—or our children—second-generation Indians there—or the questioner? Consider, for example, one of the oft-heard answers to the question about not eating beef which goes as follows: Indians are nourished by cow's milk which is akin to being breast-fed by the mother; therefore, most Indians consider the cow as their mother. Hence, they do not slaughter cows or eat beef. (Or else, cattle are crucial to the survival of the Indian peasantry; hence they do not slaughter and eat them; or, any number of such 'explanations'.) Needless to say, this answer is satisfying neither to the questioner nor to most second-generation Indian children. In India, one sees people beating cows and throwing stones at them, which is hardly an expression of 'reverence' to the mother figure that the cow is alleged to be; no Indian goes around feeding his 'mother' when he sees the cow foraging for food on the streets. Furthermore, although at first sight, it appears an irrational answer: surely, the matter of people dying of starvation is of greater consequence than abstaining from eating beef. Would it not be possible to reduce starvation and hunger in India, if people were 'allowed' to eat beef? To questions like these, one has to come up with all kinds of convoluted answers, which leave most people unsatisfied. Alternately, one takes the route of the Jews and the Muslims: we are forbidden from eating beef for 'religious reasons'; in the same way Muslims do not eat pork and Jews want only kosher' food. This answer will work only so long as one does not meet someone well-versed in the history of India. When such a person comes up with textual evidence that there was no prohibition against meat (including beef) in the early Indian 'religion', then one gets well and truly stuck.

2. However, the presence of such multiplicity of answers is itself an occasion for embarrassment. Why do different 'Hindus' give different answers to questions like the above? Here is where

the new cultural milieu exerts pressure for standardizing the answers. Some questions like, 'Why do Hindu women wear a bindi on their foreheads?' might allow some leeway regarding the answers; others like, 'Why do you worship the phallus?' do not appear to do so.

3. The standardization of answers seeks to impose uniformity across the variety that characterizes Indian traditions. Such answers not only codify but also strengthen (among some) another tendency typical to all immigrants, namely, the tendency to accentuate their practices and beliefs, and to hold them both rigidly. One tends to hold on to the real or remembered practices of one's ancestors even more rigidly than one's own ancestors (or the Indians in India) and also become a super-orthodox 'Hindu' as a consequence.

4. The codification of beliefs and a rigid attempt to transplant, into a totally different milieu, a set of local practices encourage the fossilization of human practices. Instead of being an expression of the dynamic adaptation of human beings to their environments, human practices become rigid and, as such, require justifications. Such justifications can only be provided by a highly dogmatic set of beliefs formulated by this or that institution or swami. Thus, a 'Hinduism' that resembles the Semitic religions comes into existence.

5. Needless to say, such 'Hinduism' becomes even more vulnerable to challenges from the new cultural milieu. This time around, the diversity and multiplicity of Indian traditions are counterposed to it. The same milieu which appears to force one to come up with a recognizably Semitic version of Hinduism sharply criticizes all attempts to do so.

Thus, in responding to the Western milieu the way the early intellectuals responded would merely force us in the direction taken by the reformers. However, unlike them, we do not live in a milieu generated by Indian culture. That is to say, the 'Hinduism' that we could sustain in the cultural milieu of the West would be even worse than that created by the reformers of yesteryear. It would resemble their 'Hinduism' because of the attempts to codify beliefs, but it would be worse than that because we would also end up rigidly adhering to some sets of practices. We would end up sacrificing the very vitality that characterizes Indian traditions and which allowed them to survive over the millennia and in different environments.

How can we avoid these and other assorted ills and yet continue to practise our traditions in the West? To answer this problem, let me reiterate the following question: *Why are most of these questions not raised in India by us or our fellow 'Hindus'?* As I have already said, we learn not to ask such questions about our traditions, and this learning is a part of learning to become a follower of Indian traditions. In other words, when we confront such questions in Western culture, we need to understand two things about such questions: (a) they force and compel us to provide a particular kind of answers; (b) such questions do not make sense in Indian culture but are eminently sensible in Western culture. That is, when such questions are asked of Indian traditions, we *should not assume* that these questions are intelligible to us; they are not. *It is in the nature of Western culture to raise such questions.*

Almost all of us who are successful in the West, assume that we understand Western culture. Our only reason for making this assumption is our ability to be successful in the West. Furthermore, we also assume that we know what these questions mean just because we speak and understand English (or European languages). I would like to submit to you that this assumption is false: *we have not understood Western culture at all.*

One of the most important consequences of my claim is this: when Western culture quizzes us about the nature of Indian traditions, that culture is telling us about itself. To provide satisfactory answers to our interlocutors about our traditions does not require us to read the Upanishads or Patanjali; it does not require us to come up with our own 'Ten Commandments' or a poorly spun theology. We need to understand the nature of Western culture. Simply put: *to answer questions about Indian traditions, we need to understand Western culture.*

That is what the reformers did not understand; that is what we do not understand either. The questions that the West raises are rooted in its culture. Consequently, if we want our children to confront their milieu with confidence, we need, more than anything else, to teach them about Western culture. We need to make them understand why the West raises such questions and what those questions mean. Currently, they understand neither. We need not teach them 'the' answers to such questions; they will figure out on their own which answers are appropriate. However, we need to make them understand what Western culture 'means' when its members ask us whether 'Hindus believe in God'; 'what the religious symbol of the Hindus is'; and why 'Hindus worship lifeless statues'.

To sum up: while we live in the West, much like the reformers of yesteryear, we are forced into creating a rigid and codified 'Hinduism as a religion'. However, while such constructions surely have their place in the variety and diversity that characterizes Indian traditions, they neither solve nor address the problem that our children face. Our children—much like us—understand neither the culture they are living in nor how to answer some of its challenges. This situation defines our basic task: to teach our children about the West while we pass on our traditions to them. The only question we have to ask ourselves is this: How successful have we been in doing either?

I have begun the process of seeking answers to this problem. All I can do is begin this process; it is left to others to join me in this attempt and it is for future generations to carry the task to its completion. The stakes are huge: what hangs in balance is nothing less than the survival and flourishing of Indian culture. Not only that: it is also about the future of all of us. Will this process be crowned with success? Not having a crystal ball that can predict the future, I do not know; all I have is faith in the ability of future generations. Is that enough? No one can answer this question today except those called by the future, who hear it and also heed it. To them—surely they do exist—I humbly gift this book: this is yours, do with it what you will.

Bibliography

Abu-Lughod, L. (1991), 'Writing against Culture', in R.G. Fox (ed.), *Recapturing Anthropology: Working in the Present*, Santa Fé: School of American Research Press.

Ackerman, B. (1989), 'Why Dialogue?', *The Journal of Philosophy*, 86(1), pp. 5–22.

———(1994), 'Political Liberalisms', *The Journal of Philosophy*, 91(7), pp. 364–86.

Alatas, S.H. (1990), *Corruption: Its Nature, Causes, and Functions*, Aldershot: Avebury.

Almond, P.C. (1988), *The British Discovery of Buddhism*, Cambridge: Cambridge University Press.

Ambedkar, B.R. (2002), *The Essential Writings of B.R. Ambedkar*, V. Rodrigues (ed), New Delhi: Oxford University Press.

Apffel-Marglin, F. (1999), 'Secularism, Unicity and Diversity: The Case of Haracandi's Grove', in V. Das, D. Gupta, and P. Uberoi (eds), *Tradition, Pluralism and Identity: In Honour of T.N. Madan*, New Delhi: Sage Publications.

Appleby, R.S. (2000), *The Ambivalence of the Sacred: Religion, Violence, and Reconciliation*, New York: Rowan and Littlefield Publishers.

Appleby, R.S., and M.E. Marty (2002), 'Fundamentalism', *Foreign Policy*, No. 128, pp. 16–22.

Arkes, H. (1986), *First Things: An Inquiry into the First Principles of Morals and Justice*, Princeton: Princeton University Press.

Arneil, B. (1994), 'Trade, Plantation, and Property: John Locke and the Economic Defense of Colonialism', *Journal of the History of Ideas*, 55(4), pp. 591–609.

Asad, T. (2003), *Formations of the Secular: Christianity, Islam, Modernity*, Stanford: Stanford University Press

Ashcroft, B.,G. Griffiths, and H. Tiffin (eds) (1995), *The Post-Colonial Reader*, London: Routledge.

———(2003), *Post-Colonial Studies: The Key Concepts*, London: Routledge.

Avineri, S. (ed.) (1969), *Karl Marx on Colonialism and Modernization*, New York: Anchor Books.

Balagangadhara, S.N. (1988), 'Comparative Anthropology and Moral Domains', *Cultural Dynamics*, 1(1), pp. 98–128.

———(1994), '*The Heathen in His Blindness ...*': *Asia, the West and the Dynamic of Religion*, Leiden: E.J. Brill (second revised edition, New Delhi: Manohar, 2005).

———(2005), 'How to Speak for the Indian Traditions: An Agenda for the Future', *Journal of the American Academy of Religion*, 73(4), pp. 987–1013.

Balagangadhara, S.N., and J. De Roover (2007), 'The Secular State and Religious Conflict: Liberal Neutrality and the Indian Case of Pluralism', *The Journal of Political Philosophy*, 15(1), pp. 67–92.

Barnard, A., and J. Spencer (1996), 'Culture', in A. Barnard and J. Spencer, eds, *Encyclopedia of Social and Cultural Anthropology*, London: Routledge.

Barrow, R.H. (ed.) (1973), *Prefect and Emperor: The Relationes of Symmachus, A.D. 384*, Oxford: Clarendon Press.

Barth, E.M., and E.C.W. Krabbe (1982), *From Axiom to Dialogue: A Philosophical Study of Logics and Argumentation*, Berlin: Walter de Gruyter.

Bayley, D.H. (1978), 'The Effects of Corruption in a Developing Nation', in A.J. Heidenheimer (ed.), *Political Corruption: Readings in Comparative Analysis*, New Jersey: Transaction Books.

Benhabib, S. (2002), *The Claims of Culture: Equality and Diversity in the Global Era*, Princeton: Princeton University Press.

Bennett, J.W. (1954), 'Interdisciplinary Research and the Concept of Culture', *American Anthropologist*, Vol. 56, pp. 169–79.

Bernier, F. (1671), *A Continuation of the Memoires of Monsieur Bernier concerning the Empire of the Great Mogol, Tome III & IV*, London.

Bhabha, H.K. (1994), *The Location of Culture*, London: Routledge.

Bhargava, R. (1998), 'Introduction', in R. Bhargava (ed.), *Secularism and Its Critics*, New Delhi: Oxford University Press.

Bhatnagar, S., and S.K. Sharma (eds), (1991), *Corruption in Indian Politics and Bureaucracy*, New Delhi: Ess Ess Publications.

Bidney, D. (1944), 'On the Concept of Culture and Some Cultural Fallacies', *American Anthropologist*, Vol. 46, pp. 30–44.

Boas, F. (1928), *Anthropology and Modern Life*, New York: W.W. Norton and Co.

Boggs, J.P. (2004), 'The Culture Concept as Theory, in Context', *Current Anthropology*, Vol. 45, pp. 187–208.

Bohannan, P. (1973), 'Rethinking Culture: A Project for Current Anthropologists', *Current Anthropology*, Vol. 14, pp. 357–72.

Bohman, J. (1995), 'Public Reason and Cultural Pluralism: Political Liberalism and the Problem of Moral Conflict', *Political Theory*, 23(2), pp. 253–279.

———(2003), 'Deliberative Toleration', *Political Theory*, 31(6), pp. 757–79.

Borofsky, R. (1994), 'Rethinking the Cultural', in R. Borofsky (ed.), *Assessing Cultural Anthropology*, New York: McGraw-Hill.

Bouglé, C. (1971), *Essays on the Caste System*, trans. from French by D.F. Pocock, Cambridge: Cambridge University Press.

Braibanti, R. (1962), 'Reflections on Bureaucratic Corruption', *Public Administration*, Vol. 40, pp. 357–72.

Brass, P.R. (1999), 'Secularism Out of its Place', in V. Das, D. Gupta, and P. Uberoi (eds), *Tradition, Pluralism and Identity: In Honour of T.N. Madan*, New Delhi: Sage Publications.

Breckenridge, C.A., and P. van der Veer (eds) (1993), *Orientalism and the Postcolonial Predicament: Perspectives on South Asia*, Philadelphia: University of Pennsylvania Press.

Brightman, R. (1995), 'Forget Culture: Replacement, Transcendence, Relexification', *Cultural Anthropology*, Vol. 10, pp. 509–46.

Brumann, C. (1999), 'Writing for Culture: Why a Successful Concept Should not be Discarded', *Current Anthropology*, Vol. 40, pp. S1–27.

Buchanan, A. (2000), 'Justice, Legitimacy, and Human Rights', in V. Davion and C. Wolf (eds), *The Idea of a Political Liberalism: Essays on Rawls*, Lanham, MA: Rowman and Littlefield.

Burman, J.J.R. (2002), *Hindu–Muslim Syncretic Shrines and Communities*, New Delhi: Mittal.

Carstairs, M.G. (1957), *Twice Born*, London: Midland Books.

Césaire, A. (2000), *Discourse on Colonialism*, New York: Monthly Review Press.

Chakrabarty, D. (1997), 'Post-Coloniality and the Artifice of History: Who Speaks for "Indian" Pasts?' in R. Guha (ed.), *A Subaltern Studies Reader*, Minneapolis: University of Minnesota Press.

Chandra, B. (1994), *Ideology and Politics in Modern India*, New Delhi: Har-Anand Publications.

Chandra, B., M. Mukherjee, and A. Mukherjee (2003), *India After Independence, 1947–2000*, New Delhi: Penguin Books.

Chatfield, R. (1984), *Social, Political, Historical & Commercial Review of Hindoostan, From the Earliest Period to the Present Time*, New Delhi: Bimla Publishing House.

Chatterjee, P. (1992), 'History and the Nationalization of Hinduism', *Social Research*, 59(1), pp. 111–49.

Chatterjee, P. (1993), *The Nation and Its Fragments: Colonial and Postcolonial Histories*, Princeton: Princeton University Press.

———(1996), *Nationalist Thought and the Colonial World: A Derivative Discourse?* Delhi: Oxford University Press.

———(1998), 'Secularism and Tolerance', in R. Bhargava (ed.), *Secularism and Its Critics*, New Delhi: Oxford University Press.

Chatterji, P.C (1995), *Secular Values for Secular India*, New Delhi: Manohar.

Chattopadhyaya, B. (1998), *Representing the Other? Sanskrit Sources and the Muslims (Eighth to Fourteenth Century)*, New Delhi: Manohar.

Chattopadhyaya, D.P. (1998), 'Raja Rammohun Roy: A New Appraisal', in Kalyan Sengupta (ed.), *19th Century Thought in Bengal*, Calcutta: Allied Publisher.

Chaudhuri, P.C. (1994), 'Corruption', in *Seminar*, No. 421, pp. 41–51.

Chitkara, M.G. (1997), *Hindutva*, New Delhi: APH.

Cicero (1979), *De Natura Deorum*, trans. from Latin by H. Rackham, The Loeb Classical Library, London: Heinemann.

Claes, T. (1996), 'Theorizing the West: A Second Look at Francis Hsu', *Cultural Dynamics*, 8(1), pp. 79–99.

Clausen, C. (1996), 'Welcome to Post-Culturalism', *American Scholar*, 65, pp. 379–89.

Clifford, J. (1988), *The Predicament of Culture: Twentieth-Century Ethnography, Literature, and Art*, Cambridge: Harvard University Press.

Clooney, F.X. (2010), *Comparative Theology: Deep Learning across Religious Borders*, Oxford: Wiley-Blackwell.

Cohn, B.S. (1997), *Colonialism and Its Forms of Knowledge: The British in India*, Delhi: Oxford University Press.

Collins, S. (1988), 'Monasticism, Utopias and Comparative Social Theory', *Religion*, 18(2), pp. 101–35.

Comaroff, J., and J. Comaroff (2002), 'The Colonization of Consciousness', in M. Lambek (ed.), *A Reader in the Anthropology of Religion*, Oxford: Blackwell Publishers.

Conkle, D.O. (1995–6), 'Secular Fundamentalism, Religious Fundamentalism, and the Search for Truth in Contemporary America', *Journal of Law and Religion*, 12 (2), pp. 337–70.

Courtright, P.B. (1985), *Ganesa: Lord of Obstacles, Lord of Beginnings*, Oxford: Oxford University Press.

———(2006), 'The Self-Serving Humility of Disciplining Liberal Humanist Scholars: A Response to Russell McCutcheon', *Journal of the American Academy of Religion*, 74(3), pp. 751–4.

Craufurd, Q. (1790), *Sketches Chiefly Relating to the History, Religion, Learning, and Manners of the Hindoos*, London.

D'Agostino, F., and G.F. Gaus (eds) (1998), *Public Reason*, The International Research Library of Philosophy 21, Dartmouth: Ashgate.

D'Souza, D. (2002), 'Two Cheers for Colonialism', *Chronicle for Higher Education*, 48 (35), May 10.

Dalmia, V., and H. Von Stietencron (eds) (1995), *Representing Hinduism: The Construction of Religious Traditions and National Identity*, New Delhi: Sage Publications.

Dandekar, R.N. (1971), 'Hinduism', in E.J. Bleeker and G. Widengren (eds), *Historia Religionum: Handbook for the History of Religions*, Vol. 2, *Religions of the Present*, Leiden: E.J. Brill.

Daniel, V.E. (1984), *Fluid Signs: Being a Person the Tamil Way*, Berkeley: University of California Press.

Das, S.K. (2001), *Public Office, Private Interest: Bureaucracy and Corruption in India*, Delhi: Oxford University Press.

Davies, M.W. (2002), *Introducing Anthropology*, Cambridge: Icon Books Ltd.

Davion, V., and C. Wolf (2000), 'Introduction: From Comprehensive Justice to Political Liberalism', in V. Davion and C. Wolf (eds), *The Idea of a Political Liberalism: Essays on Rawls*, Lanham, MA: Rowman and Littlefield.

Dawson, C. (1977), 'The Christian View of History', in C.T. McIntire (ed.), *God, History, and Historians: Modern Christian Views of History*, New York: Oxford University Press.

De Roover, J. (2002), 'The Vacuity of Secularism: On the Indian Debate and Its Western Origins', *Economic and Political Weekly*, 37(39), pp. 4047–53.

Dilworth, C. (2008), *Scientific Progress: A Study Concerning the Nature of the Relation between Successive Scientific Theories*, Berlin: Springer.

Dirks, N. (2001) *Castes of Mind: Colonialism and the Making of Modern India*, New Delhi: Permanent Black.

Dumont, L. (1972), *Homo Hierarchicus: The Caste System and its Implications*, London: Paladin Books.

Eagleton, T. (2000), *The Idea of Culture*, Oxford: Blackwell.

Earman, J., and J. Roberts (1999), '*Ceteris Paribus*, There Are No Provisos', *Synthese*, 118, 438–79.

Elison, G. (1988), *Deus Destroyed: The Image of Christianity in Early Modern Japan*, Cambridge, MA: Council on East Asian Studies, Harvard University.

Elst, K. (2001), *Decolonizing the Hindu Mind: Ideological Development of Hindu Revivalism*, New Delhi: Rupa and Co.

Farquhar, J. N. (1911), *Modern Religious Movements in India*, London.

Fetzer, J.H., D. Shatz, and G. Schlesinger (1991), *Definitions and Definability: Philosophical Perspectives*, Dordrecht: D. Reidel.

Feyerabend, P. (2010), *Against Method*, London: Verso Books.

Fischer-Tiné, H., and M. Mann (eds) (2004), *Colonialism as Civilizing Mission: Cultural Ideology in British India*, Anthem South Asian Studies, London: Anthem Press.

Flannery, K.V. (1982), 'The Golden Marshalltown: A Parable for the Archeology of the 1980s', *American Anthropologist*, n.s., Vol. 84, pp. 265–78.

Fodor, J.A. (1991) 'You Can Fool Some of the People All of the Time, Everything Else Being Equal: Hedged Laws and Psychological Explanations', *Mind*, 100(1), pp.19–34.

Fox, R.G., and B.J. King (2002), 'Introduction: Beyond Culture Worry', in R.G. Fox and B.J. King (eds), *Anthropology Beyond Culture*, Oxford and New York: Berg.

Franklin, A. (1986), *The Neglect of Experiment*, Cambridge: Cambridge University Press.

Friedman, J. (1994), *Cultural Identity and Global Process*, London: Sage.

Friedman, M. (2000), 'John Rawls and the Political Coercion of Unreasonable People', in V. Davion and C. Wolf (eds), *The Idea of a Political Liberalism: Essays on Rawls*, Lanham, MA: Rowman and Littlefield.

Frohock, F.M. (1997), 'The Boundaries of Public Reason', *American Political Science Review*, 91(4), pp. 833–44.

Frykenberg, R.E. (1993), 'Constructions of Hinduism at the Nexus of History and Religion', *Journal of Interdisciplinary History*, 23(3), pp. 523–50.

Gandhi, M.K. (1942), *To the Hindus and Muslims*, Karachi: Hingorani.

Gay, P. (1973), *The Enlightenment: An Interpretation, Volume 1 , The Rise of Modern Paganism*, London: Wildwood House.

Gebhardt, J. (2008), 'Political Thought in an Intercivilizational Perspective: A Critical Reflection', *The Review of Politics*, Vol. 70, pp. 5–22.

Geertz, C. (1995), *After the Fact*, Cambridge, MA: Harvard University Press.

Gelders, R. (2009), 'Genealogy of Colonial Discourse: Hindu Traditions and the Limits of European Representation', *Comparative Studies in Society and History*, 51(3), pp. 563–89.

Gelders, R., and W. Derde (2003), 'Mantras of Anti-Brahmanism: Colonial Experience of Indian Intellectuals', *Economic and Political Weekly*, 38(43), pp. 4611–17.

Gellner, E., (1985), *Relativism and the Social Sciences*, Cambridge: Cambridge University Press.

Gibbon, E. (1952), 'The Decline and Fall of the Roman Empire', in *Great Books of the Western World*, Vol. 40, London: Encyclopædia Britannica.

Gilmartin, D., and B.B. Lawrence (eds) (2000), *Beyond Turk and Hindu: Rethinking Religious Identities in Islamicate South Asia*, Gainesville: University Press of Florida.

Gould, W. (2004), *Hindu Nationalism and the Language of Politics in Late Colonial India*, Cambridge: Cambridge University Press.

Graham, B.D. (2007), *Hindu Nationalism and Indian Politics: The Origins and Development of the Bharatiya Jana Sangh*, Cambridge: Cambridge University Press.

Grover, V., and R. Arora (eds) (1997), *India: Fifty Years of Independence*, Vol. 2, New Delhi: Deep & Deep Publications.

Gupta, A. (1995), 'Blurred Boundaries: The Discourse of Corruption, the Culture of Politics, and the Imagined State', *American Ethnologist*, 22(2), pp. 375–402.

Habermas, J. (1995), 'Reconciliation Through the Public Use of Reason: Remarks on John Rawls's Political Liberalism', *The Journal of Philosophy*, 92(3), pp. 109–31.

Halayya, M. (1985), *Corruption in India*, New Delhi: Affiliated East–West Press.

Halhed, N.B. (1776), *A Code of Gentoo Laws*, London.

Hall, D.L., and R.T. Ames (1985), *Thinking through Confucius*, Albany: State University of New York Press.

Hallowell, A.I. (1945), 'Sociopsychological Aspects of Acculturation', in R. Linton (ed.), *The Science of Man in the World of Crisis*, New York: Columbia University Press.

Harris, M. (1999), *Theories of Culture in Postmodern Times*, Walnut Creek: AltaMira Press.

Hasan, M. (1993), 'Competing Symbols and Shared Codes: Inter-community Relations in Modern India', in S. Gopal (ed.), *Anatomy of a Confrontation: Ayodhya and the Rise of Communal Politics in India*, London and New Jersey: Zed Books.

Hilpinen, R. (ed.) (1981), *Deontic Logic: Introductory and Systematic Readings*, Dordrecht: Kluwer Publishers.

Hintikka, J. (1969), *Models for Modalities*, Dordrecht: Kluwer Publishers.

Holy, L. (ed.) (1987), *Comparative Anthropology*, Oxford: Blackwell.

Hopkin, J. (2002), 'States, Markets and Corruption: A Review of Some Recent Literature', *Review of International Political Economy*, 9(3), pp. 574–90.

Horvath, R.J. (1972), 'A Definition of Colonialism', *Current Anthropology*, 13(1), pp. 45–57.

Hoyningen-Huene P., and H. Sankey (eds) (2010), *Incommensurability and Related Matters*, Berlin: Springer.

Hume, D. (1964), *The Natural History of Religion*, in T.H. Green and T.H. Grose (eds), *The Philosophical Works of David Hume*, Aalen: Scientia Verlag.

Huntington, S. (1968), 'Modernization and Corruption', in *Political Corruption: Readings in Comparative Analysis*, A.J. Heidenheimer (ed.), New Jersey: Transaction Books.

Husted, B.W. (1994), 'Honor among Thieves: A Transformation-Cost Interpretation of Corruption in Third World Countries', *Business Ethics Quarterly*, 4(1), pp. 17–27.

Inden, R. (1986), 'Orientalist Constructions of India', *Modern Asian Studies*, 20 (3), pp. 401–46.

———(1990), *Imagining India*, Oxford: Blackwell.

Ingold, T. (1993), 'The Art of Translation in a Continuous World', in G. Pálsson (ed.), *Beyond Boundaries: Understanding, Translation, and Anthropological Discourse*, London: Berg.

Jenco, L.K. (2007),'"What Does Heaven Ever Say?" A Methods-Centered Approach to Cross-cultural Engagement', *American Political Science Review*, 101(4), pp. 741–55.

Jones, K.W. (1976), *Arya Dharm: Hindu Consciousness in 19th-Century Punjab*, Berkeley: University of California Press.

Jones, Sir W. (1798a), 'On the Gods of Greece, Italy and India', in *Asiatick Researches*, Vol. 1, Calcutta.

———(1798b), *Institutes of Hindu Law*, London.

Jonsen, A.R., and S. Toulmin (1988), *The Abuse of Casuistry: A History of Moral Reasoning*, Berkeley: University of California Press.

Juergensmeyer, M. (2000), *Terror in the Mind of God: The Global Rise of Religious Violence*, Berkeley: University of California Press.

Juneja, R. (1992), 'The Native and the Nabob: Representations of the Indian Experience in Eighteenth-Century English Literature', *The Journal of Commonwealth Literature*, 27(1), pp. 183–98.

Kahn, J. (1989), 'Culture, Demise or Resurrection?' *Critique of Anthropology*, 9(2), pp. 5–25.

Kaye, Sir J.W. (1859), *Christianity in India: An Historical Narrative*, London.

Keay, J. (1988), *India Discovered*, London: Collins.

Keddie, N.R. (1997), 'Secularism and the State: Towards Clarity and Global Comparison', *New Left Review*, I/226, November–December, pp. 21–40.

Keesing, R.M. (1994), 'Theories of Culture Revisited', in R. Borofsky (ed.), *Assessing Cultural Anthropology*, New York: McGraw-Hill.

King, R. (1999a), 'Orientalism and the Modern Myth of "Hinduism"', *Numen*, 46(2), pp. 146–85.

———(1999b), *Orientalism and Religion: Post-colonial Theory, India and the Mystic East*, London: Routledge.

Kripal, J. (1998), *Kali's Child: The Mystical and the Erotic in the Life and Teachings of Ramakrishna*, Chicago: University of Chicago Press.

Kroeber, A.L., and C. Kluckhohn (1952), *Culture: A Critical Review of Concepts and Definitions*, Cambridge, MA: Papers of the Peabody Museum, Harvard University.

Laclear, G.F. (1859), *The Christian Statesman and Our Indian Empire*, Cambridge.

Lakatos, I. (1980), *The Methodology of Scientific Research Programmes: Philosophical Papers*, Vol. 1, Cambridge: Cambridge University Press.

Lambek, M. (ed.) (2002), *A Reader in the Anthropology of Religion*, Oxford: Blackwell Publishers.

Larmore, C. (1990), 'Political Liberalism', *Political Theory*, 18(3), pp. 339–60.

———(1994), 'Pluralism and Reasonable Disagreement', *Social Philosophy and Policy*, Vol. 11, pp. 61–79.

———(1996), *The Morals of Modernity*, Cambridge: Cambridge University Press.

Larson, G.J., and E. Deutsch (eds) (1988), *Interpreting Across Boundaries: New Essays in Comparative Philosophy*, Princeton: Princeton University Press.

Laudan, L. (1977), *Progress and Its Problems*, Berkeley: University of California Press.

Lorenzen, D.N. (1999), 'Who Invented Hinduism?' *Comparative Studies in Society and History*, 41(4). pp. 630–659.

Lorenzen, P., and K. Lorenz (1978), *Dialogische Logik*, Darmstadt: Wissenschaftliche Buchgesellschaft.

Loy, D. (1988), *Nonduality: A Study in Comparative Philosophy*, New Haven: Yale University Press.

Lynch, M.P. (ed.) (2001), *The Nature of Truth: Classic and Contemporary Perspectives*, Cambridge, MA: The MIT Press.

Macaulay, T.B. (1836), *Critical and Historical Essays*, Vol. 1, K.C.B.

MacIntyre, A. (1984), *After Virtue*, Notre Dame: University of Notre Dame Press, 2nd edition.

MacMullen, R., (1984), *Christianizing the Roman Empire, (A. D. 100–400)*, New Haven: Yale University Press.

Madan, T.N. (1987), 'Secularism in Its Place', *The Journal of Asian Studies*, 46 (4), pp. 747–59.

Madhok, B. (1995), 'Secularism: Genesis and Development', in M.M. Sankhdher (ed.), *Secularism in India: Dilemmas and Challenges*, New Delhi: Deep and Deep Publications.

Mahoney, J., and D. Rueschmeyer (eds) (2003), *Comparative Historical Analysis in the Social Sciences*, Cambridge: Cambridge University Press.

Major, A. (2006), *Pious Flames: European Encounters with Sati 1500–1830*, New Delhi: Oxford University Press.

Majumdar, J.K. (ed.) (1988), *Raja Rammohun Roy and Progressive Movements in India*, Delhi: Anmol Publications.

Malcolm, Sir J. (1833), *The Government of India*, London.

Mani, L. (1986), 'Production of an Official Discourse on Sati in Early Nineteenth Century Bengal', *Economic and Political Weekly*, 21(17), pp. 32–40.

———(1989), 'Contentious Traditions: The Debate on Sati in Colonial India', in K. Sangari and S. Vaid (eds.), *Recasting Women: Essays in Colonial History*, New Delhi: Kali for Women.

———(1998), *Contentious Traditions: The Debate on Sati in Colonial India*, Berkeley: University of California Press.

Marriott, M. (1976), 'Interpreting Indian Society: A Monistic Alternative to Dumont's Dualism', *Journal of Asian Studies*, 36(3), pp. 189–95.

———(1990), 'Constructing an Indian Ethnosociology', in M. Marriott (ed.), *India through Hindu Categories*, New Delhi: Sage Publications.

Martin E.M., and R.S. Appleby, eds (1991–1995), *The Fundamentalism Project*, 5 vols, Chicago: University of Chicago Press.

Mason, A.D. (1990), 'Autonomy, Liberalism and State Neutrality', *The Philosophical Quarterly*, 40(160), pp. 433–52.

Massie, J.W. (1985), *Continental India*, 2 vols, Delhi: B.R. Publishing Company.

Mathur, S. (1996), *Hindu Revivalism and the Indian National Movement: A Documentary Study of the Ideals and Policies of the Hindu Mahasabha, 1939–45*, Jodhpur: Kusumanjali Prakashan.

McCutcheon, R.T. (2006), '"It's a Lie. There's No Truth in It! It's a Sin!" On the Limits of the Humanistic Study of Religion and the Costs of Saving Others from Themselves', *Journal of the American Academy of Religion*, 74(3), pp. 720–50.

Mehta, U.S. (1999), *Liberalism and Empire: India in British Liberal Thought*, New Delhi: Oxford University Press.

Memmi, A. (2003), *The Colonizer and the Colonized*, London: Earthscan Publications.

Mill, J. (1990), *The History of British India*, Vol. 1, New Delhi.

Misra, B.B. (1977), *The Bureaucracy in India: An Historical Analysis of Development up to 1947*, Delhi: Oxford University Press.

Moir, M., and L. Zastoupil (eds), 'Introduction', in *The Great Indian Education Debate: Documents Relating to the Orientalist–Anglicist Controversy, 1781–1843*, London: Routledge.

Monier-Williams, M. (1891), *Brahmanism and Hinduism*, London.

Moore, J.D. (2004), *Visions of Culture: An Introduction to Anthropological Theories and Theorists*, Walnut Creek: AltaMira Press.

Moore, J.H. (1974), 'The Culture Concept as Ideology', *American Ethnologist*, 1, pp. 537–49.

Moussaief-Masson, G. (1980), *The Oceanic Feeling: The Origins of Religious Sentiment in Ancient India*, Dordrecht: D. Reidel.

Müller, Max (1962), *The Upanishads: In Two Parts*, New York: Dover Publications, reprint edition.

Myrdal, G. (1968), *Asian Drama: An Enquiry into the Poverty of Nations*, New York: Twentieth Century Fund.

Nandy, A. (1985), 'An Anti-secularist Manifesto', *Seminar*, No. 314, pp.14–24.

———(1998), 'The Politics of Secularism and the Recovery of Religious Tolerance', in R. Bhargava (ed.), *Secularism and Its Critics*, New Delhi: Oxford University Press.

Narayanan, V. (2001), 'The Strains of Hindu–Muslim Relations: Babri Masjid, Music, and Other Areas where the Traditions Cleave', in A. Sharma (ed.), *Hinduism and Secularism after Ayodhya*, Basingstoke: Palgrave.

Needham, A.D., and R.S. Rajan (eds) (2007), *The Crisis of Secularism in India*, Durham: Duke University Press.

Nehru, J. (1986), *Selected Works of Jawaharlal Nehru*, Second Series, Vol. 4, S. Gopal (ed.), New Delhi: Oxford University Press.

———(1988a), *The Discovery of India*, New Delhi: Jawaharlal Nehru Memorial Fund and Oxford University Press.

———(1988b), *Selected Works of Jawaharlal Nehru*, Second Series, Vol. 7, S. Gopal (ed.), New Delhi: Oxford University Press.

Nietzsche, F. (1986), *Human, All Too Human: A Book for Free Spirits*, trans. from German by R. J. Hollingdale, Cambridge: Cambridge University Press.

Oddie, G.A. (1995), *Popular Religion, Elites and Reform: Hook-Swinging and Its Prohibition in Colonial India, 1800–1894*, New Delhi: Manohar.

———(2006), *Imagined Hinduism: British Protestant Missionary Constructions of Hinduism, 1793–1900*, New Delhi: Sage Publications.

Ohnuki-Tierney, E. (2005), 'Always Discontinuous/Continuous and "Hybrid" by its Very Nature: The Culture Concept Historicized', *Ethnohistory*, Vol. 52, pp. 179–95.

Oldenburg, V. (2002), *Dowry Murder: The Imperial Origins of a Cultural Crime*, Delhi: Oxford University Press.

Olson, Jr, M. (1984), *The Rise and Decline of Nations: Economic Growth, Stagflation, and Social Rigidities*, New Haven: Yale University Press.

Osterhammel, J. (1997), *Colonialism: A Theoretical Overview*, Princeton: Markus Wiener Publishers.

Page, M., and P. Sonnenburg (eds) (2003), *Colonialism: An International Social, Cultural and Political Encyclopedia*, California: ABC-Clio, Inc.

Pandey, G. (1990), *The Construction of Communalism in Colonial North India*, New Delhi: Oxford University Press.

Parekh, B. (2000), *Rethinking Multiculturalism: Cultural Diversity and Political Theory*, London: Macmillan.

Parfit, D. (1984), *Reasons and Persons*, Oxford: Oxford University Press.

Pavarala, V. (1996), *Interpreting Corruption: Elite Perspectives in India*, New Delhi: Sage Publications.

Pennington, B. (2005), *Was Hinduism Invented? Britons, Indians and the Colonial Construction of Religion*, New York: Oxford University Press.

Pennycook, A. (1998), *English and the Discourses on Colonialism*, London: Routledge.

Peterson, R.A. (1979), 'Revitalizing the Culture Concept', *Annual Review of Sociology*, 5, pp. 137–66.

Pieterse, J.N. (2001), 'Hybridity, So What? The Anti-hybridity Backlash and the Riddles of Recognition', *Theory, Culture & Society*, 18(2–3), pp. 219–45.

Pietroski, P., and G. Rey (1991), 'When Other Things Aren't Equal: Saving Ceteris Paribus Laws from Vacuity', *The British Journal for the Philosophy of Science*, 46(1), pp. 81–110.

Popper, K. (1968), *Conjectures and Refutations*, London: Routledge.

———(1972), *The Logic of Scientific Discovery*, London: Hutchinson and Co.

———(1976), 'Reason or Revolution?' in T.W. Adorno (ed.), *The Positivist Dispute in German Sociology*, London: Heinemann Educational Books.

Potter, N.T., and M. Timmons (eds) (1985), *Morality and Universality: Essays on Ethical Universalizability*, Dordrecht: D. Reidel.

Quong, J. (2004), 'The Scope of Public Reason', *Political Studies*, Vol. 52, pp. 233–50.

Radcliffe-Brown, A.R. (1940), 'On Social Structure', *Journal of the Royal Anthropological Institute*, 70, pp. 1–12.

Radhakrishnan, P. (2002), 'Conversion Politics I & II', *The Hindu*, November 6–7.

Ramaswami, M. (2002), 'Is there God and whose God is He?' *The Hindu*, October 29.

Rawls, J., (1971), *A Theory of Justice*, Harvard: Harvard University Press.

———(1996), *Political Liberalism*, New York: Columbia University Press.

———(1999a), 'The Domain of the Political and Overlapping Consensus', in S. Freeman (ed.), *John Rawls: Collected Papers*, Cambridge, MA: Harvard University Press.

Rawls, J. (1999b), 'The Priority of Right and Ideas of the Good', in S. Freeman (ed.), *John Rawls: Collected Papers*, Cambridge, MA: Harvard University Press.

Ridley, M. (1993), *The Red Queen: Sex and the Evolution of Human Nature*, Harmondsworth: Penguin.

Roland, A. (1988), *In Search of Self in India and Japan*, Princeton: Princeton University Press.

Rose-Ackerman, S. (1999), *Corruption and Government: Causes, Consequences and Reform*, Cambridge: Cambridge University Press.

Rosemont Jr, H. (1988), 'Against Relativism', in G.J. Larson and E. Deutsch (eds), *Interpreting Across Boundaries: New Essays in Comparative Philosophy*, Princeton: Princeton University Press.

Rosenberg, A. (1995), 'Laws, Damn Laws, and Ceteris Paribus Clauses', *Southern Journal of Philosophy*, Vol. 34 (Suppl.), pp. 183–204.

Roy, R.R. (1885), *The English Works of Raja Rammohun Roy*, Vol. 1, J.C. Ghose (ed.), Delhi.

Ruether, R. (1974), *Faith and Fratricide: The Theological Roots of Anti-Semitism*, New York: Wipf and Stock.

Sachau, E. (ed.) (2002), *Alberuni's India: An Account of the Religion, Philosophy, Literature, Geography, Chronology, Astronomy, Customs, Laws, and Astrology of India about A.D. 1030*, New Delhi: Rupa and Co.

Said, E. (1978; reprint 1995), *Orientalism: Western Conceptions of the Orient*, London: Penguin Books.

Salzman, P.C. (2001), *Understanding Culture: An Introduction to Anthropological Theory*, Prospect Heights: Waveland Press, Inc.

Saraswati, Swami D. (1978), *Autobiography of Dayanand Saraswati*, New Delhi: Manohar.

———(1994), *Light of Truth or an English Translation of the Satyarth Prakash*, New Delhi: Sarvadeshik Arya Pratinidhi Sabha.

Sardar, Z. (2001), 'Among Asians, *Bakshish* is Just Another Word', *New Statesman*, 28, March pp. 11–12.

Savarkar, V.D. (1969), *Hindutva: Who Is a Hindu?* Bombay.

———(1984), *Hindu Rashtra Darshan*, Bombay.

Schiffer, S. (1991), 'Ceteris Paribus Laws', *Mind*, 100(1), pp. 1–17.

Sen, A. (2005), *The Argumentative Indian: Writings on Indian History, Culture and Identity*, New York: Farrar, Straus and Giroux.

Sen, A.P. (1993), *Hindu Revivalism in Bengal, 1872–1905: Some Essays in Interpretation*, New Delhi: Oxford University Press.

Sharma, J. (2003), *Hindutva: Exploring the Idea of Hindu Nationalism*, New Delhi: Viking.

Shweder, R.A., and E.J. Bourne (1984), 'Does the Concept of the Person Vary Cross-Culturally?' in R.A. Shweder and R.A. Levine (eds), *Culture Theory: Essays on Mind, Self, and Emotion*, Cambridge: Cambridge University Press.

Shweder, R.A., M. Mahapatra, and J.G. Miller (1987), 'Culture and Moral Development', in J. Kagan and S. Lamb (eds), *The Emergence of Morality in Young Children*, Chicago: University of Chicago Press.

Silverman, S., (2002), 'Foreword', in R.G. Fox and B. King (eds), *Anthropology Beyond Culture*, Oxford and New York: Berg.

Singh, N. (1998), *The World of Bribery and Corruption: From Ancient Times to Modern Age*, Delhi: Mittal Publications.

Spinner-Halev, J. (2005), 'Hinduism, Christianity and Liberal Religious Toleration', *Political Theory*, Vol. 33, pp. 28–57.

Spurr, D. (1993), *The Rhetoric of Empire: Colonial Discourse in Journalism, Travel Writing, and Imperial Administration*, Durham: Duke University Press.

Srivastava, C.P. (2001), *Corruption: India's Enemy Within*, New Delhi: Macmillan India.

Staniforth, M., ed. and trans (1968), *Early Christian Writers: The Apostolic Fathers*, Harmondsworth: Penguin.

Stock, E. (1899), *The History of the Church Missionary Society: Its Environment, Its Men and Its Work*, Vol. 2, London.

Stolcke, V. (1995), 'Talking Culture: New Boundaries, New Rhetorics of Exclusion in Europe', *Current Anthropology*, Vol. 36, pp. 1–24.

Stout, J. (1988), *Ethics after Babel: The Languages of Morals and Their Discontents*, Massachusetts: Beacon Press.

Strachey, Sir J., (1911), *India: Its Administration & Progress*, London.

Subrahmanyam, S. (2003), 'Before the Leviathan: Sectarian Violence and the State in Pre-Colonial India', in K. Basu and S. Subrahmanyam (eds), *Unravelling the Nation: Sectarian Conflict and India's Secular Identity*, New Delhi: Penguin Books.

Sugirtharajah, S. (2003), *Imagining Hinduism: A Postcolonial Perspective*, London: Routledge.

Tambiah, S. (1998), 'The Crisis of Secularism in India', in R. Bhargava (ed.), *Secularism and Its Critics*, New Delhi: Oxford University Press.

Thapar, R. (1989), 'Imagined Religious Communities? Ancient History and the Modern Search for a Hindu Identity', *Modern Asian Studies*, Vol. 23, pp. 209–31.

——(2007), 'Secularism, History and Contemporary Politics in India', in A.D. Needham and R.S. Rajan (eds), *The Crisis of Secularism in India*, Durham: Duke University Press.

Thomas, T. (1988), 'The Impact of Other Religions', in G. Parsons (ed.), *Religion in Victorian Britain*, Vol. 3, *Controversies*, Manchester: Manchester University Press.

Tone, W.H. (1799), 'Illustrations of Some Institutions of the Mahratta People', in *The Asiatic Annual Register… For the Year 1799*, London.

Tullock, G., (1996), 'Corruption: Theory and Practice', *Contemporary Economic Policy*, Vol. 14, pp. 6–13.

Tupper, C.L., (1893), *Our Indian Protectorate: An Introduction to the Study of the Relations Between the British Government and Its Indian Feudatories*, London.

Urwick, W. (1985), *India 100 Years Ago: The Beauty of Old India Illustrated*, London: Bracken Books.

Van Den Berghe, P. (1981), *The Ethnic Phenomenon*, New York: Elsevier.

Van Den Bossche, F., and F. Mortier (1997), 'The Vajjalaggam: A Study in Virtue Theory', *Asian Philosophy*, 7(2), 7, pp. 85–108.

Van Den Bouwhuijsen H., W. Derde, and T. Claes (1995), 'Recovering Culture', *Cultural Dynamics*, 7(2), pp. 163–86.

van Eemeren, F., and R. Grootendorst (1992), *Argumentation, Communication, and Fallacies: A Pragma-dialectical Perspective*, New Jersey: Lawrence Erlbaum Associates.

van Eemeren, F., R. Grootendorst, R. Jackson, and S. Jacobs (1993), *Reconstructing Argumentative Discourse*, London: University of Alabama Press.

van Eemeren, F., R. Grootendorst, F.S. Henkemans (1996), *Fundamentals of Argumentation Theory: A Handbook of Historical Backgrounds and Contemporary Developments*, New Jersey: Lawrence Erlbaum Associates.

Vedantam, S. (2004), 'Wrath over a Hindu God: U.S. Scholars' Writings Draw Threats From Faithful', *The Washington Post*, April 10.

Verma, A. (1999), 'Cultural Roots of Police Corruption in India', *Policing: An International Journal of Police Strategies and Management*, 22(3), pp. 264–79.

Visvanathan, S., and H. Sethi (eds) (1998), *Foul Play: Chronicles of Corruption 1974–97*, New Delhi: Banyan Books.

Vittal, N. (2000), 'Combatting Corruption', *Seminar*, No. 485.

Watson, P.J. (1995), 'Archaeology, Anthropology, and the Culture Concept', *American Anthropologist*, n.s. Vol. 97, pp. 683–94.

Weightman, S.(1984), 'Hinduism', in J. R. Hinnells (ed.), *A Handbook of Living Religions*, Harmondsworth: Penguin Books.

Weiss, G. (1973), 'A Scientific Concept of Culture', *American Anthropologist*, n.s., Vol. 75, pp. 1376–413.

Westman, R.S. (ed.) (1975), *The Copernican Achievement*, Berkeley: University of California Press.

Wheeler, J.T. (1888), *College History of India: Asiatic and European*, London.

White, L.A. (1949), *The Science of Culture: A Study of Man and Civilization*, New York: Grove Press.

———(1959), 'The Concept of Culture', *American Anthropologist*, n.s., Vol. 61, pp. 227–51.

Whitehead, H. (1924), *Indian Problems in Religion, Education, Politics*, London.

Willey, M. (1929), 'The Validity of the Culture Concept', *The American Journal of Sociology*, Vol. 35, pp. 204–19.

Williams, B. (1985), *Ethics and the Limits of Philosophy*, Massachusetts: Harvard University Press.

Williams, R. (ed.) (2000), *Explaining Corruption*, Cheltenham: Edward Elgar.

Williams, R., and A. Doig, eds (2000), *Controlling Corruption*, Cheltenham: Edward Elgar.

Wittgenstein, L. (2002), 'Remarks on Frazer's *Golden Bough*', in Michael Lambek (ed.) *A Reader in the Anthropology of Religion*, Oxford: Blackwell.

Wolf, E. (1980), 'They Divide and Subdivide, and Call it Anthropology', *The New York Times*, 30 November.

———(1982), *Europe and the People Without History*, Berkeley: University of California Press.

Yengoyan, A. (1986), 'Theory in Anthropology: On the Demise of the Concept of Culture', *Comparative Studies in Society and History*, 28(2), pp. 368–74.

———, ed. (2006), *Modes of Comparison: Theory and Practice*, Ann Arbor: University of Michigan Press.

Young, R.F., ed. (1981), *Resistant Hinduism: Sanskrit Sources on Anti-Christian Apologetics in Early Nineteenth-Century India*, Vienna: Institut für Indologie der Universität Wien.

Ziegenbalg, B. (1719), *Thirty-Four Conferences Between the Danish Missionaries and the Malabarian Bramans ... in the East Indies, Concerning the Truth of the Christian Religion*, London.

Index of Names

Index of Subjects

linga/ phallus (symbol of male
    fertility) worship 87, 123–4, 136,
    139–40, 141–2, 145, 155, 160,
    239, 241
lokayata 7

man and society 62
materialism 7
Maya Panchakam (Shankara) 127
maya, avidya and *agyanaare* 138
maya' as 'illusion' 127–8, 138
Mein Kampf (Hitler) 231
metaphor, use 18
minority religions 223
modernity and nationhood 68
modernization 3, 229
Mogul rule in India 98
moral
    abhorrence 122
    awareness 49
    behavior 82
    development 49
    judgement 16
    notions 49
    philosophy 106
    violation 50–1
morality in the Indian tradition 7, 10,
    59 n6, 79, 81, 93, 102, 107, 108,
    111, 128, 167
    of middle class 129
multiculturality 32
Muslims 4, 47, 199–200, 201, 202,
    205, 207, 210, 211, 223, 240
mysticism 136, 146

Neutrality of justification 213–14
non-resident Indians (NRIs) and their
    story 233–5
non-western societies and culture 1,
    9, 40–1, 55, 62, 64–5, 67, 69–74,
    78, 85, 90, 181
normative political theory 169–96
normative epistemology 165

Obscurantism 13
Occidental 43
On Superstition (Plutarch) 175
oral communication 151
Orient
    on constructing 40–3
    a place and an idea 37
    as an experiential entity 37–9
Orientalism (Edward Said) 35–57, 95
Orientalism
    and cultures 9, 39–40, 48–56
    and social sciences 48, 49, 50, 61,
        62–4, 74, 76, 85, 89, 92
overlapping consensus 190

Pagan cultures 12, 69, 176, 206–8,
    209–13, 214, 217–19, 221, 225.
    See also Semitic religions
perverse phenomena 107–12
phallus worship. *See* linga worship
Phenomenology (George Wilhelm
    Friedrich Hegel) 36
pluralism 173, 189–90, 196, 221,
    223–4
    cultural 198, 225
    religious 11, 199, 214
political
    authority 62
    beliefs 82
    correctness 79
    economy 91–2
    ideologies and caste system 4
    liberalism 11, 169–72, 180,
        187–9, 195–6; and violence
        189–91
    sociology 223
    structures 186, 224
    theory of toleration 199
Political Liberalism (John Rawls) 170
politics 62, 84, 199
poverty and backwardness 3, 56,
    230, 231
Prajapathi 142–3